TENDING THE GARDEN

Praise for *Tending the Garden*

Jennifer Wojciechowski's *Tending the Garden: A History of Christian Mysticism* is a fascinating fresh look at mysticism and an array of mystics, especially women in the West. The book is a gentle walk through the garden of mystics and takes you deeper and deeper, pointing and guiding to eight signposts of the history of Christian mysticism. A captivating book for reflection and inspiration for anyone disenchanted with the emptiness, loneliness, despair, and lack of empathy in America. Loving relationship between humans and God is central to *Tending the Garden*. It is about finding answers to practicing contemplation of the self and deep, active love for all, especially God. Raising questions about the meaning and purpose of life, the author highlights the importance of Christian mysticism and courageously recategorizes it as a new historical renovation of mysticism.

—Moses Penumaka, director of Theological Education for Emerging Ministries and Indigenous Leaders, Pacific Lutheran Theological Seminary of California Lutheran University

This book offers a timely and necessary introduction to Christian mysticism. Through her insightful exploration of mystics ranging from patristic authors to figures like Sojourner Truth, Phoebe Palmer, and Howard Thurman, Wojciechowski invites readers to rediscover Christian mysticism as a valuable tradition and an inspiring practice that can enrich both personal and communal spiritual lives today.

—Jeehei Park, assistant professor of New Testament, Seminary of the Southwest, and author of *All Citizens of Christ: A Cosmopolitan Reading of Unity and Diversity in Paul's Letters*

Jennifer Wojciechowski's work has helped make Christian mysticism, a complex and often misunderstood subject, more accessible to readers. Her expertise has enabled Christians to better understand and appreciate the experiential aspects of Christian history and theology. Above all,

Wojciechowski illustrates the significance of embracing the unknown, and how that can guide Christians toward reorienting their lives within the context of an increasingly broken and messed-up world.

—Man-Hei Yip, assistant professor of systematic theology, Wartburg Theological Seminary, and author of *Interrogating the Language of "Self" and "Other" in the History of Modern Christian Mission: Contestation, Subversion, and Re-imagination*

In an age addicted to spiritualities with (or more often without) God, Jennifer Wojciechowski's *Tending the Garden* is an important contribution. As the great teacher she is, she teaches the reader that the mystical is a fundamentally theological practice of encountering a living, speaking, and acting God. This is a helpful book for our times.

—Andrew Root, author of *The Church in an Age of Secular Mysticisms*

Jennifer Wojciechowski has written a wonderful introduction to the history and theology of Christian mysticism. Not only does she explore the lives and writings of classic Christian mystics with highly engaging and readable prose, but she also helps us understand how we too, as modern people, might benefit from their spiritual practices and ways of tending to God's loving presence in our lives. I highly recommend this book!

—Lois Malcolm, Olin and Amanda Fjelstad Reigstad Professor of Systematic Theology, Luther Seminary

TENDING THE GARDEN

A History of Christian Mysticism

Jennifer Hornyak Wojciechowski

Fortress Press
Minneapolis

TENDING THE GARDEN
A History of Christian Mysticism

30 29 28 27 26 25 24 1 2 3 4 5 6 7 8 9

Library of Congress Control Number: 2024942770 (print)

Cover image: Compilation of vintage woodcut illustration from duncan1890/Getty Images, Jesus With Birds stock illustration from CSA Images/Getty Images, and textures from Getty Images
Cover design: Kristin Miller

Print ISBN: 978-1-5064-9702-0
eBook ISBN: 978-1-5064-9703-7

for my husband, Alec

CONTENTS

PREFACE

Love grants prophecy, miracles. It is an abyss of illumination, a fountain of fire, bubbling up to inflame the thirsty soul. It is the condition of angels, and the progress of eternity.

—John Climacus, *The Ladder of Divine Ascent*

IN AUGUST 2023, my kids and I headed to the only approved Marian shrine in the United States. It had been a bit of work to convince them, then aged twelve and eight, that going to a religious shrine, in an unincorporated village outside Green Bay, Wisconsin, would be a fun end of the summer trip. But the drive was only about four hours, and after showing them the website and telling them about the miracles associated with the shrine, they agreed. We headed out one morning with a ridiculous number of electronic devices and way too many snacks. We called it our car pilgrimage, and we managed to make the four-hour drive last about six.

The motivation for the trip was that I was in the middle of working on this book about mysticism, and I was feeling a disconnect between our modern American life, devoid of the miraculous, and the lives of the many mystics I was reading about. Over the previous year I had read so, so many mystical texts, analyses of mystical theology, and biographies and hagiographies of the saints. The mystics as a group are difficult to categorize (they really are an eclectic collection of people), and one of the few things I feel comfortable stating about them is that their faith was experiential and wild. They did not just think about God. They were in deep and loving relationships with God.

Diving into the lives of the mystics is a fascinating experience for the modern person. The oddities and miracles are ever-present in the literature, so much so that after spending time with the mystics, one starts to wonder why we aren't all having visions and levitating. Which brings me to Our Lady of Champion Shrine. In 1859, a young immigrant woman claimed to have seen an apparition of the Virgin Mary three times. This experience propelled the woman to take up a religious life, and soon the community built a shrine on the spot. In 1871, when the deadly Peshtigo Fire, still the deadliest fire in US history, was ravaging the area, the local people sought refuge from the fire and were miraculously saved. In 2010, the bishop of Green Bay decreed the apparitions authentic and worthy of belief (though not obligatory).[1] I was hoping a trip to the shrine would help me process all the mystical materials I had been reading, especially since I am particularly fond of the medieval Catholic mystics who reported experiencing the miraculous frequently. I did not have any sort of mystical experience myself, nor did my children, though the shrine is incredibly peaceful and worth the trip.[2] The shrine may have helped me understand the mystics a little better though. It helped me put my rationalism on the back burner and embrace the unexplained. After all, "for God all things are possible" (Matt 19:26), whether or not we feel comfortable with God acting in such unexpected ways.

This book project grew out of a desire to know the mystics, and therefore God, a little better. It was an excuse to read the great mystics over the course of a couple of years. While writing my previous book, which was on Christian women's history, I had been particularly

---

1 David Laurin Ricken, "Decree on the Authenticity of the Apparitions of 1859 at the Shrine of Our Lady of Good Help," December 8, 2010, https://www.gbdioc.org/images/stories/Evangelization_Worship/Shrine/Documents/Shrine-of-Our-Lady-of-Good-Help.pdf.

2 I wrote a lengthy blog post about the trip: Jennifer Hornyak Wojciechowski, "The Ecstatic and the Everyday," Faith+Lead Blog, January 17, 2024, https://faithlead.org/blog/the-ecstatic-and-the-everyday/.

fascinated with the medieval and early modern women mystics, such as Julian of Norwich and Teresa of Ávila. How does one decide to do the things these women did? What kind of experience with God propels someone to move into a doorless cell or to take on the overwhelming task of reforming a monastic order, *as a woman*, in the sixteenth century! I wanted to spend time with these people. I wanted to read what they had to say, and their writings are truly incredible.

There is another, far more practical inspiration for this book as well. Over the years of teaching the history of Christianity, I found that my students were often very interested in the mystics, but many found them a difficult subject to approach. Mystical texts can be obscure, the theology can seem complex, and the secondary literature on Christian mysticism can be excessively academic and intimidating. I struggled to find a relatively short and accessible introduction to the field for my students, which is why I structure this book as I have. I hope that this will be a way for people both to learn of the general themes found in Christian mysticism and to meet a number of the most influential and beloved mystics.

One of the things I was not expecting when I approached this project was how love would permeate everything. Of all the themes and subjects with which the varied mystics engaged over the centuries, it is love that emerges as the most prominent. Regardless of the time and place, there is a longing present in so many of texts—a longing to be near God, to love God, and to receive love from God. Bernard of Clairvaux writes of the degrees to which a person can love God. Mechthild and Hadewijch wrote love poetry, which resembles courtly love poems, about their love for God. John of the Cross wrote poems of love and longing between lovers who represent the soul and God. Julian of Norwich's book about her visions is even named *Revelations of Divine Love*, and one meets a God who loves deeply throughout. This is only scratching the surface of the mystics' writings about love. It is ever-present throughout the centuries. To engage with the mystics, one must be prepared to love. It is not an exaggeration to say that mystical texts are some of the most beautiful writings to come out of the Christian tradition.

This book would not be possible with the help of a whole host of friends and colleagues. First, I want to thank my editor at Fortress Press, Bethany Dickerson, who was part of the process from the very start—indeed, when this book was more of a vague idea than a concrete proposal. She not only helped to create a better final product but also calmed me down when I was convinced that I was not going to be able to structure the book, because how could one possibly categorize this group of people who seem to defy any sort of categorization? I would like to thank the staff at the Luther Seminary Library, who over the past couple of years checked out, then checked back in, then checked out, and so on most of the books on Christian mysticism (not to mention ordering things for me as well). I would also like to thank my colleagues and friends at Luther Seminary, especially Grace Pomroy, who helped make the introduction much better; Mark Granquist, for the support and all the books on Lutheran mystics; Lois Malcom, for checking my theology on Pelagianism; Andy Root, for the conversations and book on secular mysticism; and my teaching assistant for my mysticism class and doctoral student, Bryant Kumlin, for materials on Swedenborg and conversation on hesychasm. I want to thank the faculty, especially the History/Theology division, for being supportive of this project and offering up encouragement, conversations, and book suggestions. I also need to thank my January 2024 History of Christian Mysticism class, who engaged with these materials and helped me finish up this project. Their faith and engagement with the mystics was inspirational.

I want to thank my two wonderful children, Lucy and Emory, who have valiantly tolerated my writing schedule (and a trip to a Catholic shrine). Finally, I want to thank my husband, Alec. He not only listened to me fret about the progress, or lack thereof, on the book but offered up endless support and encouragement. Absolutely none of this would be possible without him.

TIMELINE OF HISTORICAL FIGURES

Late Antiquity

Origen (ca. 185–253), chapter 5
Anthony of the Desert (251–356), chapter 2
Evagrius of Pontus (345–399), chapter 2
Augustine (354–430), chapter 5
John Cassian (ca. 360–435), chapter 2

Early Medieval

Pseudo-Dionysius (ca. late fifth–early sixth century), chapter 1
Benedict of Nursia (480–547), chapter 3
Pope Gregory the Great (ca. 540–604), chapter 3
John Climacus (sixth–seventh centuries), chapter 2

High Medieval

Bernard of Clairvaux (1090–1153), chapter 4
Hildegard of Bingen (1098–1179), chapter 3
Guigo II (twelfth century), chapter 1
Francis of Assisi (ca. 1181–1226), chapter 3
Hadewijch (ca. 1200–1260), chapter 6
Mechthild of Magdeburg (ca. 1207–1282/1294), chapter 6
Bonaventure (1221–1274), chapter 3
Angela of Foligno (1248–1309), chapter 7
Marguerite Porete (1250–1310), chapter 8
Gertrude the Great (1256–1302), chapter 5
Meister Eckhart (ca. 1260–1328), chapter 8

Late Medieval

Birgitta of Sweden (1303–1373), chapter 4
Julian of Norwich (1342/3–after 1416), chapter 2
Catherine of Siena (1347–1380), chapter 4
Catherine of Genoa (1447–1510), chapter 7

Early Modern

Ignatius of Loyola (1491–1556), chapter 7
Teresa of Ávila (1515–1582), chapter 3
John of the Cross (1542–1591), chapter 6
Francis de Sales (1567–1622), chapter 5
Jakob Boehme (1575–1624), chapter 7
Marie of the Incarnation (1599–1672), chapter 7
George Fox (1624–1691), chapter 8
Angelus Silesius (ca. 1624–1677), chapter 7
Emmanuel Swedenborg (1688–1772), chapter 8

Modern

Sojourner Truth (1797–1883), chapter 4
Phoebe Palmer (1807–1874), chapter 7
Rufus Jones (1863–1948), chapter 8
Thérèse of Lisieux (1873–1897), conclusion
Evelyn Underhill (1875–1941), chapter 6
T. S. Eliot (1888–1965), chapter 6
Edith Stein (1891–1942), chapter 5
Dorothy Day (1897–1980), chapter 4
Howard Thurman (1899–1981), chapter 4
Simone Weil (1909–1943), chapter 8
Thomas Merton (1915–1968), chapter 2
Raimon Panikkar (1918–2010), conclusion

INTRODUCTION

> *Let the beginner think of herself as a gardener who is preparing to plant a garden for her Beloved. But the soil is barren and full of noxious weeks. His majesty himself pulls up the weeds and replaces them with good seed. Bear in mind that the minute the soul sets out on the path of prayer and service, God has already begun to cultivate her soil in this way.*
>
> —Teresa of Ávila, *The Book of My Life*

SIXTEENTH-CENTURY SPANISH NUN and mystic Teresa of Ávila uses an analogy of a garden to discuss the path of prayer that a believer may take up to grow closer to God. After spending decades of struggling in her prayer life, Teresa had a profound mystical experience in which she devoted herself to God and reportedly experienced a host of miraculous events afterward, which brought significant attention, both positive and negative. At the command of the Catholic hierarchy, she wrote about her theology and experiences in the book that is generally known as her *Vida*, or her autobiography, though considering she was still middle-aged and had decades of important monastic reforming work ahead of her, the book is more a glimpse into her life and theology while it was still in development.[1] Throughout her book, Teresa writes about prayer in what are some of the most personal and helpful reflections on the topic of any book in Christian history.

---

1 Her book, *The Interior Castle*, written toward the end of her life, presents an even more robust look at prayer, with a different analogy, one of a mansion with many rooms.

The name of this book is taken from her garden imagery. Teresa tells the beginner to think of herself as a gardener who is preparing a garden for her Beloved. Both God and the believer care for the garden. At the beginning of the journey, the garden is full of weeds, but God works the soil to prepare a place for the believer. Like a good gardener, it is the believer's job to tend to the plants in the garden with love and care. One needs to work to water the garden, a task that can happen four different ways: one can pull the water from a well, one can turn a crank of a waterwheel, one can channel water through an irrigation ditch, or one can wait for abundant rain, which is from God. She compares these stages of drawing water to stages in the life of prayer. She astutely notes, "Like good gardeners, we do whatever lies in our power and leave the rest to him."[2]

Teresa has long been a favorite Christian historical figure. Her approachability, humility, intelligence, literary skill, and humor have inspired many, both Catholic and not, through the centuries since her death. Her honest reflections, extraordinary experiences, and plaguing self-doubt have also given rise to disdain and even accusations of insanity. Such is the lot of a gifted mystic, especially a woman mystic.

Christian mysticism has become a rather popular subject today, with renewed attention being paid to a host of saints hailing from previous centuries. It is reasonable to ask, though, What do mystically inclined ancient desert monks, hermits, and medieval monastics have to offer people today? As it turns out, quite a bit. While the particulars of their historical contexts were different from today, basic human experiences and values have changed surprisingly little in the past couple of millennia. Past writings on God and theological reflections are and will continue to be profoundly moving and perhaps even life changing. To engage with the mystics is to embark on a journey of self-discovery, prayer, faith, and ultimately love.

---

2 Teresa of Ávila, *The Book of My Life*, trans. Mirabai Starr (Boston: New Seeds, 2007), 73–75.

Demystifying the Mystics

This book is an introduction to the history and theology of Christian mysticism. It provides the reader with a basic definition of Christian mysticism, offers clarity around several terms and practices related to Christian mysticism, and explores and analyzes the lives and writings of important Christian mystics. It also proposes some ways in which modern people, living in an industrialized and disenchanted society, can benefit from knowing the history of Christian mysticism and engaging in spiritual practices related to it. Another aim is to demystify the mystics—to make them understandable and relatable. Mysticism is an ancient and important aspect of the Christian faith. It is also highly misunderstood. Due to obscure language and concepts, not to mention occasionally eccentric personalities, the mystics can be difficult to approach. However, once one peels back the layers of insider language, one begins to see a highly relatable group of people who were first and foremost concerned with tending to a personal and loving relationship with God.

This book is not meant to be the penultimate study on Christian mysticism.[3] It is an approachable introduction to the field with the nonspecialist in mind. Besides the introduction and chapter 1, which are largely concerned with concepts related to the field and mystical theology, I offer this introduction primarily through the lives and stories of various Christian mystics. This is because it is through stories that human beings truly come to understand others. The mystics who are highlighted in the following pages come from a variety of times, places, and theological traditions. A timeline on page xiii breaks the figures into their historical contexts, with fairly even distribution between eras, though the medieval period (which roughly runs a thousand years) does have the most. There are mystics represented from Catholic, Orthodox, and Protestant traditions, though due to the

---

3 That distinction belongs to Bernard McGinn and his multivolume series The Presence of God.

nature of Christian mysticism and that Protestantism is only about five hundred years old, there is a larger percentage of Catholic and Orthodox mystics represented throughout the book. There is roughly equal representation of men and women.

After reading the book, the reader should have a good understanding of the Christian mystical tradition along with the knowledge and skill set to explore further through the robust bibliography and suggested reading lists at the end of each chapter. It is inevitable that the reader will connect with or enjoy certain mystical figures more than others. This largely has to do with theology, personal experience, and even taste. This book should help focus the reader's further engagement with mysticism based on those preferences.

What Is Christian Mysticism?

One of the great problems when exploring Christian mysticism is that there is not an agreed-on definition. *Mysticism* is a term that tends to get overused and misused, especially in the popular imagination. Without providing some clarity, the term is almost meaningless because it can be so many things to so many different people. A simple internet search for "mysticism" will bring up results ranging from prayer practices to New Age spirituality to a Women's National Basketball Association team.[4] Even if one gets more specific by looking at *Christian* mysticism, there is little consensus on the term—though, to be fair, there are not any sports teams named after Christian mystics—but popular imagination tends to emphasize the mysterious and miraculous elements.

Because of this general confusion around the term, it is essential to establish a definition to be used throughout this book. My definition is based on the common elements that arose after surveying

---

4 The Washington Mystics are the WNBA counterpart to the NBA's Washington Wizards. There is an interesting association here between mysticism and magic, which would *not* have been appreciated by most Christian mystics throughout history.

a large body of mystical literature (including exploring the lives of the mystics), ranging from texts that were written in the early church to texts that were written as recently as the twentieth century. With that background in mind, the basic definition of Christian mysticism used throughout this book is *an intimate and experiential relationship, set within a Christian framework, with the Triune God.* There is also a sense of spiritual progress inherent in the term that needs acknowledgment. Not everyone would define mysticism in this way, and some will certainly quibble with it. This is a broad definition that allows for much flexibility and a range of lived experience, but this broadness also necessitates explanation.

CHRISTIAN MYSTICISM: A DEFINITION

There is disagreement, debate, and confusion regarding the term *Christian mysticism.* Especially in popular culture, *mysticism* can refer to anything from occult practices to prayer. Therefore it is essential that a definition be established that will be used throughout this book. I define Christian mysticism as *an intimate and experiential relationship, set within a Christian framework, with the Triune God.* There is also a sense of spiritual progress inherent in the term that needs acknowledgment.

While it is difficult to generalize about the mystics, since they tend to be an unruly lot, they are bound by a commitment to deep, experiential relationships with God. This theme stands regardless of time, place, and denominational affiliation. The mystics were not people who just thought about God; they were in a deep relationship with God. Except in a few rare instances, the mystics identify the keys to developing a relationship with God as prayer, living a pious life, love for God, and love for neighbor. Throughout the remainder of the book, the reader will see this commitment to relationship and spiritual progress in the lives of the mystics examined.

SPIRITUAL PROGRESS AND PURGATION, ILLUMINATION, AND UNION

The term *spiritual progress* may be obscure today, but the mystics refer to it often. It can have slightly different meanings depending on time and place, but the general idea is that someone is becoming closer to God and growing in religious life, which can include going deeper with prayer, engaging in spiritual practices, overcoming sins, or even trying to imitate Christ.

For the desert monastics in the early church, spiritual progress could mean tempering the passions and overcoming sins. For mystics living in late antiquity, the Middle Ages, and early modernity, this spiritual progress often meant the process of purgation, illumination, and union.[5] Purgation is the process of understanding and purifying oneself of sins, while illumination is the process of understanding God, and union is connecting to God. This tripartite process is such a prominent theme in mystical writing that sometimes mysticism is defined by purgation, illumination, and union. Notably, many Protestants reject this framework, but for Catholic and Orthodox mystics, this process continues to be a vitally important aspect of mystical thought and practice.

5 Due to the frequency of this progression, mysticism is sometimes even defined as the process of purgation, illumination, and union. For example, this is how Harvey Egan defines mysticism in his very useful text *An Anthology of Christian Mysticism* (Collegeville, MN: Liturgical Press, 1991), xvi.

This definition does not include any reference to mystical union, various miracles, or altered states of consciousness. This is an intentional choice, though it needs explanation because these terms are often closely associated with mysticism. Mystical union will be explored in more detail in chapter 1; therefore, it is sufficient to say here that while many mystics do talk of union with God, it is not universal, especially among mystics in both the early church and the post-Enlightenment West. Thus, by defining mysticism as union with God, many religious figures who have long been considered mystics would be excluded. It is also impossible to prove that someone experienced a mystical union with God, so basing a definition on such a categorization can lead to problems.

Similarly, people often associate the mystics with miracles or envision the mystics as miracle workers, and there are reasons for this close association. Hagiographies, or writings about the saints with the purpose of promoting veneration, are filled with the miraculous, and even some biographies offer examples of miracles. Many of the mystics themselves wrote about miracles and unexplained events. Hildegard of Bingen reported her own visions (among other experiences), Teresa of Ávila levitated (among other experiences), Francis of Assisi had the stigmata (again, among other experiences), and so on. But these miraculous components of their stories are not what make them mystics. Strange and unexplained events are tangential to the core of mysticism, which is built on prayer and relationship with God. A good example of this is Teresa of Ávila. Repeatedly through her writings, she insists that these spiritual gifts are just that: gifts. They were not given because she earned them, and she comments that God sends them to her because she is weak. The true gift is a relationship with God. It is also important to note that many mystical texts do not make any references to miracles at all.

Disagreements Regarding Mysticism

Even with a basic working definition of mysticism provided earlier, it is necessary to discuss why there is so much disagreement on the term.

Mystics, scholars, and interested lay readers genuinely have different understandings of mysticism. While this diversity of thought may seem odd at first, once one starts to dive into the lives and writings of the mystics, the confusion starts to make sense. The mystics had vastly different religious experiences; they lived vastly different lifestyles; they understood God in different ways, wrote about God in different ways, and understood their own faith in different ways. It is impossible to paint a picture of a typical mystic. Mysticism is about experience and relationship with God, and this cannot be easily tamed or put into a box.

Simply put, there is no one way to be a mystic. Nor is mysticism a well-defined scholarly field of study (though of course there are plenty of scholars who deal with mysticism). Ecclesial—that is, church—definitions can be helpful, but they cannot be the sole source, especially since mystics are found in a plethora of different Christian denominations and traditions. Likely the most useful official church reference to mysticism can be found in the Catechism of the Catholic Church, since so many mystics have been Catholic. It refers to mysticism as a type of spiritual progress:

> *Spiritual progress tends toward ever more intimate union with Christ. This union is called "mystical" because it participates in the mystery of Christ through the sacraments—"the holy mysteries"—and, in him, in the mystery of the Holy Trinity. God calls us all to this intimate union with him, even if the special graces or extraordinary signs of this mystical life are granted only to some for the sake of manifesting the gratuitous gift given to all.*[6]

As helpful as this definition may be, it cannot be applied to all mystics, or even all those included in this book. Protestant and Orthodox

---

6 Catholic Church, *Catechism of the Catholic Church: Revised in Accordance with the Official Latin Text Promulgated by Pope John Paul II* (Washington, DC: United States Catholic Conference, 2000), 2014–2015.

mystics, and even some Catholic mystics, would have a different understanding, especially because of the definition's close association between mystical thought and the sacraments. There are also mystics who fall outside more established religious organizations.

Another complication is that many of the Christians we would today define as mystics would have never used that term themselves. The term *mysticism* is a modern academic invention, though the term *mystical theology* has been used for many centuries.[7] Most of the so-called mystics would have called themselves contemplatives (more on this in ch. 1) in their own times. Regardless, the word *mystical* is used extensively today, and despite its rather fuzzy boundaries, it is helpful, especially after establishing an agreed-on definition.

Why Study Christian Mysticism?

If the mystics are a varied and loosely bound group of Christians, with some tending toward eccentricity, why study them? What benefits can come from dwelling with these often-misunderstood individuals who mostly died centuries ago? What can they possibly say that would provide meaning for modern life and modern problems?

Early twentieth-century writer Evelyn Underhill writes that the benefit of engaging with mysticism is that one will "have a far deeper, truer knowledge than ever before both of the general and the individual existence; and so you are able to handle life with a surer hand."[8] This is a lofty answer, of course, but also not wrong. The question becomes, though, how can Underhill make such claims? How does mysticism supposedly empower people to handle life with a surer hand?

Christianity has a powerful tradition of mystical prayer and deep relationships between believers and God that dates back millennia,

---

7 Mark A. McIntosh, *Mystical Theology* (Malden, MA: Wiley-Blackwell, 1998), 11.

8 Evelyn Underhill, *Practical Mysticism: A Little Book for Normal People and Abba Meditations on the Lord's Prayer*, ed. John F. Thorton and Susan B. Varenne (New York: Vintage Spiritual Classics, 2003), 121.

but the era of mystical encounters with God has not ended. Mystical prayer and relationship are still available today. Through those who have come before us, Christians today can learn how to pray and how to tend a meaningful relationship with God. People can read beautiful writings that explore aspects of faith, the attributes of God, and the meaning of life. Perhaps most affecting is the understanding that these giants of the Christian faith were regular people, who had struggles and flaws, and yet they had a deep relationship with God and influenced the world around them.

This mystical tradition of prayer and relationship has had profound influence on individual believers, church institutions, and the world throughout history. Mysticism is perhaps more needed today than it has been in centuries. To fully unpack that statement, it is necessary to take a step back and recognize where Americans are today physically, emotionally, and spiritually.

The majority of Americans continue to identify as Christians, though the numbers are in decline. According to the last Pew Research Religious Landscape data, Christianity in America is waning. Between 2007 and 2014, Christians in the United States decreased from 78 percent to 63 percent. Meanwhile, the number of those who are unaffiliated has grown nearly 7 percent to 29 percent. This decline is even more stark when considering that in 1972, 90 percent of Americans identified as Christian, and only 5 percent were religiously unaffiliated.[9] Mainline Protestants have been hit the hardest, with 52 percent of Americans identifying as mainline in 2007 and a mere 40 percent in 2021.[10] There is much to be encouraged about when looking at Christianity on a global scale—Christianity is growing in many places in the

---

9 Pew Research Center, "Modeling the Future of Religion in America," Pew Research Center Report, September 13, 2022, https://www.pewresearch.org/religion/2022/09/13/how-u-s-religious-composition-has-changed-in-recent-decades/.

10 Gregory A. Smith, "About Three-in-Ten U.S. Adults Are Now Religiously Unaffiliated," Pew Research Forum, December 14, 2021, https://www.pewforum.org/2021/12/14/about-three-in-ten-u-s-adults-are-now-religiously-unaffiliated/.

world, especially in Africa, Asia, and Latin America—but that does not change the lived experience of religious decline in the United States.[11] People are leaving the church, and some have stopped believing in God, though rates of atheism remain quite low.[12] Many Americans are simply not interested in attending traditional worship services, though they have not necessarily given up on God.

Besides the oft-reported statistics of religious decline, there are deeper spiritual problems in the United States. There is a general decline of voluntary organizations, and it appears that Americans are much less likely to be involved in meaningful community.[13] Arguably, this lack of community is leading to other problems. There are countless articles and research on America's loneliness epidemic, deaths of despair, lack of empathy, and generally poor public behavior during and after the Covid-19 pandemic.[14] Americans are constantly surrounded by

---

11 Pew Research Center, "Global Christianity—A Report on the Size and Distribution of the World's Christian Population," December, 19, 2011, https://www.pewforum.org/2011/12/19/global-christianity-exec/. Globally, Christianity is not in decline; however, there is a massive shift in religious affiliation across the globe. In 1910, there were about 600 million Christians, and in 2010 there were about 2 billion. This growth is largely due to population growth, since the overall global percentage of Christians has remained similar (32 percent in 1910 compared to 35 percent in 2010). However, the distribution of Christians has changed significantly. In 1910, Europe had 66.3 percent, and the Americas had 27.1 percent (with the Middle East/North Africa at 0.7 percent, Asia-Pacific with 4.5 percent, and Sub-Saharan Africa at 1.4 percent). In 2010, Europe had 25.9 percent of Christians, Americas 36.8 percent, Sub-Saharan Africa 23.6, Asia-Pacific 13.1 percent, and the Middle East/North Africa, remaining in a similar spot, 0.6 percent.

12 Jeffrey M. Jones, "Belief in God in U.S. Dips to 81%, a New Low," Gallup, June 17, 2022, https://news.gallup.com/poll/393737/belief-god-dips-new-low.aspx.

13 The book is now a bit dated, but it is still a good resource on the general decline in American community: Robert D. Putnam, *Bowling Alone: The Collapse and Revival of American Community* (New York: Simon & Schuster, 2000).

14 U.S. Department of Health and Human Services, "New Surgeon General Advisory Raises Alarm about the Devastating Impact of the Epidemic of Loneliness and the Isolation in the United States," May 3, 2023, https://www.hhs.gov/about

noise—from television, from social media, from an endless news cycle that makes its money on the latest panic. Modern lives are so busy and fast-paced that we have forgotten what makes a good life. America's plummeting rates of connection to one another and to God have not done anyone any favors. When freedom becomes the ability to do whatever you want, whenever you want, regardless of how it affects society, something has gone horribly wrong.

True community has been replaced by individualistic quests to find one's "authentic self," a phrase that is as vague as it is vapid. This can be seen in forms of popular spirituality, including both Christian and secular varieties. Unlike these popular forms of spirituality, true Christian mysticism is not an individualistic quest to "find yourself," nor is it "living your best life," though it is possible that one will accomplish those goals while engaging in mystical prayer. Because Christian mysticism is a deep and prayerful relationship with God, studying the Christian mystics of the past can help to overcome this modern tendency toward self-obsession and navel gazing. Even the most reclusive of the mystics, who were making a conscious choice to withdraw from the world, were concerned with their neighbor's well-being. Desert monks trained eager novices, anchorites gave council from their cells, monks and nuns did a great number of works of charity, and many mystics wrote about their experiences to inspire and teach others.

/news/2023/05/03/new-surgeon-general-advisory-raises-alarm-about-devastating-impact-epidemic-loneliness-isolation-united-states.html; Juana Summers, "America Has a Loneliness Epidemic. Here Are 6 steps to Address It," NPR, May 2, 2023, https://tinyurl.com/3utuz79u; Peter Sterling and Michael L. Platt, "Why Deaths of Despair Are Increasing in the US and Not Other Industrial Nations—Insights from Neuroscience and Anthropology," *JAMA Psychiatry* 79, no. 4 (2022): 368–74; Xochitl Gonzalez, "What Happened to Empathy?," *The Atlantic*, October 12, 2023, https://www.theatlantic.com/ideas/archive/2023/10/american-empathy-digital-isolation-humanity/675615/; Olga Khazan, "Why People Are Acting So Weird," *The Atlantic*, March 2022, https://www.theatlantic.com/politics/archive/2022/03/antisocial-behavior-crime-violence-increase-pandemic/627076/.

Christian mystics were propelled by their religious experiences to seek greater engagement in the world after building up their relationship with God.

While this attention to community may come as a surprise to some, especially considering America's hyperindividualistic society, the Christian life is first and foremost concerned with God and neighbor. As Jesus taught, the greatest commandment is this: "You shall love the Lord your God with all your heart and with all your soul and with all your mind.' This is the greatest and first commandment. And a second is like it: 'You shall love your neighbor as yourself.' On these two commandments hang all the Law and the Prophets" (Matt 22:37–40). The mystics knew this, and they lived it.

Yes, there is a process of self-discovery in the journey of building a relationship with God through prayer, but one will always need to stay orientated toward God *and* neighbor. This inevitably should lead to greater and deeper engagement with a community. Connection with God and neighbor is a central theme of this book.

On a more practical level, there are some other, less lofty benefits of studying the mystics. First is learning about inspiring stories of faith from the past. The lives and writings from the mystics tend to be personal accounts. While theological treatises are important, the mystics tend to focus on love of God, neighbor, and self. Doctrinal arguments and points of theology are rarely the point of their writings, and this can be refreshing for those who are familiar with a more academic understanding of Christian history and theology.

Second is the introduction of voices that are not always included in Christian histories, especially the voices of women. The field of history in general tends to favor the wealthy, the politically powerful, and the educated. While studying the mystics cannot completely remove these tendencies, the field includes Christian figures who were not necessarily the most powerful (though there are some mystics included in this volume who were very influential and well connected). A number of the mystics included in this book wrote in the vernacular, or the language of the common people, instead of Latin. Many were monastics but not necessarily members of the aristocracy or church hierarchy, and some were even lay believers.

Third is witnessing profound change stemming from mystical experiences. Chapter 7 is devoted to dramatic life change following a mystical encounter, which deals with extreme cases, but every single person included in this book was influenced by their experiential encounters with God. There are stories of soldiers becoming monastic leaders and aristocratic women leaving their lives of privilege to nurse the sick, and there are less dramatic but still powerful stories of believers reorienting their lives toward radical love of God and neighbor. These are inspiring tales that demonstrate that Christians can wake up each morning with the goal of being a light in the world.

How Can Modern Christians Relate to Mystics of the Past When Their Lives Were So Different?

Without a doubt, most Christian mystics, especially those from the early church and Middle Ages, lived in a way that was vastly different from modern American life. It is easy to think about how the life of someone in the year 300 or 1200 would have been enormously dissimilar from today. Few people move into hermit cells or wall themselves in churches in which they can never leave (more on this in ch. 2). In fact, most today would agree that this would be fanatical and unhealthy behavior. Even the mystics who lived a more balanced lifestyle devoted their lives to prayer in ways that would be challenging for modern laypeople to do. Yes, a few mystics were spouses and parents and employees, but most covered in this book were monastics or members of the clergy, and they were able to spend far more time attending to spiritual matters than Americans today.

These outward differences are not the only factors that separate our lives from those of the mystics. There are much deeper differences in worldview between those living today and those who lived in the past. In his helpful albeit lengthy examination of our secular age, philosopher Charles Taylor posits that humanity's understanding of the world has fundamentally changed in the West. The West is a disenchanted world in which belief is no longer expected. Modern, Western people simply do not see things as many of the mystics did (especially mystics who lived before the Enlightenment). He argues that it was virtually impossible not to believe in God in the year 1500, while it is easy, or even expected, not to believe today.

A person living in the late medieval era (or any time before that) lived in a world that testified to a divine purpose; God was indicated in the very existence of society, and people lived in an "enchanted world" in which spirits, demons, and moral forces existed.[15] While Taylor's exploration of how Western humans moved from a world of enchantment to a world of disenchantment is entirely out of the scope of this project, his argument that belief is merely one option of many is of particular relevance. To believe in God is not expected. Nor is belief in God quite the same as it was in the past, especially prior to the Enlightenment.

It seems unlikely that American society will return to an enchanted-world outlook, but that does not mean that modern people do not mourn this loss, nor does it mean that on an individual level people cannot engage in belief. In fact, the twentieth-century rise of Pentecostal forms of Christianity, a type of Christianity that emphasizes that the Holy Spirit is active in the world and in the lives of believers, suggests that a significant number of people are reacting against this world of disenchantment.

Despite the differences in circumstances and even the different understanding of how God functions in our world, there is a reason that the mystics have an enduring legacy in the church and society. While many things have changed, basic humanity has not. Nor has human desire to connect with God. The mystics' lives and writings can still be both engaging and relatable. Their instructions for how to pray

---

15 Charles Taylor, *A Secular Age* (Cambridge, MA: Belknap, 2007), 25–26.

and connect with God are still relevant all these years later—perhaps even more so because connecting with the divine is not necessarily assumed anymore. Many of the mystics are brutally honest about their own struggles, which brings profound comfort when one is struggling with prayer or relationship with God. It is helpful to see that before they were saints, the mystics were regular people who lived regular lives. They dealt with conflict and controversies. They had friendships, and some had marriages and children. Some were involved in great political and religious debates, but all dealt with the trials and tribulations that come with living.

Thematic Arrangement and Outline of Chapters

There are many ways in which to categorize Christian mystics, and all have benefits and drawbacks. This book uses a thematic approach, and there are two primary reasons for doing so. First, how a mystic's relationship with God manifests itself in the world is of particular interest in this study, and the thematic approach allows for examination of religious figures in light of how their relationship with God influenced their actions, including their public persona, their relationships with other people, and their interactions with institutions. Second, this is a more accessible way to approach the mystics than a more typical study based on chronology or theological similarities. It draws on commonalities between mystics who are separated by both place and time, and it demonstrates that there have been similar motivations and manifestations of mystical thought throughout the history of the church.

The book begins with a chapter on prayer and other spiritual practices (ch. 1). This chapter explores the ways in which mystics interacted with God. It provides common language for many of the activities and writings that will be discussed in later chapters. Following the chapter on prayer, I have the mystics in the following categories: those who withdrew from the world (ch. 2, "Escape"); those who became leaders as a result of their mystical experiences (ch. 3, "Leadership");

those who became involved in politics, both church and secular (ch. 4, "Politics"); those who used intellectual pursuits as their primary method of interacting in the world (ch. 5, "Intellect"); those who are identified primarily for their literary works (ch. 6, "Literature"); those whose lives were profoundly transformed by mystical experiences (ch. 7, "A Changed Life"); and those who carved their own paths, largely outside church institutions (ch. 8, "Controversy"). Finally, the conclusion looks at how Christian mysticism is manifesting in the modern world ("Conclusion: Mystics in Modernity").

Previous books on mysticism often group mystics by time periods or by salient features of their theology. Let us take a well-known mystic, John of the Cross, as an example. A chronological study of Christian mysticism would likely group him with Teresa of Ávila and Ignatius of Loyola because they were all sixteenth-century Spanish mystics. This book, on the other hand, emphasizes John of the Cross's literary contributions and therefore groups him with other literary mystics due to his beautiful and influential poetry. Neither of these categorizations is wrong, but they do influence the interpretation of both the religious figures and their writings.

Categorizing these Christian figures thematically is not to put them in a box or define them by only one aspect of their life or work. All Christian figures, including canonized saints, were complex human beings who worshipped God in a variety of ways, interacted with the world in a variety of ways, and also struggled in a variety of ways. They cannot be reduced to one-sided characterizations of themselves. Rather, the thematic lens highlights a particular aspect of their life that will be accessible and relatable to the reader.

The downside of this approach is that human beings are indeed complex, and categorizing them by theme is an artificial construction. Because of this, some will certainly quibble with how I have arranged the historical figures. Some mystics quite obviously fall into certain chapters, while other figures are a bit more ambiguous. Hildegard of Bingen, who influenced a shocking number of academic disciplines, could have reasonably been put in the chapter on intellect. However, she is in the chapter on leadership because her mystical experiences propelled her to lead, and this was a marked change from her previous lifestyle and became a dominant theme in the second half of her life. I have had to make choices, and while some will perhaps think a particular figure belongs in a different chapter, I do not think any of these categorizations are completely off base.

The benefits of this thematic approach outweigh the downsides. This thematic approach will demonstrate how these various themes have been present throughout Christian history. It will show the diversity of the mystical tradition and how this tradition has had an impact on the institutional church, popular religion, and even secular culture throughout the centuries. The thematic approach also welcomes the reader into certain aspects of Christian mysticism, and it is likely readers will feel pulled toward certain themes to which they most relate. This volume is meant to be an introduction and a place to explore the beauty and complexity of the Christian mystical tradition. These themes are simply more relatable than lengthy discussion of theological concepts that may or not be regularly considered outside the academy.

1

PRAYER

One day when I was busy working with my hands I began to think about our spiritual work, and all at once four stages in spiritual exercise came into my mind: reading, meditation, prayer, and contemplation. These make a ladder for monks by which they are lifted up from earth to heaven. . . . Reading is the careful study of the Scriptures, concentrating all one's powers on it. Meditation is the busy application of the mind to seek with the help of one's own reason for knowledge of hidden truth. Prayer is the heart's devoted turning to God to drive away evil and obtain what is good. Contemplation is when the mind is in some sort lifted up to God and held above itself, so that it tastes the joys of everlasting sweetness.

—Guigo II, *The Ladder of Monks*

THE ABOVE QUOTE is from a twelfth-century text called *The Ladder of Monks*, written by a Carthusian monk who is known as Guigo II or Guigo the Angelic. Guigo was the ninth prior of La Grande Chartreuse and the superior general of the Carthusian Order.[1] *The Ladder of Monks* is neither the first nor the only Christian text to use the imagery

1 La Grande Chartreuse was the head monastery for the Carthusian Order. The Carthusians were established in the High Middle Ages, and their first monastic house, La Chartreuse, was established by Bruno of Cologne (d. 1101) sometime in the early 1180s. The Carthusians are an enclosed religious order, and they observe a primitive form of monasticism, modeling themselves on the desert monastics. It was under the leadership of another Guigo, Guigo I (d. 1136), that the Carthusians expanded to a full monastic order.

of a ladder to describe the path of the Christian toward God.[2] It is a rather common image because it is such a helpful structure—it represents a process of ascending toward God. These four rungs, which Guigo writes about, of reading, meditation, prayer, and contemplation, can be seen throughout the mystical tradition. While these terms may not always be used in the same way among different mystical texts, the terms are used so frequently that a common understanding of each must be established. That is what this chapter aims to do—to provide common terminology for these practices and other concepts that are foundational to the mystical life.

The most fundamental aspect of the mystical life is prayer. This chapter discusses what it means to pray, different types of prayer, and concepts of positive and negative prayer, especially within the mystical tradition. Next, the chapter turns to reading, or specifically the practice of *lectio divina*, or divine reading. This will be followed by an examination of meditation and contemplation, supplemented by terms and experiences that mystics often refer to such as union, visions, rapture, and a few miscellaneous items such as stigmata. Finally, the chapter will discuss the Eastern Orthodox Church and the mystical form of prayer called hesychasm. Hesychasm has parallels with Western mystical practices but offers a different perspective, especially around the issue of continual prayer.

Some of these concepts are abstract, and others are difficult to accept as a modern person in a world that rarely believes in things that cannot be scientifically explained. However, mystics experienced such things as part of their spirituality, and these terms frequently appear in their own writings. Thus these terms will be used throughout the rest of the book. This chapter will provide an important foundation for understanding how different mystics understood God, prayer, their experiences, and even themselves.

---

2 See John Climacus, *The Ladder of Divine Ascent*, trans. Colm Luibheid and Norman Russell (New York: Paulist Press, 1982).

What Is Prayer?

People have been praying to deities for thousands of years, perhaps since the very beginning of humanity. Prayer is a universal aspect of religion that is shared across almost all religions throughout time, and it is indeed a foundational part of Christianity. It also provides the core of the mystical tradition. So, what exactly is prayer? Simply put, prayer is a spiritual communication between a person and God (or gods, in the case of a polytheistic faith). However, within a Christian framework, it is communication between a believer and the Triune God. Importantly, it is a two-way relationship. It may be helpful to think of prayer as a conversation. When one prays, it can be free-form, or one can pray the Scriptures or other prewritten prayers. Different Christians have described prayer in different ways, but a sense of dialogue is often present.

> **PRAYER: A DEFINITION**
>
> Prayer is a spiritual communication between a person and God (or gods, in the case of a polytheistic faith). Within a Christian framework, it is communication between a believer and the Triune God.

There is not one correct way to pray; different people find different prayers or methods of prayer helpful or affirming at different times. However, there are generally accepted categories of prayer that Christians frequently use, and these categories describe different ways in which prayer is done and how it shapes one's encounter with God. There are prayers of praise or adoration, which are simply prayers that praise God. There are prayers of confession. This can be a formal process, like during the rite of reconciliation (or confession, as it is usually colloquially called), or it can be more intimate and informal. Regardless, it involves confessing sins and shortcomings and asking for forgiveness. There are prayers of thanksgiving, which recognize the good things God has given and thank God. Prayers of supplication lift up requests to God. These can be petitions (which are prayers for oneself) or intercessions (prayers on behalf of others). There are also countless prewritten prayers that are profoundly important in different Christian traditions. The Lord's Prayer is undoubtedly the most important of the Christian prayers, because it is the one Jesus taught (Matt 6:9–13); however, others are deeply meaningful as well. Within the Catholic faith, for example, other prominent prayers include the Hail Mary and the Glory Be. Within the Orthodox tradition, the Jesus Prayer, which is discussed below, is vital. Finally, there is less formal prayer, simply talking to or listening to God.

THE HAIL MARY AND THE GLORY BE

Both the Hail Mary (*Ave Maria*) and the Glory Be to the Father (*Gloria Patri*), colloquially called the Glory Be, are traditional and beloved Catholic prayers. The Hail Mary is largely derived from Scripture, while the Gloria Be is a doxology, or words of glory.

Hail Mary:
Hail Mary, full of grace. The Lord is with thee. Blessed art thou amongst women, and blessed is the fruit of thy womb, Jesus. Holy Mary, Mother of God, pray for us sinners, now and at the hour of our death, Amen.

Glory Be to the Father:

Glory be to the Father,
and to the Son,
and to the Holy Spirit.
As it was in the beginning, is now,
and ever shall be,
world without end.

Prayer is a theme to which the mystics return again and again. Depending on the mystic, there are different understandings of the practice, but one can find commonalities throughout the literature. For the mystic, prayer becomes more than just a simple conversation between Creator and creature. Communication is an essential part of it, but there is a commitment to deep connection, devotion, and transcendent love—an inbreaking of the divine into the believer's being.

MYSTICS ON PRAYER

These quotes demonstrate that while there is variance in thought regarding prayer and prayer practices, there are also overarching commonalities despite these individuals having lived in vastly different times and contexts.

Desert recluse and eventual abbot John Climacus writes, "Prayer is by nature a dialogue and a union of man with God. It achieves a reconciliation with God."[3]

The epigraph from Guigo II at the beginning of this chapter describes prayer as "the heart's devoted turning to God."

Seventeenth-century French Catholic Francis de Sales explains that prayer "places our intellect in the brilliance of God's light and exposes our will to the warmth of his heavenly love, nothing else so effectively purifies our intellect of ignorance and our will of depraved affections. It is a stream of holy water that flows forth and makes the plants of our good desires grow green and flourish and quenches the passions within our hearts."[4]

3 Climacus, *Ladder of Divine Ascent*, 274.

4 Francis de Sales, *Introduction to the Devout Life*, ed. and trans. John K. Ryan (New York: Image Books, 1989), 81.

In a more modern take on prayer, American Baptist Howard Thurman describes it as "the *method* by which the individual makes his way to the temple of quiet within his own spirit and the *activity* of the spirit within its walls. Prayer is not only the participation in the communication with God in the encounter of religious experience, but also the readying of the spirit for such communication."[5]

Thomas Merton, a Catholic monk and social commentator who was a contemporary of Thurman, writes, "Prayer in not only the 'lifting up of the mind and heart to God,' but it is also the response to God within us, the discovery of God within us; it leads ultimately to the discovery and fulfillment of own true being in God."[6]

German philosopher, theologian, and Carmelite nun Edith Stein compares prayer to a ladder: "Prayer is a Jacob's ladder on which the human spirit ascends to God and God's grace descends to people. The stages of prayer are distinguished according to the measure in which the natural efforts of the soul and God's grace participate. When the soul is no longer active by virtue of its own efforts, but is simply a receptacle for grace, one speaks of a mystical life of prayer."[7]

Finally, Spanish Roman Catholic priest Raimon Panikkar asserts, "Prayer is the highest activity of the intellect, which does not just petition for private favors but connects with the Source of all intelligibility."[8]

---

5 Howard Thurman, *The Creative Encounter* (New York: Harper & Row, 1954), 34.

6 Thomas Merton, "Preface to a Collection of Prayers, 1961," quoted in *Thomas Merton: Essential Writings*, ed. M. Bochen, Modern Spiritual Masters Series (Maryknoll, NY: Orbis Books, 2000), 82.

7 Edith Stein, *Essential Writings*, ed. John Sullivan, OCD (Maryknoll, NY: Orbis Books, 2002), 123.

8 Raimon Panikkar, *The Rhythm of Being*, Gifford Lectures (Maryknoll, NY: Orbis Books, 2010), 62–63.

Apophatic and Cataphatic Prayer

With a basic description of prayer established, there are two concepts closely related to prayer and how one prays that hold significance when studying Christian mysticism. The words *cataphatic* (sometimes spelled *kataphatic*) and *apophatic* run throughout the literature on mysticism and mystical theology, and they are useful to think about how one is praying and what type of prayer in which one is engaged. Simply put, cataphatic prayer has content, and apophatic does not. Perhaps another way of thinking about it is that cataphatic emphasizes the knowable aspects of God, while the apophatic emphasizes the unknowable aspects of God (or God's transcendence).

For many, cataphatic prayer, which is sometimes also referred to as "positive prayer," is the most familiar and comfortable type of prayer. This type of prayer affirms things about God. It uses thoughts, words, images, and symbols. The Lord's Prayer is cataphatic. So is the Hail Mary and the Glory Be. If you pray while looking at an icon or a religious picture, this is cataphatic prayer. Even imagining talking to Jesus while praying would be cataphatic. The Ignatian *Spiritual Exercises*, which will be discussed further in chapter 7, is an example of using this type of prayer for spiritual progress.

In contrast to cataphatic is apophatic, also called "negative prayer," which emphasizes the unknowable nature of God. God is mystery, and the human mind cannot truly understand God's nature. This is a much more difficult concept than cataphatic. Trying to understand God by asserting God's unknowability is inherently abstract. The question is, then: How does one pray if God is unknowable? Of all the classic works of Western Christian mysticism, the anonymous author of *The Cloud of Unknowing* may best express this sense of apophatic, the mysterious and unknowable nature of God. The author writes about the darkness and the complete otherness of God. The author emphasizes how the believer needs to be at home in this darkness:

> *For in the beginning it is usual to feel nothing but a kind of darkness about your mind, or as it were,* a cloud of unknowing. *You will seem to know nothing and to feel nothing except a naked intent toward God in the depths of your being. Try as you might, this darkness and this cloud will remain between you and your God. You will feel frustrated, for your mind will be unable to grasp him, and your heart will not relish the delight of his love. But learn to be at home in the darkness.*[9]

Later, the author writes simply, "For the intellect of both men and angels is too small to comprehend God as he is in himself."[10] This type of understanding, or nonunderstanding, of God is often more associated with Eastern religions, but it has been an important aspect of Christianity since the early church. The benefit of apophatic theology is that God's transcendence is safeguarded, though the downside is that God may be seen as abstract and impersonal.

On the surface, these approaches of knowing or not knowing God may seem contradictory. However, these two types of prayers need not be in complete opposition. There is a sense in which God is both knowable—especially through the Scriptures and the Second Person of the Trinity, Jesus Christ—and beyond human understanding. Different mystics lean toward positive or negative understandings of God, and this aspect of their theology influenced their prayer life.

The terminology of apophatic and cataphatic in reference to God was first used by the author known as Pseudo-Dionysius. Pseudo-Dionysius takes his name from the Athenian who converted to Christianity after listening to St. Paul in Acts 17: "But some of them joined [Paul] and became believers, including Dionysius the Areopagite and

---

9 Anonymous, *The Cloud of Unknowing and the Book of Privy Counseling*, ed. William Johnston (New York: Image Books, 1996), 48–49.

10 Anonymous, *Cloud of Unknowing*, 50.

a woman named Damaris, and others with them" (17:34). The name is a pseudonym, and virtually nothing is known of the person behind the writing, who was active in the late fifth and early sixth centuries.[11] Regardless, this mysterious writer left an important legacy regarding mystical theology, another term he coined.

Pseudo-Dionysius intertwines positive and negative imagery beautifully in his writing *The Divine Names*:

> *God is therefore known in all things and as distinct from all things. He is known through knowledge and through unknowing. Of him there is conception, reason, understanding, touch, perception, opinion, imagination, name, and many other things. On the other hand he cannot be understood, words cannot contain him, and no name can lay hold of him. He is not one of the things that are and he cannot be known in any of them. He is all things in all things and he is no thing among things.*[12]

After stripping away the theological language, there remains the idea that one can know certain things about God, but one cannot know everything. There will always be a sense of mystery. One can dwell on the knowable but also the unknowable aspects of God through prayer.

While Pseudo-Dionysius was the first to use the terms *apophatic* and *cataphatic*, he did not invent the concepts. Chapter 2 discusses Evagrius of Pontus, a fourth-century monk and theologian, whose prayer life and theology was heavily influenced by the idea that God was unknowable. As Evagrius explains, "Never give a shape to the

---

11 Andrew Louth, "Apophatic and Cataphatic Theology," in *The Cambridge Companion to Christian Mysticism*, ed. Amy Hollywood and Patricia Z. Beckman (Cambridge: Cambridge University Press, 2012), 137.

12 Pseudo-Dionysius, *The Divine Names*, in *Pseudo-Dionysius, The Complete Works*, trans. Colm Luibhéid (New York: Paulist Press, 1987), 108–9.

divine as such when you pray, nor allow your mind to be imprinted by any form, but go immaterial to the Immaterial and you will understand."[13] There are many other examples of theologians employing a similar understanding or lack of understanding regarding God. One can find the beginnings of this theology in Plato; although not speaking of the Christian Triune God, he does refer to the highest reality as beyond being.[14]

While these concepts are particularly important when studying Christian mysticism and thinking about how one prays, the concepts are useful theologically in a broader sense as well. Whether one believes God to be essentially knowable or unknowable is going to profoundly affect how one prays and how one interacts with others, and it will even influence one's basic understanding of the Christian faith. Regarding mystical thought, an apophatic or cataphatic understanding deeply affected how mystics conveyed theological truths to others. To use a few particularly well-known mystics as examples, in examining the anonymous author of *The Cloud of Unknowing*, Julian of Norwich, and Hildegard of Bingen, one can see these differences play out in their theology and imagery. The author of *The Cloud of Unknowing* says one needs to become comfortable in the darkness. While the work is deeply mystical, there are no visions of the divine. There is intimacy, but it is not rooted in more conventional images. The book is primarily focused on the process of contemplation and abandonment. Julian of Norwich, who has a much more cataphatic understanding of God, provides incredible images of a relatable God. She writes of a God who longs to be known. Julian provides her readers with an image of God holding and preserving all of creation and loving that creation deeply. Hildegard of Bingen provides an interesting example of a cataphatic theology that is also deeply other. She uses language to describe the

---

13 Evagrius of Pontus, "On Prayer," in *Evagrius Ponticus*, by A. M. Casiday (London: Routledge, 2006), 193.

14 Louth, "Apophatic and Cataphatic Theology," 137.

things she witnessed, but the images are so strange and completely other that they can be profoundly difficult for readers to understand. For example, in her vision of the Trinity, which is discussed further in chapter 5, she writes of a sapphire man surrounded by fire and light. This is something that *can* be imagined, but it feels unfamiliar and strange.

Lectio Divina

One of the more important spiritual practices relating to Christian mysticism is the medieval practice of *lectio divina*, which is the prayerful study of Scripture. The term literally means "divine reading" or "sacred reading" in Latin, and Christians in a variety of traditions all around the world practice it. It is not the same as simply reading the Bible, nor is it the same as a Bible study. It is a particular type of prayer in which a believer *encounters* God through the reading of Scripture.

Lectio divina has its roots in Scripture and ancient practices. Reading sacred texts devotionally was part of religious life in both Judaism and early Christianity. There are plenty of examples of the Bible encouraging meditation on Scripture. The book of Deuteronomy, for example, extols the necessity of reading Scripture all the days of one's life to learn to fear God: "When he has taken the throne of his kingdom, he shall write for himself a copy of this law on a scroll in the presence of the Levitical priests. It shall remain with him, and he shall read in it all the days of his life, so that he may learn to fear the Lord his God, diligently observing all the words of this law and these statutes" (Deut 17:18–19). Or another excerpt, this time from the Psalms, emphasizes the importance of reading the sacred texts:

Oh, how I love your law!
    It is my meditation all day long.
Your commandment makes me wiser than my enemies,

for it is always with me.
I have more understanding than all my teachers,
for your decrees are my meditation.
I understand more than the aged,
for I keep your precepts.
I hold back my feet from every evil way,
in order to keep your word.
I do not turn away from your ordinances,
for you have taught me.
How sweet are your words to my taste,
sweeter than honey to my mouth!
Through your precepts I get understanding;
therefore I hate every false way. (Ps 119:97–104)

These passages demonstrate a type of reading that imprints on the body and soul; it transforms the reader. While these do not command *lectio divina* explicitly, this transformative nature is deeply connected to the practice.

The tradition of *lectio divina* developed in the early Middle Ages, though it likely is even older, and grew out of this general atmosphere of Scripture reading and reflection. Specifically, *lectio divina* is a key activity in the Rule of Benedict (Benedict and his Rule are discussed more deeply in ch. 3). Chapter 48 of the Rule, which deals with daily manual labor, states: "Idleness is the enemy of the soul. Therefore, all the community must be occupied at definite times in manual labor and at other times in *lectio Divina*."[15] In the Middle Ages, the Psalms were especially important because the Benedictine tradition organized each day around the Divine Office, or eight prayer services that ran throughout the day. All 150 Psalms were sung each week, and these were an essential part of monastic

15 Benedict, *Saint Benedict's Rule*, trans. Patrick Barry, OSB (Mahwah, NJ: Hidden Springs, 2004), 117.

spirituality.[16] While it is true that the origins of *lectio divina* have a strong footing in the monastic world, one can practice *lectio divina* in other settings. One can easily sit down to prayerfully dwell on the Scriptures anywhere.[17] *Lectio divina* can be a communal practice or an individual one.

LECTIO DIVINA

Lectio divina traces its roots back to early Christian communities, though it was particularly important in the Benedictine monastic tradition. It consists of four steps: *lectio*, or reading; *meditatio*, or meditation, *contemplatio*, or contemplation; and *oratio*, or prayer. *Lectio* consists of a slow and reflective reading of a short Scripture passage. This leads to *meditatio*, in which one is to reflect, or ruminate, on what was read. *Contemplatio* then is an openness to experiencing God. Last, one responds to God through prayer.

Set within this practice is the understanding that Scripture is a deep well. When one goes to Scripture, one must be open to the idea that an encounter with God is possible and that there are layers of different interpretations and experiences. This is unlike

16 E. Anna Matter, "Lectio Divina," in Hollywood and Beckman, *Cambridge Companion to Christian Mysticism*, 147–56.

17 For a helpful guide to practicing *lectio divina*, see Stephen Barany, "How to Practice Lectio Divina, Pray with Scripture," McGrath Institute for Church Life, University of Notre Dame, May 2, 2019, https://mcgrathblog.nd.edu/how-to-practice-lectio-divina-praying-with-scripture. Also, at the seminary where I work, Luther Seminary, we often practice dwelling in the word, an adaptation of *lectio divina* that focuses on reading Scripture in community. See: Faith+Lead, *Faithful Innovation Leader Companion* (St. Paul, MN: Faith+Lead of Luther Seminary, 2021), 16–19.

many modern methods of biblical interpretation, such as literal interpretation or the historical-critical method. Scripture is a place of active encounter. *Lectio divina* is at its core a mystical practice because Scripture becomes the place where one *experiences* God—and this experience is critical to understanding the practice. It is not necessarily about "correct" interpretation but how one experiences the text in that moment and how one can encounter God through the text. For some, this understanding of Scripture reading may be difficult to accept, especially if one is trained in modern biblical interpretation, which is an academic field, not necessarily a spiritual practice (though, of course, intellectual study can be a form of spiritual practice). If that is the case, one must set aside the tendency to analyze the text and open oneself to the possibility of encounter.

Meditation

Meditation is a term frequently used in the modern world, and in its more secular form it simply refers to thinking deeply or carefully, or focusing one's mind. The practice of mindfulness meditation is particularly popular today. In fact, retreat centers, wellness programs, articles, and even phone apps are ready to help people reach a variety of outcomes through the practice. A *New York Times* article even suggests that meditation can reduce blood pressure, ease anxiety, reduce the number of respiratory illnesses one experiences, help with hot flashes for women, and even ease the symptoms of irritable bowel syndrome.[18] The cure-all potential takes on an air of absurdity. It is best to acknowledge the modern understandings of meditation and then leave these behind because meditation in a Christian—especially medieval mystical—sense has very little overlap with the modern wellness idea of meditation.

---

18 Roni Caryn Rabin, "Ask Well: The Health Benefits of Meditation," *New York Times*, November 10, 2015, https://archive.nytimes.com/well.blogs.nytimes.com/2015/11/10/ask-well-the-health-benefits-of-meditation/.

The term *mystical meditation* is not entirely straightforward. Meditation has long been considered an important aspect of the contemplative life. It is usually seen as a training for prayer and contemplation—not an end in itself but a preparation. Early monks recited memorized biblical texts both in community and alone. This practice was called *meditatio*, or "meditation" in Latin. In the early Middle Ages, meditation was generally found in a monastic setting and was seen as a spiritual exercise connected with the private recitation of a text with the intention of memorization.[19] Guigo II says, "Meditation is the busy application of the mind to seek with the help of one's own reason for knowledge of the hidden truth."[20] This application of the mind can take on different forms. Twelfth-century English Cistercian monk Aelred of Rievaulx defines three types of meditation: "on the memory of Christ in the past, the experience of things in the present, and the expectation of what lies ahead in the future."[21] Meditation emphasizing self-knowledge is another important tradition that has carried through to the present day and can be seen in a variety of different mystical works and practices. Yet even meditation emphasizing self-knowledge is for the ultimate purpose of knowing God.

Meditation and the contemplative life were practiced by monks, nuns, and priests for much of Christian history. However, in the High Middle Ages, the term *meditation* began to be applied to devotional writings, and there was increased interest among the laity, especially among educated women. Therefore, there was an increase in meditative works written for the laity, which became an important part of medieval spirituality. The most popular of these medieval works was Bonaventure's *Meditations on the Life of Christ*.[22]

---

19 Thomas H. Bestul, "*Meditatio*/Meditation," in Hollywood and Beckman, *Cambridge Companion to Christian Mysticism*, 157.

20 Guigo II, *The Ladder of Monks: A Letter on the Contemplative Life and Twelve Meditations*, trans. Edmund Colledge and James Walsh (Kalamazoo, MI: Cistercian Publications, 1981), 68.

21 Bestul, "*Meditatio*/Meditation," 161.

22 Bestul, "*Meditatio*/Meditation," 165.

Contemplation

Most of the people considered Christian mystics today would not have used the term *mystic* to describe themselves. They would have called themselves *contemplatives* or referred to what they were doing as *contemplation.* The quote below comes from the preface to an 1860 version of the *Spiritual Exercises* and is a helpful definition of contemplation. Somewhat amusingly, the author notes that since so few people practice contemplation nowadays, it needs to be defined, which demonstrates that people always tend to think that those in the past were more religious, more faithful, or perhaps just better at prayer:

> *We contemplate rather than meditate when, after the memory has recalled the whole, or some detail, of the life of our Lord Jesus Christ, the soul, in a state of profound recollection, employs itself in seeing, hearing, considering the different circumstances of the mystery, for the purpose of being instructed, edified, and moved by it. . . . Thus, in meditation, it is the* understanding *which is exerted on an abstract truth, of which it seeks to be convinced; in* contemplation, *it is the soul that applies itself to the Incarnate Truth, which represents to itself the practical teachings of the Man-God, which applies itself to see, to hear, the Word made flesh—to* "contemplate" *Him; such is the word which has been chosen to express these acts.*[23]

The author of this passage highlights the difference between understanding and experiencing, which is a critical point in understanding contemplation. To contemplate, God needs to be the center of attention and the sole concern of the mind and heart. One should forget *all else.*

---

23 Ignatius of Loyola, *The Spiritual Exercises of St. Ignatius* (London: Burns & Lambert, 1860), xii–xiii.

Another quote, from modern scholar of mystical theology Mark McIntosh, provides a definition of contemplation that again emphasizes its extraordinary nature. Like in the previous definition, contemplation is not the same as thinking or even meditation. It is a practice that involves encounter:

> *Contemplation is not like normal thinking only muddled and tentative, on the contrary it is seen as an activity in which the mind is liberated to perceive clearly, freed from the usual constraints of distraction, self-preoccupation or prejudice. If what is perceived in the mind's clear vision is dark and mysterious this is not because pious emotions have muddled things to a murk, but because of the shocking intensity of the vision of reality that has broken through.*[24]

Later McIntosh notes that contemplation is not something one does but something to which one is invited.[25] While one does work to engage in a life of contemplation, it is ultimately God's action that makes it possible. While mystics talk of a process in which they grow in both their prayer life and relationship with God, they see contemplation as an invitation—something God gives a believer. It is not earned. A common misconception about the mystics is that they promote a works-righteousness that emphasizes human action, but the mystical life is about invitation, not works. One does nothing to deserve these spiritual gifts, and contemplation is not something one can do without God's help.

Contemplation is different from thinking about or understanding something, which is admittedly a little confusing for modern readers because today the word *contemplation* generally refers to thinking about something deeply in modern American usage. However, regarding prayer and spiritual practices, contemplation transcends

---

24 McIntosh, *Mystical Theology*, 11.

25 McIntosh, *Mystical Theology*, 12.

understanding; it is a way of *experiencing* God, especially in relation to the Second Person of the Trinity, Jesus Christ. Contemplation as experience is key to why mysticism is defined primarily as relationship in this book. One cannot have a relationship by simply thinking about another person. To have a relationship, one needs to interact with and experience the other. This is also the case for one's relationship with God. Thinking about God is not the same as having a relationship with God.

Miraculous Experiences

Prayer, meditation, and contemplation with the purpose of building a relationship with God are the primary aspects of Christian mysticism, but concepts and experiences such as union, visions, raptures, stigmata, and levitations are often associated with it. These miracles have always caught people's attention, and many people have reduced the mystical tradition to these phenomena. Even if this book's definition of mysticism places these occurrences in an auxiliary role in Christian mysticism, these are terms that pop up frequently through the literature, and thus having a shared understanding of them is helpful.

Mystical Union

Mystical union is the most important of these concepts. Like so many things related to Christian mysticism, the idea is complex, and people understand it differently. For simplicity, there are two broad understandings of mystical union: indistinct union and a mingling of the wills. Indistinct union is when the believer and God are completely joined. While this understanding has had precedence since the early church, it is less common within mystical literature and largely considered less orthodox. The type of union referred to as a mingling of the wills refers to believers' retaining their own sense of being after union with God. There is diversity of thought within each of these broad categories.

For some mystics, the ultimate goal of the Christian life is to completely and totally join with God. Sometimes this type of union is referred to as an annihilation of the self because the believer's goal is to completely lose oneself in God. This type of union is not possible within one's lifetime, but it is the ultimate goal of the mystic's life to prepare for it. Evagrius of Pontus, in *The Great Letter*, describes the process of becoming one with God through an analogy of rivers flowing into a sea. This analogy makes the difficult concept easier to grasp:

> *Do not be surprised that I said concerning the unification of rational beings with God the Father that they will be one nature in three persons without addition or alteration. If this visible sea (which is one in nature, colour and taste), when many rivers of different taste join it, not only is not changed to their qualities, but instead easily changes them completely to its own nature, colour and taste—how much more so the intelligible, infinite and immutable sea, that is, God the Father? When like torrents to the sea the minds return to him he completely changes them to his own nature, colour and taste: in his endless and inseparable unity they will be one and no longer many, since they will be united and joined to him.*[26]

Here God is compared to a sea, and believers are rivers that flow into the sea. Once a river flows into the sea, the river is for all intents and purposes lost; it has become one with something bigger, greater, more powerful. Evagrius describes the torrents of the sea changing the rivers into the sea's own nature. So too with believers and God in this understanding of mystical union. Does the believer retain any sense of self after becoming one with God? That depends on the mystic, though that sense of self would at least be profoundly changed.

Numerous mystics have held ideas of indistinct union throughout Christian history. A few examples are Meister Eckhart, some of whose writings were condemned by the Catholic Church; Margarete

---

26 Evagrius of Pontus, "The Great Letter," in Casiday, *Evagrius Ponticus*, 69.

Porete, often associated with the beguine movement, who was burned at the stake for her writings; and Jeanne Guyon, who was imprisoned after publishing a mystical text around the turn of the eighteenth century. As is evident from these references, religious authorities have often been suspicious of this particular understanding of mystical union, and the mystics who fell into this category often faced scrutiny.

The other major category of mystical union, called a mingling of the wills, is one in which there is a uniting of God and believer through bonds of love, but God and believer remain distinct. Another way to understand this concept is an alignment of the wills between Creator and creature. Marriage is a common analogy to describe this understanding of mystical union. In a marriage, two people are joined, but they do not become one being—they remain two distinct persons bound by love. Most of the mystics examined in this book, though the specifics of their theological understanding of union vary, fall within this category. While mystical union is a prominent theme throughout Christian history, it is not universal. In fact, early mystics often do not refer to union at all; the concept became common in the Middle Ages. While prayer and relationship with God are two concepts that bind the mystics as a group, becoming one with God—especially in its most extreme form, which can even advocate for annihilation of the self—is certainly not.

Other Miraculous Occurrences

Various other phenomena are associated with mysticism, though, again, these are not universal. However, they show up in enough writings and are sufficiently obscure to the modern reader that explanations are helpful. These include ecstasies, raptures, and flights of the spirit. The term *ecstasy* is often associated with a short-term union with God. The meaning of the word *rapture* has changed significantly over time. Most modern Americans will likely associate the word with the Left Behind series that was popular in the 1900s and 2000s.[27] However, in the medieval/

---

27 Tim LaHaye and Jerry B. Jenkins, *Left Behind* (Carol Stream, IL: Tyndale House, 1995).

early modern period, raptures were similar to ecstasies, but the experience would come on suddenly, even violently. Finally, a "flight of the spirit" is like a rapture or ecstasy but with an out-of-body experience. Like so many aspects of mysticism, these terms are somewhat flexible, but these short definitions provide an adequate understanding of these phenomena.

Finally, there are experiences associated with mysticism that are largely self-explanatory but still worthy of note. Visions are common in the mystical literature, and mystics reported seeing a variety of miraculous things, including Christ, angels, demons, and the dead. Julian of Norwich had a vision of the crucifixion. Teresa of Ávila, who had a plethora of visions, reported experiencing a few excruciating moments in hell. Catherine of Siena had a vision in which she was married to Christ. Marie of the Incarnation had a vision of the world that prompted her to turn to missionary work. Related is the experience of intellectual visions, in which knowledge is given to the mystic, almost like a computer download. Both Hildegard of Bingen and Teresa of Ávila, for example, reported this type of experience.

Sometimes mystics claimed bodily changes resulting from mystical experiences. Francis of Assisi was reportedly given the stigmata, which are the wounds of Christ—wounds on the hands, feet, side, and the wounds from a crown of thorns—after an extremely powerful mystical vision. Catherine of Siena also claimed to have had the stigmata, but unlike in the case of Francis, in which others testified that they saw the wounds, Catherine's were invisible. These miraculous experiences may be difficult for a modern reader to accept as real, though mystics found these to be both powerful and occasionally burdensome parts of life. The experiences were frequently seen as signs of their relationship with God, but they could also bring unwanted attention and scrutiny from skeptical church authorities.

Hesychasm

Much of this book is concerned with Western manifestations of mystical thought, but the Eastern Orthodox tradition has a mystical tradition that traces back to the earliest days of Christianity. An important Eastern mystical concept that has even had some impact on Western thought is hesychasm. This practice, which focuses on stillness and continual prayer, has its roots in desert monasticism. It will be particularly important when examining Eastern Orthodox mystics, such as John Climacus (ch. 2), and the Russian devotional novel *The Pilgrim's Tale* (ch. 6).

The idea that one can and should pray unceasingly is one that few modern Westerners would accept, but in late antiquity and at other times and places since, it was considered a defining trait of a Christian life, especially for monastics. This idea has its roots in Scripture. In Luke's Gospel, Jesus tells a "parable about their need to pray always and not to lose heart" (Luke 18:1). In 1 Thessalonians, Paul says to "pray without ceasing" (5:17), and in his Letter to the Ephesians, he says to "pray in the Spirit at all times in every prayer and supplication" (6:18).

The word *hesychasm* comes from a Greek word meaning "silence, tranquility, stillness," and it "denotes a major current in Greek Christian spirituality that fosters an intimate, contemplative relationship with God, typically, through fasting, vigilance, and prayer."[28] The specific "term *hesychia* is found in monastic literature since the fourth century to designate the mode of life chosen by hermits, dedication to contemplation and constant prayer."[29] Evagrius of Pontus and fourth-century desert hermit Macarius of Egypt were important early figures in the development of hesychasm. The prayer associated with hesychasm is often the Jesus Prayer. There are variants of the prayer, but the most common form is "Lord Jesus Christ, son of God, have mercy on me, a sinner." Since it is so short and simple, repetition of the prayer is easy.

---

28 Augustine Casiday, "Hesychasm," in *The Cambridge Dictionary of Christian Theology*, ed. Ian McFarland et al. (Cambridge: Cambridge University Press, 2012), 211.

29 Gregory Palamas, *The Triads*, ed. John Meyendorff, trans. Nicholas Gendle (New York: Paulist Press, 1983), 1.

There have been four major historical periods that can be identified in the development of the modern concept of hesychasm, and a brief examination of this history will help explain the importance of this particular mystical practice. The first period is of the desert fathers, which spanned from roughly 250 to 400. This was a time in which Christians went to the desert to seek out God in the wilderness, often in solitude. It seems that in its earliest form, the Jesus Prayer was simply repeating the words "Lord have mercy" (*Kyrie eleison*), which still is part of both Orthodox and Catholic liturgies. Macarius of Egypt, for example, is recorded as having said there was no need to waste time with words in prayer, and it was enough to simply say: "Lord according to your desire and to your wisdom, have mercy." [30] Regardless of variance, the Jesus Prayer is always a short and memorable phrase that invokes Christ and petitions for mercy.

The second period of development is associated with the monastery of Sinai in the seventh and eight centuries. John Climacus makes mention of reciting the Jesus Prayer in *The Ladder of Divine Ascent*. In step 27, which is of particular relevance, he teaches: "Stillness (*hesychia*) is worshipping God unceasingly and waiting on Him. Let the remembrance of Jesus be present with your every breath. Then indeed you will appreciate the value of stillness."[31] In the eight century, a priest known as Hesychios wrote a method of hesychastic prayer in *On Watchfulness and Holiness*.[32] He emphasizes attentiveness, the importance of stillness, and invoking Jesus Christ:

> *Attentiveness is the heart's stillness, unbroken by any thought. In this stillness the heart breathes and invokes, endlessly and without ceasing, only Jesus Christ who is the Son of God and Himself God. It confesses Him who alone has power to forgive*

30 John Meyendorff, *Gregory Palamas and Orthodox Spirituality*, trans. Adele Fiske (New York: St. Vladimir's Seminary Press, 1974), 24.

31 Climacus, *Ladder of Divine Ascent*, step 27, pp. 269–70.

32 Casiday, "Hesychasm," 211.

> *our sins, and with His aid it courageously faces its enemies. Though this invocation enfolded continually in Christ, who secretly divines all hearts, the soul does everything it can to keep its sweetness and its inner struggle hidden from men, so that the devil, coming upon it surreptitiously, does not lead it into evil and destroy its precious work.*[33]

The Jesus Prayer is bound up with the attentiveness and watchfulness mentioned. Hesychios specifically writes, "Watchfulness and the Jesus Prayer, as I have said, mutually reinforce one another; for close attentiveness goes with constant prayer, while prayer goes with close watchfulness and attentiveness of intellect."[34] Watchfulness or stillness and the Jesus Prayer reinforce each other. In this practice there is both the internal transformation and the external, physical practice of continual prayer.

The third period of the development of hesychasm is associated with Mount Athos in the fourteenth century. The two figures most tied to this movement are Gregory of Sinai, who was a proponent of "inner prayer," and Gregory of Palamas, who was heavily involved in public debates surrounding the practice.[35] Gregory of Palamas is of particular importance. As a monk, the archbishop of Thessalonica, and a skilled theologian, he was committed to hesychasm. After entering the monastic life, he practiced a hesychastic life, in which he spent five days of the week reciting the "prayer of Jesus" in his hermitage and rejoined his community on Saturdays and Sundays. He later became an abbot and was drawn into the arena of theological controversy.[36] Against theolog-

---

33 St. Hesychios the Priest, "On Watchfulness and Holiness," in *Philokalia: The Eastern Christian Spiritual Texts, Selections, Annotated and Explained*, trans. G. E. H Palmer, Philip Sherrard, and Bishop Kallistos Ware (Woodstock, VT: Skylight Paths), 105.

34 Hesychios, "On Watchfulness and Holiness," 107.

35 For a full explanation of the theological debates and Palamas's role in these debates, see Meyendorff, *Gregory Palamas and Orthodox Spirituality*.

36 Palamas, *Triads*, 5–6.

ical detractors, Palamas wrote a defense of the practice. According to scholar John Meyendorff, Palamas's intention, in his work *The Triads*, was to formulate a theological foundation justifying the hesychastic monks and their goal, which was the deification of human beings in Christ. "The main concern of Palamas is to affirm that this goal is not reserved to isolated 'mystics,' but is, in fact, identical with the Christian faith itself and, therefore, offered to all members of the church, in virtue of their baptism."[37] This was his critical move: this lifestyle was no longer for the spiritual elite, for those who could move to the desert and pray for five days a week, but was open to everyone.

Finally, there was a more modern revival of hesychasm in the nineteenth century. This revival was also rooted at Mount Athos, and a number of old texts relating to hesychasm were published. An excellent example of this particular movement, especially its influence on lay Christians, can be found in the nineteenth-century Russian text *The Pilgrim's Tale*, which I will examine in further detail in chapter 6.

Today hesychastic prayer is enjoying another revival of sorts. There are online resources and videos that can teach believers about this ancient practice.[38] Perhaps a practice that emphasizes stillness, watchfulness, and silence speaks profoundly to a people who rarely have the opportunity to be still or silent.

Prayer for a Modern World

This chapter has examined different types of prayer and spiritual practices, from the mundane to the extraordinary. After spending time

---

37 Palamas, *Triads*, 8.

38 One particularly helpful resource is from St. Vladimir's Orthodox Theological Seminary and focuses on the recitation of the Jesus Prayer. I have used this as a resources for students who want to learn more about this particular Orthodox practice. Albert S. Rossi, "Saying the Jesus Prayer," St. Vladimir's Orthodox Theological Seminary, accessed May 1, 2024, https://www.svots.edu/saying-jesus-prayer#:~:text=We%20are%20to%20breath%20naturally,slowly%20and%20reverently%20and%20attentively.

considering all this, it may appear that Christian prayer is highly complex. After all, there are some rather complicated theological concepts, historical debates, and obscure practices. And all of that is true; prayer and the study of prayer can be exceedingly complicated. Yet, at the root of it, prayer is simple. It is perhaps even ingrained in human nature. With a longing to connect with God, one engages in prayer in doing just that. Whether reciting an ancient prayer, engaging in contemplation in which we experience God, or even the simple plea "Lord have mercy"—it is all prayer. It is all an attempt to reach God, all an attempt to connect with something bigger than ourselves.

Suggested Reading List

Anonymous. *The Cloud of Unknowing and the Book of Privy Counseling*. Edited by William Johnston. New York: Image Books, 1996.

Benedict. *Saint Benedict's Rule*. Translated by Patrick Barry, OSB. Mahwah, NJ: Hidden Springs, 2004.

Guigo II. *The Ladder of Monks: A Letter on the Contemplative Life and Twelve Meditations*. Translated by Edmund Colledge and James Walsh. Kalamazoo, MI: Cistercian Publications, 1981.

Palamas, Gregory. *The Triads*. Edited by John Meyendorff. Translated by Nicholas Gendle. New York: Paulist Press, 1983.

Philokalia: The Eastern Christian Spiritual Texts, Selections, Annotated and Explained. Translated by G. E. H. Palmer, Philip Sherrard, and Bishop Kallistos Ware. Woodstock, VT: Skylight Paths, 2006.

2

ESCAPE

And so for nearly twenty years [Anthony] continued training himself in solitude, never going forth, and but seldom seen by any. After this when many were eager and wishful to imitate his discipline, and his acquaintances came and began to cast down and wrench off the door by force, Anthony, as from a shrine, came forth initiated in the mysteries and filled with the Spirit of God. . . . Through him the Lord healed the bodily ailments of many present, and cleansed others from evil spirits. And He gave grace to Anthony in speaking, so that he consoled many that were sorrowful, and set those at variance at one, exhorting all to prefer the love of Christ before all that is in the world. And while he exhorted and advised them to remember the good things to come, and the loving kindness of God towards us, "Who spared not His own Son, but delivered Him up for us all" (Rom. 8:32), he persuaded many to embrace the solitary life. And thus it happened in the end that cells arose in the mountains, and the desert was colonized by monks, who came forth from their own people, and enrolled themselves for the citizenship in the heavens.

—Athanasius of Alexandria, *Life of Anthony*

HISTORY IS NOT lacking examples of Christians who left secular society either to live in religious communities or to live as religious recluses. In either form of monasticism, Christians made a choice to seclude themselves to one degree or another. A monastic life, however, does not necessarily mean total separation from the world; in fact, many monks and nuns were actively engaged in the world. But for others, monasticism, especially its more solitary versions of hermit and anchorite, was indeed a form of escape. A cave, a hut, a cell, or even joining a monastic community could be a way to leave the world behind to focus on God.

The root of the word *monasticisms* is "alone"—so even the name itself implies solitude and escape. Indeed, the first monastics were generally solitary. Both men and women fled from the world, often going to the desert, to devote themselves to a life of prayer and penance. The question you may have is: What exactly were these pious Christians fleeing from? Accounts vary depending on the person, but societal changes were unquestionably at the root of the proliferation of monasticism in the fourth century. For about the first three hundred years of its existence, Christianity was illegal in the Roman Empire, which was the place of the faith's greatest growth during late antiquity. Persecution was sporadic but an ever-present danger. The act of committing to Jesus put someone in peril, so early Christians were serious about their faith. Early church literature is filled with harrowing tales of martyrdom, and persecution was a defining trait of the era.

At the beginning of the fourth century, Christianity became legal in the Roman Empire, and the church was free to flourish without threat of persecution. Despite the benefits of legalization, of which there were many, the church did face an existential problem. How could one be a true Christian when the church and the world seemed to be merging into one entity? For some, the solution to this problem was monasticism. A commitment to chastity and asceticism became a new type of sacrifice, and rejecting society to embrace solitude or communal living became increasingly popular.

As time marched on, new types of monasticism developed. Cenobitic forms arose, in which monks and nuns lived in community. Urban forms of monasticism developed soon after.[1] In

---

1 For more information on a monastic community of women founded by a patrician woman named Marcella, see Jennifer Hornyak Wojciechowski, *Women and the Christian Story: A Global History* (Minneapolis: Fortress, 2022), 37–38.

the West, the Rule of Benedict, which I will examine further in chapter 3, became dominant. In the High Middle Ages the mendicant orders emerged, with their emphasis on living out in the world that would reshape monasticism once again. Regardless of the type, monks and nuns experienced a duality of community and seclusion.

There are a couple of terms that are often used interchangeably but have distinctions that are important when studying this lifestyle. The term *hermit* generally refers to a person who withdraws from society "at liberty," which means they lived alone but could travel or move around freely. An anchorite (or anchoress, as women anchorites are often called) is solitary like a hermit but bound to live in a particular place.[2] Julian of Norwich, an anchoress, lived decades walled into a cell in a church. These monastic roles could be quite fluid in practice. Evagrius and John Cassian, both of whom I will discuss below, spent time in communal monastic communities and time as hermits.

It should come as little surprise that the monastic lifestyle lent itself well to mystical experiences. Religious recluses spent hours a day in prayer, and they kept intense fasts. Since they devoted their lives to building a strong relationship with God, eager Christians flocked to these recluses for training and advice. The mystics included in this chapter did escape the world, but they did not abandon it.

Anthony of the Desert (251–356)

The quote that began this chapter comes from a mid-fourth century book titled *Life of St. Anthony*. It was written by Athanasius of Alexandria, who served as the bishop of Alexandria and is best known for

2 Cate Gunn and Liz Herbert McAvoy, "Introduction: 'No Such Thing as Society'? Solitude in Community," in *Medieval Anchorites in Their Communities*, ed. Cate Gunn and Liz Herbert McAvoy (Rochester, NY: Boydell & Brewer, 2017), 5.

his relentless defense of Nicene Christianity against the early church heresy called Arianism, which claimed that Jesus Christ was created (and therefore not fully God). Through the course of his eventful life, Athanasius was exiled five times for a total of seventeen years. During one of his exiles Athanasius met Anthony and then wrote of his life. The book became a bestseller in the ancient world. Anthony was not the first monk, but he serves as both a prototype and an exemplar specifically regarding desert monasticism.

As a young man, Anthony was inspired by a passage in the Gospel of Matthew: "Jesus said to him, 'If you wish to be perfect, go, sell your possessions, and give the money to the poor, and you will have treasure in heaven; then come, follow me'" (Matt 19:21). That is what Anthony did. First Anthony trained with another man who had previously retreated to the desert, a spiritual father or abba. After this he moved to a tomb, where he lived on alms and battled demons (the account emphasizes that these were literal, not figurative, demons). Then he moved farther into the desert, where he continued to battle demons and experience visions.

MIRACLES, ANGELS, AND DEMONS

While miracles and miraculous events are not included in my definition of mysticism, it is difficult for one to truly and deeply engage with the history and theology of Christian mysticism without believing that miraculous events are at least *possible*.[3] This is not to say a reader must believe every single miraculous event; rather, the miraculous is so prevalent in mystical literature that to completely deny that

3 For a fascinating history of the impossible and how we are supposed to make sense of reports of the miraculous, see Carlos Eire, *They Flew: A History of the Impossible* (New Haven: Yale University Press, 2023).

aspect of so many mystics' experiences would be to deny an indispensable aspect of their faith. Later mystics, especially those who lived after the Enlightenment, tended to have fewer miraculous experiences, though there are still plenty even in the modern era. The other side of that coin was the presence of the demonic. For many mystics, especially mystics in late antiquity, the devil and demons were a real and present threat to both their spiritual life and their soul. Sometimes the demonic could take on bizarre forms. In one quote from Evagrius's text *On Prayer*, he tells of a monk whose experience with the demonic seems completely unfathomable to a modern reader: "I mean the monk John the Little, or rather, the Mighty, who remained unmovable from his communion with God, though a demon in the form of a dragon coiled around him and chewed his flesh and belched in his face."[4] While accounts like this are difficult to understand today, to entirely dismiss the spiritual battles so many mystics describe in great detail would be to dismiss an important part of their faith and experience.

In many ways, Anthony epitomizes the figure of the recluse—seeking holiness in solitude. Anthony detached himself from society to become a holy person worth emulating. He did not abandon his Christian concern for the neighbor. Anthony eventually emerged from solitude and agreed to train other eager Christians in his spiritual ways (provided they did not bother him too much), as is demonstrated in quote that opens the chapter. He taught his disciples about discipline, the love of God, and the benefits of contemplative life. He showed concern for the wider church and correct theological interpretation. He went to Alexandria twice—once during a particularly harsh

4 Evagrius, "On Prayer," 197.

persecution of Christians by the state under the reign of Emperor Diocletian and a second time to defend the divinity of Christ.

Anthony did not write about Christian mysticism, nor is there any systematic understanding of his theology per se. He was not a scholar or a theologian in the academic sense. He was a practitioner, and thus he left no writings behind; the sources that exist are those written *about* him. However, aspects of his story are easily identifiable as mystical, and his life served as an example to many others who desired to be mystics. He devoted himself to relationship with God through solitude, fasting, and prayer. His faith serves as an example of spiritual progress. As in stories of other holy people in the desert, Anthony is credited with healings, miracles, and interactions with otherworldly beings.

The popularity of *Life of St. Anthony* helped promote the monastic lifestyle in the fourth century. Monastic communities in Greece, Syria, Persia, Egypt, Nubia, Ethiopia, Sinai, Palestine, Arabia, and Asia Minor began to develop. After the fifth century, there was a growing tradition of monasticism in Western Europe as well. While monastic communities existed in a wide variety of contexts, there is something profoundly moving, perhaps romantic, about the early monastics who left the world in search of God in the harshness of the desert.

While Anthony's story was particularly famous, many others followed a similar path of holy lifestyle, controlling the passions, and devoting their lives to prayer in similar desert settings. Three of these monks were Evagrius, John Cassian, and John Climacus. All of these men were educated, and their writings address spiritual growth, relationship with God, and, in the case of Evagrius, sophisticated mystical theology. However, each provides more than just an example—they all had a long-term impact on mystical thought, prayer, and monasticism.

Evagrius of Pontus (345–399)

One of the most influential theologians of mystical thought, Evagrius of Pontus, was born nearly one hundred years after St. Anthony.

Before he was a hermit and a mystic, Evagrius was an extremely well-connected young man, who had a tendency, according to the sources, toward "vainglory and pride."[5] He secured an impressive ecclesial post in the capital city of the Roman Empire, Constantinople. He later fled to the desert as a means of escaping a tricky situation of his own making, and he eventually devoted his life to God in solitude. While his path to forsaking society may not have been the most pious, his became an important, albeit controversial, voice in desert Christianity.

Evagrius was born in the town of Ibora, which is now located in Turkey. He was the son of a bishop, and he was connected with prominent theologians and church officials. He was ordained as a lector by Basil of Caesarea, and Gregory of Nazianzus ordained him as a deacon. Evagrius went with Gregory of Nazianzus to Constantinople when the latter was installed as bishop of the city. Never wanting the appointment, Gregory quickly quit, but Evagrius stayed and continued to serve the next bishop, Nectarius, who was devout and of the senatorial class but unprepared for the position, especially considering he was not yet baptized at the time of his appointment.[6]

THE CAPPADOCIANS

Basil of Caesarea (also known as Basil the Great) and Gregory of Nazianzus (also known as Gregory the Theologian), along with Basil's brother, Gregory of Nyssa, are collectively known as the Cappadocian fathers. Each was a bishop—Gregory of Nazianzus even briefly occupying the prestigious post of bishop of Constantinople—and their

5 Robert E. Sinkewicz, "Introduction," in *Evagrius of Pontus: The Greek Classic Corpus*, ed. and trans. Robert E. Sinkewicz (Oxford: Oxford University Press, 2003), xvii.

6 Casiday, *Evagrius Ponticus*, 8.

theology was profoundly important in defending Nicene Christianity and developing the doctrine of the Trinity. Basil was an adept monastic organizer and is frequently referred to as the father of Eastern monasticism. Basil and Gregory of Nyssa also had an older sister named Macrina, whom Gregory writes about in his *The Life of Macrina*. They referred to her as "the teacher," and it seems likely she also was influential in the development of Eastern monasticism.

While in Constantinople, Evagrius became involved in a scandal. He fell in love with a married woman of aristocratic rank. It is unclear whether Evagrius had an affair or merely had fallen in love, but the situation had dire ramifications for his career. Sources state that Evagrius had a vision or a dream of being arrested as a result of this liaison. In the vision, an angel told him to leave the city. Likely there were also some concrete political signs that leaving would be advantageous, and Evagrius fled the city for Jerusalem, probably around the year 382.

In Palestine he met Melania the Elder, another prominent monastic leader of the era, and he was welcomed into the dual monastery she ran with her companion, Rufinus. Apparently Evagrius then began to doubt his commitment to a monastic life and returned to his old ways until he was struck down by illness. Melania, suspecting his illness was spiritual in nature, instructed him to set aside his worldly ways and become a monk. Once he agreed, he was cured within a few days. He took the habit from Rufinus (or in more modern terms, he became a monk), and then departed for the deserts of Egypt. He settled first in Nitria for two years before heading deeper into the desert to Kellia, where he spent the rest of his life. In Egypt he studied under two different monastic teachers, Macarius of Egypt and Macarius of Alexandria.[7]

7 Sinkewicz, "Introduction," xvii–xviii.

Evagrius brought a sophisticated intellectualism with him to the desert. He is particularly well-known for his system of categorizing evil thoughts (or sins) that block the way to God. Evagrius's list included gluttony, fornication, avarice, sadness, anger, acedia, vainglory, and pride.[8] This list was a precursor to the better-known seven deadly sins.[9] For Evagrius, Christians need asceticism to overcome these evil tendencies. Once this is obtained, the believer can pursue the contemplative life. It is worth noting the order here—it is necessary to aim for a perfect life *before* engaging in contemplation. This is in sharp contrast to other mystics who more readily accepted the limitation of human sin.

Another important aspect of Evagrius's mystical theology is the negative, or apophatic, aspect of it. For Evagrius, true prayer has no form at all because God is beyond form. This may seem like mere advice at first, rooted in his own opinions or prayer preferences, but he is explicit in his writings about the dangers of associating an image or shape with God:

> *Look out for the snares of the enemies. It may happen when you are praying in purity and without disturbance that some strange and foreign shape suddenly appears to you to lead you into the notion of rashly putting the giving in a place, so that you will be persuaded that the quantity which has suddenly revealed itself to you is the divine. But the divine admits of neither quantity nor shape.*[10]

Later, he argues even that yearning to see angels or Christ can make one go insane. There is little doubt in his writing that visual prayer is seen as negative. This runs in sharp contrast to many other mystics throughout the centuries. While visual prayer has long been considered

8 Sinkewicz, "Introduction," xxv–xxvi.

9 The seven deadly sins are lust, gluttony, greed, sloth, wrath, envy, and pride.

10 Evagrius, "On Prayer," 193.

a genuine way to pray, there is value in his warnings that other mystical voices have echoed. Evagrius does not want the Christian to be fooled by demonic creatures masquerading as angels or even God. Discerning between mystical experiences that are gifts from God and those that are hallucinations from Satan is a common theme throughout much of Christian mystical literature. One could argue that one's own imagination might be just as concerning and perhaps more relevant to modern Christians since many no longer believe in the devil and demons to the extent that people did in the past.

One final aspect of Evagrius's theology must be addressed, and that is his understanding of mystical union with God. His is not the view of the intermingling of wills that is far more common among mystical thinkers but a more extreme understanding of union as becoming one with God. His thought around this issue borders on self-annihilation (as briefly discussed in ch. 1). Those who held this type of understanding of union often faced criticism, and Evagrius is no exception. Evagrius was condemned at the Fifth Ecumenical Council in 553; his condemnation was largely based on his reliance on Greek philosophy and the theologian Origen (discussed more in ch. 5). While today many scholars respect Evagrius for his important contributions, he has had a cloud of suspicion follow him through the ages.[11]

Evagrius had a more literal escape to the desert than most. It was not just a desire to be free from the trappings of society; he needed to escape from a scandal. Even then, his transformation to a monk was gradual and prompted by an extreme illness. Once he made the commitment, he seemed to be all in, and he left his mark on the tradition. His mystical writings are foundational, and even though aspects of his theology were condemned, strains of his thought proved to be highly influential, particularly relating to a more apophatic understanding of mystical prayer.

---

11 For more on the condemnation, see Julia S. Konstantinovsky, *Evagrius Ponticus: The Making of a Gnostic* (Burlington, VT: Ashgate, 2009), 20–22.

John Cassian (ca. 360–ca. 435)

John Cassian, who was a near contemporary of Evagrius, had an eventful life. While there is a great deal historians do not know about this monk, and there are questions and debates among Cassian scholars on specific aspects of his life, there is still much from his biography that can be pieced together. He belonged to the Latin-speaking West (Latin was likely his native language), but he was also at home in the Greek-speaking East, and he served as a sort of bridge between the two diverging traditions. He lived as a monk in the desert, was an envoy for the patriarch of Constantinople, knew the pope well, was a founder of two monastic communities in Marseilles in Gaul (present-day France), and was a writer. He sought the solitude of the desert but was then forced back into the world. Due his own personal misfortunes and inability to continue a life of desert spirituality, he brought knowledge of desert monasticism and spirituality to the West, particularly through his books, *Institutes* and *Conferences*.

Cassian was likely born in the early 360s, but his birthplace is unknown. He describes the place of his birth as wooded, fruitful, cold, and without many monks. This description leaves quite a few questions.[12] Around 380, he went to Palestine with a friend and companion named Germanus, and they lived in a monastic community in Bethlehem. Cassian describes his community there as struggling with discipline, and it seems he was only there for a few years before he left for the Egyptian desert. While Cassian is reticent about many personal details, his information from Egypt is plentiful. He and Germanus likely lived there from the mid-380s to about 400. He spent time in the Nile Delta, in Scetis, and at Kellia.

Cassian was theologically indebted to Evagrius and Origen, and due to a theological controversy in which Origenism was condemned, many monks who were associated with Origen's theology had to leave

12 Columba Stewart, *Cassian the Monk* (Oxford: Oxford University Press, 1998), 4–5.

the desert, Cassian and Germanus included. From there the two went to Constantinople, where they sought refuge with John Chrysostom, the patriarch of Constantinople. After Chrysostom was deposed and exiled, Cassian went to Rome. At some point Cassian was ordained a deacon and Germanus a priest. Cassian's biography gets particularly fuzzy between 405 and 415. It seems likely Germanus died around 405.[13]

Cassian likely arrived in Marseilles sometime around 415. There he established a monastery for men named after the martyr who was buried there, Saint Victor. Cassian established another monastery for women, though the location and name are unknown, but his sister was a nun there. In fact, it is possible he founded the community for his sister. It was no secret that Cassian found the monasticism in Gaul unimpressive. He thought it was poorly organized and the monks to be lacking in discipline. He believed his new home to be a far cry from the superior Egyptian model. In Gaul Cassian wrote the *Conferences* (likely in the mid- to late 420s), which describes twenty-four conversations with notable abbas from the Egyptian desert about their spiritual practices. This was followed by the *Institutes*, likely written shortly thereafter, which describes the practices of cenobitic monks.[14]

Like many of the early mystics, Cassian does not describe miracles or altered states of consciousness. In fact, he explicitly writes against focusing on miracle stories and instead emphasizes fixing faults and aiming for a life of Christian perfection.[15] His foundation is his attention to prayer and relationship with God. A quote from *Conferences* in which he offers advice on how to pray without ceasing drives home this point:

> *Therefore, before we pray we should make an effort to cast out from the innermost parts of our heart whatever we do not wish*

---

13 Stewart, *Cassian the Monk*, 4–24.

14 Bernard McGinn, *The Essential Writings of Christian Mysticism* (New York: Random House, 2006), 89.

15 Stewart, *Cassian the Monk*, 17.

> *to steal upon us as we pray, so that in this way we can fulfill the apostolic words: "Pray without ceasing" (1 Thess 5:17). And: "In every place lifting up pure hands without anger and dissention" (1 Tim 2:8). For we shall be unable to accomplish this command unless our mind, purified of every contagion of vice and given over to virtue alone as to a nature good, is fed upon the continual contemplation of almighty God.*[16]

Like Evagrius, Cassian writes against vice and promotes prayer and contemplation of God. There is an attention to asceticism and perfection in this quote that highlights his understanding of what makes a good Christian life. This perfectionism may not appeal or be relatable to many modern Christians, but it is a prominent element among these desert monastics. Cassian, having lived in both the East and West, both in the desert and in cities, is an example of a bridge figure, a person who was able to walk in different lifestyles. He wanted to escape from the world, yet he kept being drawn back into it. Even when he finally founded his own monastic communities, he wrote for the purpose of helping his fellow monastics, and these works have been particularly important in the history of Western monasticism.

John Climacus (Sixth–Seventh Centuries)

The last desert monastic to be explored is John Climacus, or John of the Ladder, sometimes also called John the Scholastic. Climacus is the author of the wildly influential text—at least in the Eastern Orthodox tradition—*The Ladder of Divine Ascent*. He also has the rather unique experience of living three different types of monastic life in the deserts around Mount Sinai.

The details of his life are sparse, though scholars have managed to piece together a basic outline. It is unknown where he was born,

---

16 John Cassian, *The Conferences*, trans. Boniface Ramsey, OP (New York: Paulist Press, 1997), 331.

though it was around the year 579. He likely came from an upper-class family, and he had a good education, though it is unclear exactly when or where he received it. The skill with which he composed *The Ladder* demonstrates education and intelligence at a minimum.[17]

Sources say he went to Sinai when he was sixteen years old and placed himself under the instruction of a spiritual guide named Abba Martyrius. After the death of Martyrius, Climacus lived as a hermit in a place called Tholas. This was not a time of total solitude, however; he continued to see and give direction to visitors. After some amount of time, Climacus assumed the "third way" of monasticism, sometimes called semicenobitic or semi-eremitic, in which a small group of monastics live together under the guidance of a spiritual leader. After roughly forty years of living as a hermit, he was elected against his will as abbot of the central monastery at Sinai. This is a rather fascinating development, and one wonders how Climacus received such news. It is unclear exactly how long he held this office. During this time, however, he wrote *The Ladder of Divine Ascent* at the request of a superior at another monastery.[18]

The image of the ladder was not novel when Climacus wrote his text. For example, Gregory of Nyssa too uses the image of the ladder in his *Life of Ephraim*. However, Climacus leans heavily on the biblical imagery. In step 30, his final step, he directly addresses Jacob's ladder in the book of Genesis. He writes: "I long to know how Jacob saw you fixed above the ladder (cf. Gen. 28:12). That climb, how was it? Tell me, for I long to know. What is the mode, what is the law joining together those steps that the lover has set as an ascent in his heart? (cf. Ps. 83:6). I thirst to know the number of those steps, and the time required to climb them."[19]

---

17 John Chryssavgis, *John Climacus: From the Egyptian Desert to the Sinaite Mountain* (Burlington, VT: Ashgate, 2004), 16.

18 Chryssavgis, *John Climacus*, 16–19.

19 Climacus, *Ladder of Divine Ascent*, 289.

Climacus is linking his steps of mystical ascent with Scripture, though he draws on far more than the Bible throughout his work. The text is broken down into thirty different steps—thirty rungs on a spiritual ladder, imagery that has long captured the imagination of Christians. The thirty rungs consist of renunciation, detachment, exile, obedience, penitence, remembrance of death, sorrow, anger, malice, slander, talkativeness, falsehood, despondency, gluttony, lust, avarice, insensitivity (which gets three chapters), fear, vainglory, pride (and blasphemy), simplicity, humility, discernment, stillness, prayer, dispassion, and love. The final rung of Climacus's ladder is titled "On Faith, Hope, and Love." As he states at the beginning of step 30, "And now at last, after all that has been said, there remains that triad, faith, hope, and love, binding and securing the union of all."[20]

A criticism that is sometimes leveled at works such as *The Ladder* is that it emphasizes human works. Climacus is no Pelagian.[21] The ability to imitate Christ and grow in the holy life is only possible because of the incarnation, and Climacus is explicit that progress is only possible because of God. In step 15, "On Chastity," Climacus makes it clear that humanity is not able to overcome evil through any effort of its own. He states, "For they will then discover that deep down in their hearts, like a snake in dung, is the notion that by their own efforts and enthusiasm they made great advances in purity. Poor wretches!" Later, in step 23, "On Pride," Climacus states emphatically that "it is sheer lunacy to imagine that one has deserved the gifts of God."[22]

Medieval Anchorites/Anchoresses

As noted, hermits, anchorites, and anchoresses were common in the early church, and it is one of the oldest forms of monastic life, but there was a revival of anchoritic living in the late medieval era. One

20 Climacus, *Ladder of Divine Ascent*, 286.

21 For more on Pelagianism, see pages 149–50.

22 Climacus, *Ladder of Divine Ascent*, 183, 208–9.

unique aspect of this medieval movement is the overwhelming participation of women. These medieval anchorites did not flee to the desert; in fact, many were enclosed in urban spaces where they regularly interacted with people, both clergy and lay. In many cases, anchorites occupied a liminal space—neither in the world nor out of it, neither living nor dead.

Becoming an anchorite was a process, and there is considerable historical evidence for the anchoritic vocation, including ceremonies of enclosure, wills, court documents, bishop's registers, ecclesiastical documents, and personal correspondence.[23] One needed to gain approval from the bishop and demonstrate an ability to financially support oneself while enclosed. Once the anchoritic hopeful gained approval, then the anchor-hold needed to be either acquired or built. Then there was a ceremony in which the anchorite made vows, was given a requiem Mass (or at least final rites), and was sealed into the anchor-hold. "At that time, the anchorite was declared liturgically 'dead to the world,' and the cell became, in essence, a tomb."[24]

Yet, despite the connection between the anchoritic vocation and death, the medieval manifestation of the anchoritic life was geared toward engagement with society. Anchorites withdrew to their cells, but they were not cut off from society. Becoming an anchorite was a public proclamation, and anchorites performed a particular function in the church—a ministry offering intercessory prayer and council.[25] For women, who had few opportunities to engage in public ministry in the Middle Ages, this could ironically open doors to providing others with spiritual care and counsel. People assumed anchorites were especially wise and devout because of their religious commitments, and their

---

23 Mari Hughes-Edwards, *Reading Medieval Anchoritism: Ideology and Spiritual Practices* (Cardiff: University of Wales Press, 2012), 4.

24 Michelle M. Sauer, "Introduction: Anchoritism, Liminality, and the Boundaries of Vocational Withdrawal," *Journal of Medieval Religious Cultures* 42, no. 1 (2016): vi.

25 Hughes-Edwards, *Reading Medieval Anchoritism*, 6.

religious authority stemmed from their holy lifestyle. Depending on how old the person was when he or she entered seclusion, they could spend decades enclosed. English anchoress Elizabeth Scott, for example, likely spent thirty years in her anchor-hold, and another named Julian Lampett may have spent fifty years as an anchoress.[26]

Despite the bizarreness of the practice, "anchoresses of this type gained unprecedented esteem and greatly influenced religious life in the later Middle Ages. Dozens, more likely hundreds, of devout women converted to this way of life."[27] They were both isolated and in community. Julian of Norwich, discussed below, is a perfect example of this balance between seclusion and engagement. She was isolated in her doorless cell, yet she received visitors and offered counsel. She gained a level of fame and likely influenced a generation of anchoresses in the Norwich area.

There was no one way to be an anchorite, and different historical accounts feature different lifestyles. An anchor-hold was generally small, consisting of only one or two rooms. Though they did not typically have doors, there were windows so the inhabitant could receive food, get rid of waste, and interact with visitors. The anchoritic tradition was particularly prominent in England, where the height of its popularity was in the fourteenth century,[28] but there is ample evidence of anchorites and anchoresses elsewhere in Europe as well. Anchorholds were constructed in a variety of places, though they typically were somewhat public. In one study of five different urban anchoresses from the Low Countries in the twelfth and thirteenth centuries, one anchoress withdrew to an anchor-hold in what appeared to be a family monastery, one was enclosed in a chapel in a leper colony, two others were enclosed together in a lepers' monastery, and one girl of twelve

26 Hughes-Edwards, *Reading Medieval Anchoritism*, 7.

27 Anneke B. Mulder-Bakker, *Lives of the Anchoresses: The Rise of the Urban Recluse in Medieval Europe* (Philadelphia: University of Pennsylvania Press, 2005), 6.

28 Hughes-Edwards, *Reading Medieval Anchoritism*, 6–7.

was enclosed "in the street" and later moved to a Dominican convent.[29] Other studies have found that anchorites lived in cells constructed near or in gates, bridges, churchyards, and even church rafters.[30] All these places have a common theme of existing in fairly high-traffic areas.

Julian of Norwich (1342/3–after 1416)

The most famous of the medieval anchorites is Julian of Norwich. Historians do not know why Julian chose the life of anchoress; in fact, there is very little known about her in general, even though she is without question one of the most popular mystics today. Historians do not even know her real name—the name by which she is known, Julian, was likely taken from the church at which she was enclosed, St. Julian's in Norwich. That said, as one dives into her mystical experiences and theological reflections, she becomes relatable. For many, a lack of biographical information is eclipsed by a feeling of understanding as she shares her reflections on God.

Because her writings were profoundly personal, there is information we can glean about her life from her writings as well as her context in medieval England. Historians can confidently state that she was born in either 1342 or 1343; based on her skill as a writer, she was likely from a wealthy family. She was probably raised in or around Norwich, which at the time was a vibrant city in England known for its trade, industry, and commerce. Julian lived during a difficult time in history. She was a child when the round of plague known as the Black Death ravaged Eurasia. Julian would have felt this loss sharply, as there is evidence that the population of Norwich shrank from an estimated twenty-five thousand people in 1333 to as few as eight thousand in the 1370s.[31] Julian's life would have also been affected by war. She

---

29 Mulder-Bakker, *Lives of the Anchoresses*, 8–9.

30 Sauer, "Introduction," vi.

31 Julian of Norwich, *Julian of Norwich: Revelations of Divine Love*, ed. Barry Windeatt (Oxford: Oxford University Press, 2016), xvi.

lived during the Hundred Years' War between England and France. Violence, disease, and death were defining features of her time.

THE BLACK DEATH

The most significant event of the fourteenth century was a catastrophic outbreak of the bubonic plague, caused by the bacterium *Yersinia pestis*. The disease was transmitted by fleas, with black rats acting as the intermediate hosts. There was an outbreak of the plague in central Asia in 1347, and it spread to Italy in 1348. By 1350 all of Europe was affected, and it is estimated that a third of the population died. Within about five days of showing symptoms of the disease, most people were dead. Within about three years the plague waned, but resurgences swept through Europe every dozen years or so, generally killing the young. The effects of this pandemic cannot be exaggerated, and the impact was felt socially, economically, and even religiously for centuries.

As for the particulars of her life, there is debate. It is unclear whether she entered a Benedictine monastery young or married and had children but later entered a monastic life after losing them. There are references in her works that have made readers think she was a mother who experienced the loss of children, but she never explicitly states that she had children. Either option is plausible, and there is not enough evidence to say definitively either way.[32] It is also unclear when Julian became an anchoress, but there are four different wills that

32 Julian of Norwich, *The Writings of Julian of Norwich: A Vision Showed to a Devout Woman and A Revelation of Love*, ed. Nicholas Watson and Jacqueline Jenkins (University Park: Pennsylvania State University Press, 2006), 4.

provide evidence for her enclosure at St. Julian's between 1393/4 and 1416. She could have been enclosed before 1393, and she may have lived past 1416, but at a minimum she was enclosed in her cell for more than two decades.[33] While it is natural to think of an anchoress sitting in quiet and solitude, St. Julian's Church sat on a busy street in an industrial part of town, and Julian would have heard the hustle and bustle of urban life from her cell. It appears that Julian may have started a bit of a trend of anchoritic living in Norwich. She was the first recorded anchorite in Norwich since 1313, but "between thirty-five and forty-seven anchorites and hermits are reckoned to have lived in Norwich between c. 1370 and 1549 (of whom between twenty-four and thirty-five have been identified as women)."[34] Unfortunately, her cell was destroyed during the Protestant Reformation, but it was reconstructed after the church was hit by a bomb during the Second World War, and it is open to visitors today.[35]

While the biographical components of Julian's life are sparse, there is far more information on her spiritual life, her mystical visions, and her theology. When she was young, she prayed for three things: First, she wanted a vivid perception of Christ's passion. Second, she wanted to experience an extreme bodily illness—a sickness so severe it would push her to the point of death. Finally, she prayed for three "wounds": the wound of contrition, the wound of compassion, and the wound of earnest longing for God.[36] She experienced all three. In May 1373, when she was thirty years old, she became sick to the point that she and everyone else believed she would die, and she was even given last rites. During this illness she received sixteen showings or visions.

---

33 Julian, *Julian of Norwich*, xiii.

34 Julian, *Julian of Norwich*, xix.

35 David Ross, "Church of St Julian and Shrine, Norwich," Britain Express, accessed May 1, 2024, https://www.britainexpress.com/counties/norfolk/norwich/st-julian.htm.

36 Julian of Norwich, *Revelations of Divine Love, the Short Text*, trans. Elizabeth Spearing (London: Penguin Books, 1998), 1.

From these visions, Julian composed *Revelations of Divine Love*, which exists in two different versions—an early, short text, which consists mainly of an account of the visions she experienced in 1373, and a later, longer text, the result of a lengthy time of theological reflection. Even though women were not able to pursue a theological education at universities, wealthy women and nuns did often receive solid educations, and the longer text demonstrates Julian's skill as a theologian.

The dominant theme of Julian's writings is God's love for humanity. One better-known example of this divine love occurs in the fifth chapter of *Revelations of Divine Love*. God showed her something the size of a hazelnut lying in the palm of her hand, and God explained that *it is all that is made*. When she wondered how something so small could last, God explained: "It will last forever for God loves it. And so shall all things that are loved by God."[37]

Love runs throughout both the shorter and the longer text. In fact, this love is so abundant that while Julian does recognize both sin and suffering, there is a sense of universalism, that all will be saved. Her most famous, and often-quoted, line, "All things shall be well," is not some sort of platitude but a radical promise to creation. She explains that during one of her visions, God told her *all* would be saved, which was certainly not the prevailing belief during her lifetime. Yet, she very clearly states this universalist message:

> *Our faith is grounded in God's word, and it is part of our faith that we should believe that God's word will be kept in all things; and one point of our faith is that many shall be damned—like the angels who fell out of heaven from pride, who are now fiends, and men on earth who die outside the faith of Holy Church, that is, those who are heathens, and also any man who has received Christianity and lives an unChristian life and so dies excluded from the love of God.*

---

37 Julian of Norwich, "A Revelation of Love," in Norwich, *Writings of Julian of Norwich*, 139. I have modernized the language for ease of reading.

> *Holy Church teaches me to believe that all these shall be condemned everlasting to hell. And given all this, I thought it impossible that all manner of things should be well, as our Lord revealed at this time. And I received no other answer in showing from our Lord God but this: "What is impossible to you is not impossible to me. I shall keep my word in all things and I shall make all things well."*[38]

The quote is quite remarkable because the first part states what the medieval church taught about salvation—without being an active member of the church, one is destined to hell. Yet, in the visions, God told Julian that this was not the case. She was so surprised she asked God how this could be possible, and God replied that nothing was impossible for God, a possible echo of Luke 1:37. The God portrayed in her text is overwhelmingly concerned with creation, and Julian is to bring her revelation to the world so people can know God's love. In one example, toward the end of her longer text, Julian explains that there are types of goodness that God offers us, which highlight God as the source of our lives, God as our protector, and that God loves us and wants to us to unite with him.

When considering Julian's writings, it is easy to forget about the context in which she lived. The fourteenth and fifteenth centuries were not an easy time to be alive. As roughly one-third of the population of Europe and as many as two-thirds of Norwich died of a horrific disease, many wondered about God's role in such a tragedy. God likely did seem distant and vengeful. Julian's visions and writings instead show a loving God who very likely appeared radically different from the God that most people imagined.

Although times have changed, Julian's writings have remained popular. Her writings are highly approachable, in sharp contrast to some of her contemporaries. Some mystical texts are extremely difficult

---

38 Julian of Norwich, *Revelations of Divine Love, the Long Text*, trans. Elizabeth Spearing (London: Penguin Books, 1998), 86.

to get through. Some are highly abstract (Hildegard's *Scivias* comes to mind); others use language and terminology that are difficult for nonspecialists (and sometimes even specialists!) to grasp. Still other texts are just difficult to follow, such as Catherine of Siena's *Dialogues*. But Julian's language is straightforward. Her theology is articulate and mature, especially considering she did not receive any formal training, and she explains concepts in such a way as to make them understandable. That her writings are over six hundred years old makes this all the more remarkable. The overarching themes of her writings are still relatable to modern people. God is loving and active in the lives of those he has created.

Thomas Merton (1915–1968)

The impulse to escape from society never completely disappeared from Christianity, though manifestations of this impulse inevitably look different in the modern world compared to the ancient or even the medieval world. The last mystic included in the chapter is a Cistercian monk, specifically a member of the Trappists, who longed for solitude and contemplation. This is well-known twentieth-century writer Thomas Merton. On the one hand, Merton did live as a recluse (sometimes). On the other hand, he was continually drawn back into the world because of his care for it. Even after he became a hermit, he traveled, received guests, and continued to engage in the world around him.

There is a fascinating dichotomy to Merton's life. Merton was a modern-day mystic who persuaded his monastic order to reinstitute the practice of allowing monks to become hermits, and he lived the last years of his life in a hermitage. This is reminiscent of the monks in the desert and the anchorites in their cells. He physically left the world to go to Gethsemani Abbey, his monastic community, and then he retreated from his monastic community to live alone. Yet, for Merton, this life was not one of isolation or apathy to what was happening in the world. Merton's faith was interwoven with the affairs of the world despite his impulse for escape. As he explains in his book *Seeds of Destruction*, "I believe that Christianity is concerned with human crises, since Christians are called to manifest the mercy and truth of God in history."[39] To understand this tension within his life, between solitude and community, between contemplation and action, a look at his background is helpful.

Merton was the son of artists. His father, Owen Merton, was from New Zealand, and his mother, Ruth Jenkins, was American. By the time Merton was sixteen, both of his parents were dead, and he was left in the care of a physician and friend of his father who lived in England. Merton attended Cambridge, but his wild lifestyle, including fathering a child he never met, soon prompted his exasperated guardian to send him to the United States. There he attended Columbia University, where he connected with other students who were passionate about writing, and earned a master's degree in English in 1939. At Columbia he became interested in Catholicism. While reading a book on the life of English poet and Jesuit priest Gerard Manley Hopkins, Merton heard a voice asking him why he was waiting. He knew what he needed to do. This prompted Merton to walk nine blocks to Corpus Christi Church rectory and tell the priest he wanted to be a Catholic.[40] Two months later, he entered into the Catholic Church, and the following year he felt a calling to be a priest.[41] After spending Holy Week at a retreat at the Abbey of Gethsemani, Merton decided to become a Trappist monk in 1941.[42] In 1949, he was ordained to the priesthood,

---

39 Thomas Merton, *Seeds of Destruction* (New York: Farrar, Straus & Giroux, 1987), 10.

40 Thomas Merton, *Seven Story Mountain* (New York: Harcourt, Brace & World, 1948), 215–16.

41 Christine M. Bochen, "Introduction: Awakening the Heart," in *Thomas Merton: Essential Writings*, ed. Christine M. Bochen (Maryknoll, NY: Orbis Books, 2000), 23–25.

42 The Trappists are Cistercians of the Strict Observance. The name comes from La Grande Trappe, which was a Cistercian monastery in Normandy where reforms began in the middle of the seventeenth century. For more information, see "Our

and following this he was responsible for the spiritual formation of monks.

In addition to his religious vocation, or perhaps intertwined with his religious vocation, Merton was a prolific writer. While he had thought that entering the monastery would end his old life as a writer, his superiors encouraged it and gave him writing assignments. Through the course of his life, he published nearly fifty books, including works of poetry, essays, biography, autobiography, meditations, and social criticism.[43] In the early 1960s, he became a proponent of nonviolence in the face of nuclear armament and the escalation of the Vietnam War. In 1966, when Buddhist monk Thich Nhat Hanh came to the United States, Merton met with him, wanting to speak to him about what was happening in Vietnam.[44] Merton had a Christian understanding of nonviolence, which he explains in a letter he wrote in 1966: "Christian nonviolence and meekness imply a particular understanding of the power of human poverty and powerlessness when they are united with the invisible strength of Christ."[45] Seemingly at odds with his increased involvement in politics, Merton longed for more solitude, and in 1965 he was given permission to live as a hermit on

---

History," Trappist Brothers & Sisters: Cistercians of the Strict Observance, accessed July 13, 2023, https://www.trappists.org/history-of-the-trappists/history-trappists/.

43 Albert J. Raboteau, *American Prophets: Seven Religious Radicals and Their Struggle for Social and Political Justice* (Princeton: Princeton University Press, 2016).

44 Gregory Hillis, "Remembering Thich Nhat Hanh, the Buddhist Monk Who Thomas Merton Called a Brother," *America the Jesuit Review*, January 24, 2022, https://www.americamagazine.org/faith/2022/01/24/thich-nhat-hanh-thomas-merton-242268. Merton was also interested in conversing with Nhat Hahn about Buddhism because Merton had come to believe that Catholic monks had much to learn from an open dialogue with Buddhists. This fact is somewhat tangential to our investigation in Christian mysticism, but it is certainly worth noting. Merton saw the similarities and value in other faith traditions, which indeed speaks to his general commitment to the neighbor. More on this in ch. 9.

45 Thomas Merton, "The Way of Nonviolence," in Bochen, *Thomas Merton's Essential Writings*, 126.

the grounds of the monastery.[46] This time of being a hermit was short-lived; he died in Thailand in 1968 in what appeared to be an accidental electrocution.

Merton is a particularly interesting and relevant figure today because he balanced an ancient way of faith with modern engagement in the world. His writings on contemplation demonstrate a strong connection to past contemplatives within in the Catholic tradition, and a need to live within the modern world. In *Contemplation in a World of Action*, he discusses what the contemplative life is in the modern age. This serves as a defense of the monastic life but also provides a framework for modern contemplation for Christians both inside and outside monastery walls. His musing are helpful descriptions of what mysticism can look like today. He begins by recognizing his context, identifying humanity's place in the atomic age and that humanity now has the ability to completely destroy itself. He then asks a most pertinent question for modernity: "What does the contemplative life or the life of prayer, solitude, silence, meditation, mean to man in the atomic age? What can it mean? Has it lost all meaning?"[47]

The answer is that no, the contemplative life has not lost meaning. However, to truly gain an awareness of God, one needs to renounce selfishness and be open to radical transformation. The following quote from Merton looks like many other mystical reflections; this is not a new theology created to reach a modern person. He is going back to classic mystical theology and presenting the themes of purgation, illumination, and union, followed by a radical transformation:

> *To reach a true awareness of [God] as well as ourselves, we have to renounce our selfish and limited self and enter into a whole new kind of existence, discovering an inner center of motivation and love which makes us see ourselves and*

46 Bochen, "Introduction," 25–26.

47 Thomas Merton, *Contemplation in a World of Action*, 2nd ed. (Notre Dame: University of Notre Dame Press, 1998), 154.

> *everything else in an entirely new light. Call it faith, call it (at a more advanced stage) contemplative illumination, call it the sense of God or even mystical union: all these are different aspects and levels of the same kind of realization: the awakening to a new awareness of ourselves in Christ, created in him, redeemed by him, to be transformed and glorified in and with him.*[48]

While he is writing of classic mysticism here, he is bringing it to an audience who, as modern people, largely had little interaction with the mystics of old, and so in a sense the old becomes new.

While Merton sought this path to contemplation and transformation in a monastery, he makes is clear elsewhere that the contemplative life is not, and cannot be merely turning one's back on the world. He argues that it is impossible to completely withdraw from society.[49] This fact is even more true today than when he originally wrote those words. Even if the world seems overwhelming, it is simply impossible to ignore it. This is not to mention that ignoring suffering and injustice runs counter to the Christian message of loving God and neighbor.

In 2018, the *New Yorker* ran an article on Merton commemorating the fiftieth anniversary of his death. The article argued that Merton was just as relevant as ever. The final paragraph sums up well Merton's value for a society that has continued to experience violence, division, and declining religious engagement:

> *[Merton] sought the peace of pure and silent contemplation, but came to believe that the value of that experience is to send us back into the world that killed us. He is perhaps the proper patron saint of our information-saturated age, of we who live and move and have our being in social media, and*

---

48 Merton, *Contemplation in a World*, 157–58.

49 Merton, *Seeds of Destruction*, xiii.

> *then, desperate for peace and rest, withdraw into privacy and silence, only to return. As we always will.*[50]

The world is not peaceful or calm, but it never has been. Merton's path may help Christians find a way forward. Solitude and quiet time with God can prepare and refresh us to better meet the world and neighbor. It can help us be the type of person who can offer comfort and love in the face of animosity.

Escape for a Modern World

Perhaps this is the great lesson that can be learned from the mystics who left society: while one cannot run away and hide from the world forever, it is possible to retire from society for a while. Just as Jesus went to the wilderness for forty days and nights before he started his active ministry (Matt 4:1–11), modern people too can escape for a time to grow closer to God. After a time away, one can enter back into the world refreshed and ready for what awaits. During a time of solitude, it is possible to connect with God. It is through this relationship with God that we learn to look outside ourselves and our own wants and needs so we can concentrate on and care about others.

The desert mystics provide a glimpse at a lifestyle that is all but gone. Christians now rarely run to the desert to escape the hustle and bustle of worldly living. Yet this impulse to escape from society continues to manifest itself in different ways depending on the time and the context of Christian believers. Even today, there are those who want to go to nature to connect with God and recharge, and this movement includes not only Christians but those who identify as adherents of other religions or even no religion at all. The importance of camp

50 Alan Jacobs, "Thomas Merton, the Monk Who Became a Prophet: Fifty Years after His Death, Merton's Contradictions Have Made His Work All the More Instructive," *The New Yorker*, December 28, 2018, https://www.newyorker.com/books/under-review/thomas-merton-the-monk-who-became-a-prophet.

ministry and outdoor retreats also speaks to the continued interest that Christians have in escaping, if only for a little while, the trappings of urban life. While these modern ministries undoubtedly are different from committing to a solitary life in the desert, they do demonstrate the continued drive to seek God in creation.

The modern world is not made for quiet or stillness. Modern life is noisy and busy, and people are constantly just trying to get by. This is not good for the soul, and it is not good for our relationship with God. One of the great gifts the Christian monastic tradition has given the world is this history of prayer, contemplation, and service. While most will not leave society for a monastery or hermitage, we can learn from this tradition anyway. Some can go on short, retreat-style weekends or even some sort of do-it-yourself mini-retreat. Everyone can employ different types of monastic prayer and silence, and emphasize community and caring for the neighbor. No, we are not going to follow Julian's lead and wall ourselves away, but taking some quiet time to work on our prayer life could be a critical part of finding both ourselves and God in this chaotic modern world.

Suggested Reading List

Athanasius of Alexandria, *Life of St. Anthony*. Translated by E. Ellershaw. Philadelphia: Dalcassian, 2019.

Casiday, A. M. *Evagrius Ponticus*. London: Routledge, 2006.

Cassian, John. *The Conferences*. Translated by Boniface Ramsey, OP. New York: Paulist Press, 1997.

———. *The Institutes*. Translated by Boniface Ramsey, OP. New York: Paulist Press, 2000.

Climacus, John. *The Ladder of Divine Ascent*. Translated by Colm Luibheid and Norman Russell. New York: Paulist Press, 1982.

Julian of Norwich. *Revelations of Divine Love*. Edited by Barry Windeatt. Oxford: Oxford University Press, 2016.

Merton, Thomas. *Contemplation in a World of Action*. 2nd ed. Notre Dame: University of Notre Dame Press, 1998.

———. *Seeds of Destruction*. New York: Farrar, Straus & Giroux, 1987.

———. *Seven Story Mountain*. New York: Harcourt, Brace & World, 1948.

3

LEADERSHIP

I did "not come to be ministered unto, but to minister," says the Lord (Matt 20:28). Let those who are set above others glory in this superiority only as much as if they had been deputed to wash the feet of the brothers; and if they are more perturbed by the loss of their superiorship than they would be by losing the office of washing feet, so much the more they lay up treasures to the peril of their own soul.

—Francis of Assisi, *The Writings of St. Francis*

IN 1136, A thirty-eight-year-old German nun named Hildegard of Bingen was elected the leader of a community of women housed in a men's Benedictine monastery. Until this moment, she had lived in the shadow of her teacher, but everything would change within a few years. Hildegard and her monastic sisters eventually left Disibodenberg (against the wishes of the male leadership), and she established not one but two different monastic houses for women. Deeply rooted in Hildegard's identity as a leader were her mystical experiences. She did not leave her first monastic house on a whim. She believed that God was calling her to lead this group of women to a new religious calling in a new location. She spent the rest of her life as an abbess.

Chapter 2 focused on mystics who escaped from the world, finding solace in separation and sometimes solitude. This chapter discusses a number of individuals whose mystical experiences propelled them to leadership positions, especially within religious communities, though others found their leadership skills were put to best use out in the world. A particularly interesting trait that many of these mystic shared was a reluctance to lead. These were not people who craved power and influence. Their eventually leadership skills seemed to be born out of a genuine desire to follow God.

This chapter explores the dynamic leadership of Benedict of Nursia, Pope Gregory the Great, Hildegard of Bingen, Francis of Assisi, and Teresa of Ávila, and how all of each of these religious figures were propelled into leadership positions by their faith and spiritual lives. For some of these figures, their mystical faith pushed them toward a particular type of Christian leadership call, though they likely would have been leaders of some sort regardless. For others, especially the two women who are examined in this chapter, it was their experiences with mystical prayer that propelled them to lead despite a world that was not quite ready for them.

The Benedictines

In October 1943, in the midst of the Second World War, an Austrian officer named Lieutenant Colonel Julius Schlegel, along with a German officer named Captain Maximilian Johannes Becker, convinced the abbot of Monte Cassino, Gregorio Diamare, to move the abbey's library and archive. According to Schlegel, they moved around eighty thousand documents and seventy thousand volumes in addition to other artifacts such as works of arts, ancient vases, tapestries, reliquaries, and crucifixes. Over three weeks, monks, Italian refugees, and German soldiers transported around one hundred trucks worth of materials. What would prompt such a move? The Allied forces were advancing, and there was concern that the abbey would be destroyed. This operation proved to be worth the effort; Monte Cassino was bombed by the Allied Forces on February 15, 1944. After the war, the international community worked to rebuild the monastery, and it was reconsecrated in 1964 by Pope Paul VI.[1] The bombing of Monte

1 Kriston R. Rennie, "Second World War Fight to Protect Monte Cassino Abbey Was a Battle of Europe's History," The Conversation, August 4, 2020, https://

Cassino was not the first time the monastery had been destroyed by war, though hopefully it will be the last. What is so special about this abbey? Why was an Austrian officer willing to launch such an operation to save the treasures inside, and why did the international community come together to rebuild? Not only does the abbey have a long and important history housing countless historical treasures, but it was founded by one of the most important figures in Western Christianity, Benedict of Nursia.

The lives, faith, and religious calls to leadership of Benedict and Gregory the Great are examined together because the lives of these saints were intertwined, though the two never met. The only contemporary biography of Benedict was written by Gregory the Great in his four-volume work, *Dialogues*, in 593.[2] According to Gregory, the biography of Benedict was based on the reminiscences of monks who had fled Benedict's monastery, Monte Cassino, for Rome when the abbey was destroyed in a different war, by the Lombards, around 580.[3]

Benedict and Gregory were both called to be leaders, though both were hesitant, to say the least. Yet, both men rose to the challenge, and both had a profound impact on the church—Benedict in the establishment of Benedictine monasticism, the primary form of monasticism in the West for centuries, and Gregory in the shape of the papacy for centuries to come. They were both mystics, though Gregory, as Benedict's sole biographer, undoubtedly influences how Benedict's mystical thought is interpreted.

---

theconversation.com/second-world-war-fight-to-protect-monte-cassino-abbey-was-a-battle-over-europes-history-138697.

2 Carmen Acevedo Butcher, *A Life of St. Benedict: Man of Blessing* (Brewster, MA: Paraclete, 2006), 21.

3 Luke Dysinger, "Beholding Christ in the Other and in the Self: Deification in Benedict of Nursia and Gregory the Great," In *Deification in the Latin Patristic Tradition*, ed. Jared Ortiz (Washington, DC: Catholic University of America Press, 2019), 265.

Benedict of Nursia (ca. 480–547)

Benedict, a member of an old Roman family, was born around 480 in Nursia in central Italy. It was a chaotic and violent time in history. The Roman Empire was collapsing, and war, disease, and famine were constant companions of the era. Perhaps the chaos of the world drove people to embrace the order of Benedict's Rule, which he would eventually write for the monastic communities he established.[4] When he was a teenager he moved to Rome, and at seventeen he enrolled in a school of rhetoric, though he later left both school and Rome, disgusted by the moral depravity he found. In doing so he not only rejected his education but his status and family. He headed for Enfide (modern Affile), where he lived for a time before taking up the life of a hermit in a cave in Subiaco. He spent three years living as a hermit, with a monk named Romanus bringing him food.

Despite Benedict's reclusive nature, his fame as a holy man grew, and the monks of a nearby monastery named Vicovaro asked him to become their abbot. At first he declined, but he reluctantly agreed after they continued to pressure him. This proved to be a poor arrangement. In fact, Benedict's time as abbot must be one of the more disastrous calls in Christian history. The monks found him too strict, and their response was to try to murder him. The event is framed as miraculous; the monks put poison in his wine, and when Benedict went to bless the wine, the glass shattered, and he knew what they had done. He calmly reprimanded them and left for his cave.[5]

Benedict could not stay away from the world, though. People flocked to his cave to learn from him. Understanding his call to lead, he left his cave once more and built thirteen monasteries, each of which housed twelve men each, and became the abbot of all thirteen. During this time he began to work on his Rule. When high-ranking

4 Butcher, *Life of St. Benedict*, 39.

5 Butcher, *Life of St. Benedict*, 67; Gregory the Great, *The Dialogues of Gregory the Great: Book Two: Saint Benedict*, trans. Myra L. Uhlfelder (Indianapolis: Bobbs-Merrill, 1967), 8–9.

Roman officials started bringing their children to him, he began to build schools. Some time later, he and some followers founded the abbey at Monte Cassino, where he spent the rest of his life. The traditional date given for Benedict's death is March 21, 457.[6]

There are numerous reasons why Benedict is of interest in the study of Christian mysticism. The first is that he lived a life that should be categorized as mystical. His biography recounts a transformation he experienced later in life, in which he embraced a more mystical way of relating to God. Gregory's biography "depict[s] the transformation of Benedict from a spiritually powerful ascetic and miracle worker into a contemplative whose 'widened heart' can behold the ascent of saints into heaven and the whole universe scintillating within a ray of divine light."[7] Of particular note is his famous mystical experience, which included a vision of the world. The account, which appears nearly at the end of Gregory's section about Benedict, is told in dramatic fashion, but the basic premise is that Benedict saw both the entire world and the soul of a bishop being carried to heaven by angels:

> *Long before the night office began, the man of God was standing at his window, where he watched and prayed while the rest were still asleep. In the dead of night he suddenly beheld a flood of light shining down from above more brilliant than the sun, and with it every trace of darkness cleared away. Another remarkable sight followed. According to his own description, the whole world was gathered up before his eyes in what appeared to be a single ray of light. As he gazed at all this dazzling display, he saw the soul of Germanus, the Bishop of Capua, being carried by angels up to heaven in a ball of fire.*[8]

---

6 Butcher, *Life of St. Benedict*, 15.

7 Dysinger, "Beholding Christ," 265.

8 Gregory the Great, *Dialogues of Gregory*, 45.

Following the vision, Benedict learned that Germanus, the man he had seen taken up to heaven, had died at the moment he experienced the vision. With this additional information, both a mystical vision and prophetic knowledge were miraculously given to the saint.

Second, though not any less important for the study of Benedict, is the Rule of Benedict.[9] This is one of the most important texts for Western Christianity written. It was not the first monastic rule, nor the last, but it is the one that dominated Western monasticism from the Middle Ages to the present.[10] The Rule provides the outline for monastic life based on the virtues of humility, silence, and obedience.[11] As a former abbot writes in his introduction to the Rule, "St. Benedict writes as though speaking in a personal way to a fellow Christian who is seeking God in the context of monasticism. . . . What he writes is essentially an attempt to convey to others his own vision of the path of life that leads eternally to goodness, truth, and fulfillment."[12] The Rule is a practical text that gives order and guidance to a community. It is strict but not fanatical; it balances a life of communal prayer, reading

---

9 Benedict, *Saint Benedict's Rule*, trans. Patrick Barry, OSB (Mahwah, NJ: Hidden Springs, 2004). There are many different translations and versions of the Rule.

10 While outside the scope of this book, it should be noted that Benedict's rule did not immediately start transforming European society. A second Benedict, Benedict of Aniane (ca. 747–821), is largely credited with shaping monastic practices in the Middle Ages. He founded numerous monasteries based on the Rule of Benedict, and when Charlemagne's heir, Louis the Pious, took the Frankish throne, monastic reform was on his agenda. He called on Benedict of Aniane for the task. Councils in 817 and 818–819 resulted in the adoption of the Rule of Benedict for all monasteries within the Frankish kingdom. It unknown to what degree the requirements were enforced, but it is clear that the Rule did gain preeminence. For more information, see Greg Peters, *The Story of Monasticism: Retrieving an Ancient Tradition for Contemporary Spirituality* (Grand Rapids: Baker Academic, 2015), 119–23.

11 "The Rule," Order of Saint Benedict, accessed July 13, 2023, https://tinyurl.com/48sbcy2t.

12 Patrick Barry, OSB, "Introduction to the Rule of St. Benedict," in Benedict, *Saint Benedict's Rule*, 1.

(*lectio divina*), devotion, and physical labor. The book also emphasizes the presence of God within the community. Many of the other mystics in this book, such as Hildegard, Gertrude the Great, and Bernard of Clairvaux, learned and grew in their faith by following the Rule of Benedict.

THE FALL OF ROME

Historians debate whether Rome fell in the fifth century—a valid conversation, considering that the eastern portion of the Roman Empire, with its capital in Constantinople, continued to stand for another millennium. However, the city of Rome was sacked in the year 410, and the last western Emperor, Romulus Augustulus, was overthrown in 476. These events were signals that the glory of Rome, that eternal city, was in decline, and at least in the West, the medieval era was born.

Pope Gregory the Great (540–604)

The person who wrote the story of Benedict's life, Gregory the Great, was arguably one of the greatest popes of the Catholic Church. He was a scholar, monk, mystic, and leader. He expanded the office of the bishop of Rome, and he brought stability to people in a time of political chaos. Born around 540, Gregory, like Benedict, lived during the time when Rome was crumbling, but the Byzantine emperors still expected some degree of loyalty from the Western portion of the empire, though they could only loosely claim it.

Like Benedict, Gregory was born to an aristocratic Roman family, and he received a proper Roman education; he was one of the last of the Western leaders to be educated in that old system. His family had long been Christian. His great-great-grandfather, Pope Felix III, had also been the bishop of Rome,[13] and his widowed mother and three of his aunts all became nuns. When Gregory was young, he served as the prefect of Rome, but then he donated his properties to the church, turned his family's estate into a monastery, and became a Benedictine monk.[14] His time of peace and seclusion was not to last. He was pulled out of his monastery by the current pope, Benedict I, made a deacon, and put in charge of the church's charitable work. Gregory proved successful in his position, and the next pope, Pelagius II, appointed him as the papal ambassador to the imperial court in Constantinople. After six years, he was called home to become Pelagius's chief adviser until Pelagius died of the plague after a devastating flood in 590.[15] Considering the level of competence Gregory had already demonstrated through his career, perhaps it was inevitable that he would be elected the next pope. He did not want the job, but he did reluctantly take on the burden of both the office and the title of *servus sevorum Dei* ("the servant of God's servants").[16]

We must spend a moment on the context for popes during this time; it was challenging. Due to crumbling social structures, these church leaders became responsible for the city. They needed to ward off attacking enemies, pay imperial troops, ransom captives, and feed and clothe both refugees and the growing number of destitute Roman citizens. It is incredible how many different activities Gregory was involved in as pope. Some were typical, such as filling bishopric vacancies, promoting clerical celibacy,[17] and administering papal lands. Other activities were certainly a result of the power vacuum created by

---

13 Bernard McGinn, *The Growth of Mysticism: Gregory the Great through the 12th Century* (New York: Crossroad, 1994), 34.

14 Eamon Duffy, *Ten Popes Who Shook the World* (New Haven: Yale University Press, 2011), 51.

15 Duffy, *Ten Popes*, 52.

16 Duffy, *Ten Popes*, 52.

17 During this era, clerical celibacy was preferred but not required for priests.

the crumbling Roman empire such as organizing food lines, rebuilding infrastructure, negotiating with opposing armies, and interestingly "cultivating Catholic wives for pagan rulers."[18] Gregory famously sent a mission to England led by Augustine of Canterbury, which was one of the more successful missions of the era. He was also a scholar, and he wrote more than 850 extant letters. He also wrote longer works, including *Moralia on Job*, *Homilies on Ezekiel* (which contains some of his most mystical teachings), *Forty Gospel Homilies*, commentaries on the Song of Songs and on 1 Kings, the *Book of Pastoral Rule* (or *Liber regulae pastoralis* in Latin), and, of course, the four-volume *Dialogues*, which features the biography of Benedict.[19]

Like other patristic scholars, Gregory was not a systematic theologian; however, his theology was both competent and influential. He was most influenced by Augustine of Hippo, though he was more mystical than Augustine. It is not possible to provide a full analysis of Gregory's theology here,[20] but what is critical is his understanding that human beings were made to contemplate God. He writes: "For man was made to contemplate his Creator, that he might ever be seeking after His likeness, and dwell in the solemnity of His love."[21] For Gregory, this idea of humanity's primary function as contemplation goes back to creation, but the ability to connect with God was marred by the introduction of sin into the world. Bernard McGinn explains this connection with creation and contemplative life well: "For Gregory, Adam was first and foremost a contemplative, and a contemplative

18 Duffy, *Ten Popes*, 54. While this may sound like a bizarre activity to modern readers, royal and aristocratic women would often bring their Catholic faith with them into a political marriage and then influence both their husbands and future children. For more on this transference of religious belief in the early medieval period, see Wojciechowski, *Women and the Christian Story*, ch. 3.

19 McGinn, *Growth of Mysticism*, 37–38.

20 For those interested in digging deeper into Gregory's theology, McGinn has a fabulous chapter on him (*Growth of Mysticism*, ch. 2).

21 Gregory the Great, *Morals on the Book of Job*, trans. John Henry Parker, JGF, and J. Rivington (Oxford: Oxford University Press, 1844), 8.18.34.

who enjoyed continuous interior loving sight of God because he had been given . . . inborn firmness of station. The fall, first and foremost, was the loss of the ability to contemplate owing to Adam's turning to the exteriority of sin."[22]

Gregory's belief is more than just the view that contemplation is important; it names contemplation as the core human trait that was lost as a result of the fall. According to Gregory, God desires to restore Adam's contemplation at least in part, and it is through Christ that humans gain *soliditas caritatis*, or the bond of love found in the church. "Therefore, whatever contemplative experience . . . is granted to believers in this life will be less than Adam's—a partial, imperfect, but still precious restoration to what was once enjoyed in paradise."[23]

A few additional aspects of Gregory's theology are helpful to highlight. For Gregory, contemplation was humanity's state before the fall, but humanity's true nature was lost through sin. Even with Christ, humans cannot fully return to this state. The contemplative experiences open to people are found *in the church*. Considering his life, his experiences, and his ecclesiastical career, it is not surprising that he would think of contemplation as so deeply intertwined with the church. Gregory operated in perhaps the most privileged position within the church; while he originally wanted to be a monk, he was continually sought out as a leader. Therefore, he had a hand in shaping both theology and practice within the Catholic Church.

This view is not shared by all Christian mystics. For other mystics, the relationship between their mystical experiences and church hierarchy was more adversarial, even when the mystic was firmly orthodox in belief and housed within a monastic community. This tension, for example, was glaringly evident in the life of Teresa of Ávila, discussed later in this chapter. For someone like her, who faced difficulties due to both being a woman and living at a particularly contentious point in history, the church hierarchy posed challenges. Yet, for Gregory, the

22 McGinn, *Growth of Mysticism*, 50–51; Gregory, *Morals* 8.10.19.

23 McGinn, *Growth of Mysticism*, 51.

head of the Catholic Church, this intertwining makes perfect sense. His life and theology are a testament to how mystical thought, which on the one hand can be so unruly, can also flourish within a more structured setting. Gregory's faith propelled him to answer a call and lead in a traditional manner within a hierarchical institution, providing stability while the world around him held much instability.

Hildegard of Bingen (1098–1179)

Hildegard of Bingen, another Benedictine, who lived hundreds of years after Benedict and Gregory, was a bit of a late bloomer in terms of her leadership skills, though she was a mystic from childhood. She was also one of the most brilliant figures of the Middle Ages, leaving her mark in a wide variety of disciplines including theology, music, medicine, and literature. She corresponded with members of the aristocracy and leaders within the church, launched a successful preaching tour in a time when it was exceedingly rare for women to do so, and established two different monastic houses. Firm in her belief in her calling, she was not afraid to publicly disagree with both political and ecclesial leadership. She wrote extensively, so there is an unusual amount of information about her, including both biographical information and, more pertinent for this study, her mystical writings.

Her position as a monastic leader and a scholar is surprising considering how her life began. She was born in a village south of Mainz, in what is now Germany. She was the tenth child of noble parents and was given to the church as a child, though the details are a bit unclear. Historians know she was turned over to the care of a young noblewoman named Jutta of Sponheim when Hildegard was eight, and when Hildegard was fourteen, she and Jutta—and likely another woman also named Jutta, who acted as their servant—entered an anchor-hold at the newly constructed men's Benedictine monastery at Disibodenberg.[24] Today the monastery lies in ruins, but archaeologists

24 Honey Meconi, *Hildegard of Bingen* (Champaign: University of Illinois Press, 2018), 4.

have found evidence that Hildegard's anchor-hold consisted of two small rooms with perhaps a garden or yard.[25]

If Hildegard had stayed an anchoress, she would likely have been put in chapter 2 with the other religious recluses, but she did not, and it seems unlikely that being an anchoress was something Hildegard ever felt called to do. It was her teacher and companion, Jutta of Sponheim, who seemed to embrace a fanatical anchoritic life. Jutta was a practitioner of extreme forms of penance. In modern society, her activities would be considered self-harm, but in her time, people were impressed by what they thought of as Jutta's holy behavior. Visitors came to their cell, and Jutta offered counsel, prayer, and healing. It was one of the great ironies of being a medieval anchoress—by confining herself, Jutta was able to take on a public ministry. As her reputation as a holy woman spread, people asked Jutta to take their daughters to train in the holy life. The small anchor-hold could not accommodate the additional girls and women, so at some point, the cell was opened so others could join. From that point forward, the small community under Jutta's guidance operated more like a monastery within a monastery than a group of anchoresses.[26]

Jutta died in 1136, when Hildegard was thirty-eight years old. Immediately after, the women in her small community voted that Hildegard should replace Jutta as their leader.[27] Five years later, Hildegard had a mystical experience that changed her life and the lives of her nuns. Through this vision, which is recorded in the preface (which she calls her declaration) of her book *Scivias*, she gained an understanding of divine revelation.[28] The quote below articulates a phenomenon known as an intellectual vision. In an intellectual vision, the recipient

---

25 Fiona Maddocks, *Hildegard of Bingen: The Woman of Her Age* (New York: Doubleday, 2001), 35.

26 Meconi, *Hildegard of Bingen*, 6–7.

27 Meconi, *Hildegard of Bingen*, 7–8.

28 Carmen Acevedo Butcher, *St. Hildegard of Bingen: A Spiritual Reader* (Brewster, MA: Paraclete, 2013), 10–11.

receives a supernatural understanding of a topic, which in Hildegard's case was mainly a profound understanding of the Bible. There have been other mystics to claim such an experience, though this is a particularly explicit explanation of this type of vision.

> *It happened that, in the eleven hundred and forty-first year of the Incarnation of the Son of God, Jesus Christ, when I was forty-two years and seven months old, Heaven was opened and a fiery light of exceeding brilliance came and permeated my whole brain, and inflamed my whole heart and my whole breast, not like a burning but like a warming flame, as the sun warms anything its rays touch. And immediately I knew the meaning of the exposition of the Scriptures, namely the Psalter, the Gospel and the other catholic volumes of both the Old and the New Testaments, though I did not have the interpretation of the words of their texts of the division of the syllables or the knowledge of cases or tenses. But I had sensed in myself wonderfully the power and mystery of secret and admirable visions from my childhood—that is, from the age of five—up to that time, as I do now.*[29]

Not only did Hildegard receive the intellectual vision, but she also received a direct command from God in which she was told that she must share her visions with others.[30] Even with the direct command, Hildegard was scared to do so. Sharing mystical visions could be dangerous if church leadership believed the visions to be false, and she had reason to tread carefully. It was only after bouts of extreme illness and seeking approval from ecclesial authorities, which included the supervisors of her monastery, Bernard of Clairvaux, *and* the pope, that she begin to write.

---

29 Hildegard of Bingen, *Scivias*, trans. Mother Columba Hart and Jane Bishop (New York: Paulist Press, 1990), 59.

30 Hildegard, *Scivias*, 59.

Once Hildegard started to write, however, she did not stop. *Scivias*, her best-known work, consists of twenty-six visions and a theological explanation of each. The visions can seem wonderous and strange, even with her theological explanations. Below is an example of one of her visions, a description of the Trinity. It is an example of the otherness of her visions and the otherness of God, though she is still rooted in a cataphatic understanding. In it, the three persons of the Trinity appear as a man of sapphire, as a gentle, glowing fire, and as bright light. The Trinity is three but also one: "Then I saw a bright light, and in this light the figure of a man the color of a sapphire, which was all blazing with a gentle glowing fire. And that bright light bathed the whole of the glowing fire, and the glowing fire bathed the bright light; and the bright light and the glowing fire poured over the whole human figure, so that the three were one light in one power of potential."[31] *Scivias* is filled with images that are sometimes difficult to understand, even with her theological reflection, but they encourage awe.

Hildegard's visions prompted her to lead. In 1150, while she was writing *Scivias*, she felt God calling her to establish her own monastery, so she took twenty nuns and their priest and confessor, named Volmar, and moved to Rupertsburg, overlooking Bingen on the Rhine, where she lived for the next thirty-three years.[32] By 1165, her convent was so crowded that she established a second one at Eibingen, east of Bingen. She crossed the Rhine twice a week and visited the nuns in her other convent until her death fourteen years later.[33]

When Hildegard was young, she had very little control over her own life, though that was not unusual for girls and women of that era. From the available sources, it seems that her parents chose a religious life for her, and Jutta chose the life of an anchoress for her. Then she lived nearly two and a half decades in Jutta's shadow. Following Jutta's death,

---

31 Hildegard, *Scivias*, 161 (book 2, vision 2).

32 Butcher, *St. Hildegard of Bingen*, 11–12.

33 Butcher, *Hildegard of Bingen*, 22.

she led within her own community of women in Disibodenberg, but it was only after a profound mystical vision, which included a direct command, that Hildegard started to emerge as a powerful force in the church of the time. It must be emphasized how brave Hildegard was in choosing to leave the Disibodenberg monastery. She had literally spent decades walled into a two-room cell with other women—unable to leave, unable to make her own choices. Yet, following powerful mystical visions, she had the confidence to take her women and leave, trusting that doing so was what God wanted for their community. All her incredible accomplishments can distract us from the role she played as a monastic leader. She established two Benedictine monasteries for women, despite pushback from the male leadership at Disibodenberg. She was responsible for the leadership and pastoral care of over one hundred women in two different communities.

THE BENEDICTINES, THE FRANCISCANS, AND THE CARMELITES

There are numerous monastic orders within the Catholic Church. This chapters deals with people who were specifically members of the Benedictines, the Franciscans, and the Carmelites. The Benedictines (officially the Order of St. Benedict) are largely a contemplative order that follows the Rule of Benedict, written in the sixth century. The Benedictine life is devoted to prayer, manual labor, and study. The Franciscans (which consist of three different orders), a medicant order, were founded by Francis of Assisi in the early thirteenth century. They are committed to the ideals of poverty and charity. The Carmelites, who were approved in 1226, originally were a group of hermits located on Mount Carmel. However, losses during the Crusades forced the group to move to Europe, where they became a mendicant order.

The Franciscans

Francis of Assisi (ca. 1181–1226)

As with Benedict and Gregory, the lives of two important early Franciscans, Francis and Bonaventure, are intertwined. Francis was the great visionary, the one who founded a new religious order based on the radical idea of voluntary poverty. Bonaventure brought stability and unity to the conflict and chaos following Francis's death. Like Gregory writing about Benedict, Bonaventure wrote a biography of Francis, and so Francis partly can be understood through the eyes of Bonaventure (though, unlike with Benedict, there are other early accounts of Francis's life).

Francis is one of the most popular of all the Catholic saints, and he has a classic Christian saint biography—a sinner who became a saint and reformed the church. He was a mystic by any definition of the word, and his spirituality influenced countless others, including, of course, the many who joined the Franciscans. Francis was born to an affluent family in late twelfth-century Italy. To understand Francis's life, a brief explanation of his world is necessary. Francis lived in the Italian states during a time when the old feudal system in Europe was breaking down. The landed aristocracy was losing wealth and importance, and a new, wealthy middle class was emerging as a powerful force in Europe (sometimes members of this "middle class" were wealthier than the aristocracy). For centuries, land equaled wealth, but money was becoming a major economic force—in other words, capitalism was emerging. This economic system is important for Francis's story for two reasons. The first is that Francis's forceful rejection of wealth was tied to the economic factors that surrounded him. The second reason is that Francis's own father, named Pietro, was a member of the nouveau riche. He was a merchant who acquired a fortune through his business ventures. Francis, as his son, was not a noble, but he was wealthy enough to pass for one.

As a young man, Francis delighted in the finer things in life, such as fancy clothing and parties. But political instability, which was a regular occurrence in medieval Italy, brought war between Assisi and nearby Perugia, and Francis went to fight. He was captured and spent a year as a prisoner of war before Assisi negotiated the release of its missing soldiers. One would assume this would be the point in the story when Francis converted to a religious life, but he returned home and took up his old life of carousing, perhaps slightly less enthusiastic about it.[34] His conversion to the religious life was gradual, though Bonaventure describes a dramatic and mystical scene that took place while Francis was at Saint Damian's, a church outside Assisi, praying before the crucifix. This mystical moment had all the drama and excitement that one would hope for as Francis received a direct command from God:

> *And as with eyes full of tears he gazed upon the Lord's Cross, he heard with his bodily ears a Voice proceeding from that Cross, saying thrice: "Francis, go and repair My House, which, as thou seest, is falling utterly into ruin." Francis trembled, being alone in the church, and was astonied at the sound of such a wondrous Voice, and, perceiving in his heart the might of the divine speech, was carried out of himself in ecstasy.*[35]

On this side of history, God's words can be understood as a more general command toward church reform, but Francis took it quite literally—he decided to rebuild Saint Damian with his own hands. He also realized he could not stand to have money. The mere thought of possessing wealth, even for an hour, felt burdensome, even oppressive, and he rushed to be rid of it. He rejected his wealth and his family, to their dismay, and took up the life of a wandering beggar. He

34 Adrian House, *Francis of Assisi: A Visionary Life* (Mahwah, NJ: Hidden Springs, 2001), 41–46.

35 Bonaventure, *The Life of Saint Francis* (London: J. M. Dent and Co, and Aldine House, n.d.), 14.

was mocked, ridiculed, and beaten. He also began to gain followers, who were drawn into his life of voluntary poverty, and they formed a community.

In 1209, Francis went to Rome to receive papal approval for a new monastic order, which was anything but a guaranteed success, as there had been several religious groups in the era who bore some resemblance to Francis's small community who had been condemned as heretics. However, Francis's meeting with Pope Innocent III and the curia went well. Francis was given papal approval for his new order.[36] Francis and his brothers lived simply; their community did not acquire any wealth, and they spent much of their time preaching. Often this preaching was done outside church walls, especially in the early days, when priests were hesitant to invite the Franciscans to preach from their pulpits.

There is little question that Francis was one of the prominent mystics of the Middle Ages. After his conversion, he led an active prayer life, seeking to be in a deep and loving relationship with God. Throughout his life, he had visions and heard voices or music miraculously. Witnesses reported effusion of light, shared visions, and his ability to heal. However, there was one mystical experience that was rare, even by the standards of other medieval mystics, and it occurred in September 1224. This was more than a fleeting vision but rather a profound change to Francis's body:

> *One morning two years before his death, about the feast of the Exaltation of the Cross, while he was praying on the side of a mountain named Alverna there appeared to him a seraph in the beautiful figure of a crucified man, having his hands and feet extended as though on a cross, and clearly showing the face of Jesus Christ. Two wings met above his head, two covered the rest of his body to the feet and two*

36 House, *Francis of Assisi*, 89–99.

> *were spread as in flight. When the vision passed, the soul of Francis was afire with love and on his body there appeared the wonderful impression of the wounds of our Lord Jesus Christ.*[37]

This was the first, though certainly not the last, time in Christian history that someone reported experiencing the stigmata—wounds that appeared on the hands, feet, head, and side that corresponded to the wounds of Christ at the crucifixion.

Francis tried to imitate Christ as closely as possible, and, inspired by his example, his followers did the same. People saw his sincere faith and wanted to join this new monastic movement that rejected the wealth and comforts of the world. By the time Francis died, in 1226, it is estimated that there were over five thousand Franciscan friars. By the end of the century, there may have been thirty or forty thousand friars throughout Europe.[38] That type of Christian witness is astounding. That one life well lived could prompt so many others to devote their lives to God is perhaps miraculous.

Prompted by church reform enacted in the thirteenth century, the Catholic hierarchy grew increasingly reliant on the Franciscans to perform essential functions of the church. The Fourth Lateran Council, held in 1215, established a renewal program for Christian life. The council decreed that every Catholic should go to confession at least once a year and receive Communion at least once a year during the season of Easter. There was also a renewed emphasis on preaching. To accomplish these goals, the church needed clergy and increasingly looked to the Franciscans and the Dominicans (another mendicant

---

37 *The Legend of St. Francis by Three Companions* (London: J. M. Dent and Co, and Aldine House, n.d.).

38 Christopher M. Cullen, *Bonaventure* (Oxford: Oxford University Press, 2006), 6.

order, founded slightly before the Franciscans). These pastoral duties required an education.[39]

Francis had been wary of education. While some have emphasized his lack of education, it is not quite accurate to say he had none. Francis, being the son of a wealthy merchant, would have received a proficient education, and he apprenticed with his father, learning the skills needed to run a successful business, plus his writings demonstrate a brilliant mind. However, Francis did not attend one of the new universities that sprang up during the High Middle Ages, and he was concerned that the accumulation of knowledge could lead to pride. Despite his concerns, following his death, the Franciscans increasingly received higher education, and a network of Franciscan theological centers were established. While the general level of education did increase, only a few of the friars were sent to a university to study. Bonaventure was among those few.[40]

Bonaventure (1221–1274)

Bonaventure was the minister general of the Franciscans and later a bishop and cardinal. He was a scholastic theologian and philosopher, a canonized saint, and a doctor of the church. He is also considered one of the great mystics of the medieval period. The first biography of Bonaventure was written nearly two hundred years after his death, but there is still enough information about him to put together a reliable account of his life. He was born with the name Giovanni in a small Italian town. It appears his father practiced medicine, but little else is known about his family. In his own writings, Bonaventure states that when he was a child, he suffered from a grave illness, and through his mother's prayers to St. Francis, he was healed. According to canonization testimony, he was educated as a child by the Franciscans at their friary. In his teenage years, he went to the University of Paris to study.

---

39 Cullen, *Bonaventure*, 7.

40 Cullen, *Bonaventure*, 7.

He entered the Franciscan Order in either 1238 or 1243 and received his master's degree one year later. In 1254, he likely received his license to teach theology. Three years later, he and his colleague Thomas Aquinas received their chairs in theology. Bonaventure's appointment ended up being a moot point because he was elected the minister general of the Franciscans. When Bonaventure took the reins, the Franciscan Order consisted of thousands of friars divided into thirty-six provinces.[41]

In the years after Francis's death, the Franciscans faced internal division over the direction of their ministry. The situation grew worse after Bonaventure's tenure as minister general, but it was still factor during his time. Bonaventure moderated Francis's extreme stance on absolute poverty. For Francis, to imitate Christ, one had to be poor. It was *the* defining factor in his imitation of Christ. Bonaventure, on the other hand, "recontextualized poverty in the whole Christian life. Poverty is carefully presented, not as an end in itself, but as a particularly effective means in insuring two essential Christian values: (1) the fundamentally humility that every Christian should have before God, and (2) the charity that is the Christian life."[42]

Critical to understanding Bonaventure's mysticism is his text *The Mind's Journey into God.* Not only is it his most famous, but it connects beautifully to the life of Francis, thus providing an example of a truly Franciscan mystical experience and guide. Bonaventure wrote it in 1259 while on retreat to Mount Alverna, which is where Francis received the stigmata. Bonaventure explains:

> *While I was there, meditating on the different ways of the mind's ascent to God, there came to me among other thoughts the memory of the miracle which had occurred in this very*

41 Cullen, *Bonaventure*, 10–13.

42 Cullen, *Bonaventure*, 13.

> *place to blessed Francis himself: the vision of a six-winged Seraph in the likeness of the Crucified. In my meditation, it was at once clear to me that this vision represented not only the contemplative rapture of our father, but also the road by which this rapture is attained.*[43]

Within this text, Bonaventure structures the path to God around six levels of contemplation, which are symbolized by the six wings of the seraph that appeared in Francis's vision.

Particularly interesting about both Bonaventure's life and mystical theology is their close dependence on Francis. Bonaventure was educated by Franciscans, joined the Franciscan Order, led the Franciscan Order, and his theology and visions were tied to Francis. However, Bonaventure did not take everything from Francis uncritically. He adapted some of Francis's theology and became a prominent theologian of the era. Together the two men demonstrate both the continuation and the adaptation of early Franciscan ideals and theological perspectives.

A Carmelite: Teresa of Ávila (1515–1582)

Teresa of Ávila did not establish her own monastic order like Francis did, but she did reform the Carmelite Order, and her ability to lead these changes was a dominant theme in the later part of her life. Also like Francis, her spirituality influenced many people, both the men and women who followed her monastic vision in life and the countless others who learned from her writings over the centuries. Reading her books feels like receiving advice on prayer from an old friend, but they contain the wisdom of a brilliant woman who had one of the most

---

43 Saint Bonaventure, *Works of Bonaventure: Journey of the Mind to God; The Triple Way, or, Love Enkindled; The Tree of Life; The Mystical Vine; On the Perfection of Life, Addressed to Sisters* (N.p.: Mockingbird, 2020), prologue, section 2.

vibrant prayer lives recorded in Christian history. Her mystical experiences were intense, and she did not always knew how best to react to them.

That she lived during one of the most brutal periods of the Inquisition added another layer of anxiety and scrutiny to her life. For example, she wrote her first book, her autobiography, commonly referred to her as *Vida*,[44] because the Catholic Church wanted to examine her theology and mystical visions to make sure they were orthodox. She was ordered to write her third book, *The Interior Castle*, because the church wanted her to provide a guide on prayer for other nuns. She did not want to write the book, a point she makes abundantly clear, but it proved to be one of the great classics of Spanish literature. All three of her books, as well as her letters, show her incredible mystical experiences and her ability to rise to the occasion and lead others when necessary.

She was born Teresa de Cepeda y Ahumada in the city of Ávila in 1515, which proved to be a rather turbulent time to be alive. By the time she was an adult, the Protestant Reformation was in full swing, and while it is unlikely that she was ever able to read any Protestant writings in her Spanish convents, she certainly knew of the events happening in other European countries. She even comments on the Lutherans in France at the beginning of her second book, *The Way of Perfection*.[45] More pertinent to her own life was the increased activity of the Inquisition and the Spanish conquest of the Americas. The Inquisition was prevalent in Spanish society, and she had brothers leave for America in hopes of making their fortunes.

---

44 Literally "life" in Latin.

45 Teresa of Ávila, *The Way of Perfection*, trans. Paula Hutson (Brewster, MA: Paraclete, 2009), 7. It is unclear whether she actually means Lutherans specifically here or whether it is just the term she is using for Protestants in general.

> **THE INQUISITION**
>
> While the Catholic Church had long investigated incidents of heresy, starting in the thirteenth century, the powers of investigation became centralized and vested in an ecclesial office known as the Inquisition. This amounted to a special court system, which included investigators, examiners, security forces, and judges (inquisitors). In 1229, the Office of the Inquisition was turned over to the Dominican Order.
>
> The Spanish Inquisition, which began in the fifteenth century, was notoriously fanatical and horrifically brutal even by the standards of the medieval Inquisition. In 1478, Pope Sixtus IV issued a bull that authorized the Spanish monarchs, Ferdinand and Isabella, the right to name inquisitors, which essentially gave the state power over the office. The result was so brutal that the pope tried to limit the power of the Inquisition, but to no avail. The Inquisition was used not only to hunt down supposed heresies but also for political and personal gain and even vengeance. It has long been remembered as an example of the dangers of religious extremism.

Both sides of her family were members of the nobility,[46] and Teresa lived a comfortable childhood. As a teenager, she seemed to

---

46 Teresa's mother was from an old Christian family that happened to be one of the leading families in Ávila, but Teresa's father was not. His father, Juan, had been the son of a *converso* (a Jewish person who converted to Catholicism) and had been convicted by the Inquisition as a Judaizer in Toledo. He had confessed to his alleged crimes and was given a pardon and a relatively lenient punishment, for the time, of public shaming. After the ordeal, Juan moved his family out of Toledo to Ávila, and the family began to use his wife's name. Juan obtained a court document to affirm his nobility, and the family hid their Jewish roots and entered fully into the old

have a wild streak, and her father sent her off to an Augustinian convent in 1536 at the age of fifteen. While she was there, she decided she wanted to become a nun; however, she deemed the Augustinians too strict. Instead she joined the Carmelite Convent of the Incarnation in Ávila, which was wealthy, not cloistered, and allowed her to receive guests into the convent; she was also able to leave to visit family and friends. Shortly after she took her final vows, she became ill, and by the following fall her father had removed her from the convent and brought her to her older sister's house. By 1539 she was so sick that he took her home to Ávila to die. Following a seizure, Teresa fell unconscious for four days, and things were so dire that her family believed she actually did die.[47]

Teresa regained consciousness, but she was bedridden, paralyzed, and in need of constant care. Four long years later, she was finally well enough to resume regular life, though certain ailments plagued her for the rest of her life. She spent the next twelve years in a state of rather lukewarm religiosity. It was not that she did not desire a more robust spiritual life, but she struggled for a variety of reasons. In the following quote, she explains how she did the best she could, but without an adequate spiritual guide, she could only go so far in her prayer life. Her situation of desiring a more robust relationship with God but being without the tools to achieve it is still relatable:

> *I set out on the path of contemplation with all my might. By now, God had begun to give me the gift of tears, and I would spend hours in solitude, reading and crying. I went to confession frequently. With only my book to guide me, I did the best I could. I couldn't find a spiritual master who understood me, though I spent the next twenty years searching*

Christian society. It has been a point of scholarly debate whether Teresa knew about this family history. For more information, see Carlos Eire, *The Life of Saint Teresa of Avila* (Princeton: Princeton University Press, 2019), 4–5.

47 Teresa, *Book of My Life*, 29.

> *for one. This lack of guidance hurt me; I was constantly backsliding and almost lost completely.*[48]

It is easy to gloss over this twenty-year span in which she struggled spiritually because her miracles and accomplishments later are so profound. But this time of frustration is very much part of her story, and it is a part of her story that many need to hear. While the saints are often portrayed as perfect, they too were human beings with their own problems. Seeing these frustrations and struggles can show others that a holy life and a robust prayer life is a process. If even someone as well-regarded as Teresa spent two decades struggling, others should not expect perfection immediately.

After her long season of frustration, things changed dramatically for Teresa in 1554 when she had a radical conversion experience. She had a vision of Christ in which she came to understand how he had suffered for her, and she was transformed. She still struggled with prayer and being misunderstood by confessors, but her life took on new meaning. She had a vibrant prayer life, and she reported a variety of mystical experiences, including visions of Jesus, angels, demons, and the dead. She had intellectual visions that gave her theological knowledge. She also reported miraculous physical experiences—specifically, she levitated, something she found embarrassing and prayed to God to stop. Her most famous mystical experience is known as the transverberation, which was immortalized in the sculptural altarpiece *Ecstasy of St. Teresa* by Gian Lorenza Bernini, in which an angel pierced her heart with a flaming lance. All this activity brought attention from some and scorn from others—but it also brought suspicion from church authorities, thus the writing of her autobiography so she could be examined. The church found her experiences to be genuine miracles and her theology to be orthodox.

Teresa was propelled by her relationship with God to become a monastic leader and reform the Carmelite Order. She believed that

---

48 Teresa, *Book of My Life*, 20.

God was calling her to return her order to its original interpretation of its monastic rule, which included enclosure, poverty, and a commitment to silent prayer. Her nuns were to be discalced, which meant wearing sandals instead of shoes, to show their commitment to poverty. A critical aspect of her reforms was to accept women of all social classes. Dowries were welcomed but not required, and a faithful woman seeking a monastic life would not be turned away due to lack of funds.[49] There was considerable opposition to her first monastic house in Ávila. Her commitment to absolute poverty was also a concern, just as it had been with Francis of Assisi centuries before. In fact, there was additional concern for her convents because they were to be enclosed, and thus the nuns could not beg for food as the Franciscan friars could do. However, Teresa went ahead and opened the Convent of St. Joseph in 1562. After this she spent the rest of her life establishing fourteen new Discalced Carmelite convents and two monastic houses for men.

In addition to her reforming activity, she showed profound spiritual leadership to her monastic sisters throughout her literary works. Her books are filled with guidance and advice meant to encourage and educate. Her autobiography, *The Way of Perfection*, and *The Interior Castle* all deal with prayer and the religious life. She teaches her readers to surrender to God and to detach themselves, though it should be noted that elsewhere she does talk about the benefits of friendship and other relationships as long as they do not interfere with one's relationship with God. After all, Teresa did not hide away from the world. Her mysticism propelled her into it, and it propelled her to reform and lead despite her own hesitations and struggles with feeling inadequate.

In the final analysis, Teresa was a brilliant woman who reformed the church, founded over a dozen monastic houses, and wrote profound religious books that have helped guide countless people, both Catholic and not, to a fruitful relationship with God. In 1970 she was

---

49 Many convents required a dowry, which was generally less than a marriage dowry but was still prohibitive for women who were not from wealthy families.

formally recognized by the Catholic Church as a doctor of the church, only one of four women to receive the honor.[50]

Leadership for a Modern World

One fascinating trait that nearly everyone in this chapter shared was a reluctance to take on positions of leadership or power. Benedict returned to his cave; Gregory did not want to be pope. Hildegard only took on her leadership role after a direct revelation from God; Francis rejected his wealth and position only to become a leader as men and women began following his lifestyle; Teresa was an unlikely leader who never gave herself the credit she deserved but believed in God's call. Also true about each of these individuals is that a deep personal relationship with God, direct revelations, or even external forces pushed them into these positions, whether they were comfortable with them or not. Once they took on these roles, they led with humility and grace.

One of the lessons we can take from their examples is the importance of motivation when assessing modern leaders. Does someone's desire to lead stem from a genuine call or a genuine desire to serve whatever office they are taking? Or is someone motivated by a desire for power or influence based on their own pride? Christian history is also filled with leaders who cared more for power and prestige than for people or ideals. Their stories are never as inspiring and often have led to tragedy.

Today is no different. Whom are we calling to lead our communities? In a time of increased polarization, viral sound bites, and a perceived erosion of human decency in the public arena, are we as a society looking for leaders who will act on behalf of others or for their own glory? Many of the leaders in this chapter led during times of

---

50 Pope Paul VI, "Proclamacíon de Santa Teresa de Jesús como Doctora de la Iglesia," The Vatican, September 27, 1970, https://www.vatican.va/content/paul-vi/es/homilies/1970/documents/hf_p-vi_hom_19700927.html.

change and chaos. Benedict and Gregory provided stability while the old Roman order crumbled around them. Francis offered a faithful witness and commitment to poverty. Teresa provided much-needed reform efforts to a church that was facing its biggest-ever challenge in the Protestant Reformation. These individuals did not lead for their own sake. They did not desire power; in fact, they generally wanted the opposite.

Suggested Reading List

Bonaventure. *Works of Bonaventure: The Soul's Journey into God, The Tree of Life, The Life of Francis.* Translated by Ewert Cousins. New York: Paulist Press, 1978.

Francis of Assisi. *The Writings of St. Francis.* Translated by Father Paschal Robinson. Philadelphia: Dolphin, 1906.

Gregory the Great. *The Dialogues of Gregory the Great: Book Two: Saint Benedict.* Translated by Myra L. Uhlfelder. Indianapolis: Bobbs-Merrill, 1967.

———. *Morals on the Book of Job.* Translated by John Henry Parker, JGF, and J. Rivington. Oxford, 1844.

Hildegard of Bingen. *Scivias.* Translated by Mother Columba Hart and Jane Bishop. New York: Paulist Press, 1990.

The Legend of St. Francis by Three Companions. London: J. M. Dent and Co, and Aldine House, n.d.

Teresa of Ávila. *The Book of My Life.* Translated by Mirabai Starr. Boston: New Seeds, 2007.

———. *The Interior Castle.* Translated by Kieran Kavanaugh, OCD, and Otilio Rodriguez, OCD. Washington, DC: ICS, 2020.

———. *The Way of Perfection.* Translated by Paula Hutson. Brewster, MA: Paraclete, 2009.

4

POLITICS

By the very law of man's desire which makes him want what he lacks in place of what he has and grow weary of what he has in preference to what he lacks, once he has obtained and despised all in heaven and on earth, he will hasten toward the only one who is missing, the God of all. There he will rest, for just as there is no rest on this side of eternity, so there will be no restlessness to bother him on the other side.

—Bernard of Clairvaux, *On Loving God*

MYSTICAL PRAYER HAS empowered Christians to call out wrongs in both the church and society. Augustine battled many political and theological foes. John Chrysostom walked a dangerous line between the tenets of his faith and the desires of the imperial class who were members of his flock. Teresa of Ávila navigated complex church politics to found monastic houses. The list could go on and on—there are so many Christian mystics who were propelled by their faith to engage in the messy politics of the world. On the surface, this may seem surprising. Christians tend to romanticize mystics of old, believing they were able to sit in their monasteries contemplating the great divine mysteries. Truthfully, most of the mystics, those included in this chapter and in other chapters, were busy people who balanced their prayer life with plenty of real-world problems. This chapter begins with a quote from Bernard of Clairvaux because of his endlessly relatable comment, "There is no rest on this side of eternity." Bernard knew this truth well. Perpetually drawn into the affairs of the church and the world, he longed for a monastic life he had all but abandoned.

This chapter is broken into two distinct sections: political mystics of the Middle Ages, which include Bernard of Clairvaux, Birgitta of Sweden, and Catherine of Siena, and political mystics of the modern era, which include Sojourner Truth, Howard Thurman, and Dorothy Day. These six mystics, separated by centuries and religious affiliation, represent a strong engagement with political affairs. However, to call these individuals politicians would be misleading. All six mystics were engaged in the world and cared deeply about addressing corruption and societal ills. However, they were first and foremost religious figures, not secular politicians.

Three Political Mystics of the Middle Ages

Bernard of Clairvaux (1090–1153)

There is a pattern of sorts that one can see when looking at the history of Christian monasticism, and it is one of decay and renewal. Throughout history, monasteries or even monastic orders fell into laxity and corruption. In response, a leader came along to reform a movement or begin an entirely new movement to combat these declining morals. This was the case in the eleventh century with the founding of the Cistercian Order. The order can be traced back to a man named Robert of Molesme (1028–1111), who wanted to establish a monastic house where the Rule of Benedict would be observed strictly. He was given a house at Cîteaux, France, which at that time was called the New Monastery. Molesme did not stay at Cîteaux, but the community to continued to grow under different leadership and eventually gave rise to major monastic reforms.[1] Within a couple of decades, four daughter houses had been founded, including one at Clairvaux in 1115. The new movement became known as Cistercian because the name for Cîteaux was *Cistertium* in Latin.[2]

---

1 Peters, *Story of Monasticism*, 138–39.

2 Justo González, *The Story of Christianity*, vol. 1, *The Early Church to the Dawn of the Reformation* (New York: HarperOne, 2010), 333.

The best-known of the Cistercians was Bernard of Clairvaux; he was a monk, abbot, preacher, ecclesiastical reformer, skilled politician, and promoter of the Second Crusade. He was a mystic who was devoted to the humanity of Christ. Historian Justo González refers to him as the enemy of all theological innovation, which likely speaks to his conflict with Peter Abelard, whom he had a primary role in excommunicating, though the assessment is far too harsh. It is true that Bernard was concerned about theology being right, not innovative. He was a conventional theologian of Western theology of his era. He was not on the cutting edge of scholastic theology, but his concerns were pastoral. His commitment to teaching others about the contemplative life permeates his writings, though he spent much of his own life active in the world. He had incredible influence within his own era; his writings are astoundingly beautiful, and his contributions to mystical Christianity were profound.

Bernard can seem paradoxical and difficult for modern readers to understand. His own assessment of his dual life of contemplation and action is worth noting because it seemed to cause dissonance within himself, and others have looked at this tendency with suspicion. He writes of his own actions, "I have kept the habit of a monk but I have long ago abandoned the life. I do wish to tell you what I dare say you have heard from others: what I am doing, what are my purposes, through what dangers I pass in the world or rather down what precipices I am hurled."[3] This tension between contemplation and action is one reason modern readers sometimes find him difficult, though this tension was not entirely of his own choosing. He is one of the most highly regarded mystical minds in Christian history, and his influence on other mystics is significant. As one scholar states, "Bernard of Clairvaux orientated the whole first movement of the twelfth-century culture toward the contemplative ideal."[4] However, it may seem like one

---

3 Quoted in Brian Patrick McGuire, *Bernard of Clairvaux: An Inner Life* (Ithaca, NY: Cornell University Press, 2020), 61.

4 Duncan Robertson, "The Experience of Reading: Bernard of Clairvaux 'Sermons on the Song of Songs,'" *Religion & Literature* 19, no. 1 (1987): 1.

of many cases of "do as I say and not what I do." Even when he was at his monastery, he was leading, but often he was being pulled into the affairs of the church and the world instead.

Bernard was born in 1090, the third of seven children, in Fontaines-lès-Dijon, Burgundy. His mother, Aleth, was from the high nobility, and his father, Tescelin, was a knight. His father's profession as a knight is of particular interest since Bernard did not seem to have had any sort of aversion to military activity, and later in life he actively intertwined monasticism and military activity with his role in the creation of the Knights Templar.[5] Like so many other saints, the story of Bernard's early life has elements of the miraculous. While pregnant with him, his mother reportedly had a vision of a white dog in her womb, and she interpreted it as communicating that the child would be a great guardian of God's house and an outstanding preacher. Another story tells of how a young Bernard had a vision of the Christ child. His mother was a strong force in his life, and his biographers write of her piety, though she died when Bernard was a teenager. Following her death, Bernard found a strong connection to the Virgin Mary, and there is an oft-told story of his devotion to her. He was praying before a statue of Mary when she pressed one of her breasts and sent milk into his mouth. This signified the wisdom he received from the Virgin and also showed that he had found a spiritual mother. Whether this event happened is somewhat irrelevant; the interesting element is how the story gives a miraculous underpinning to his great devotion to the Virgin Mary.[6]

Bernard was a force to be reckoned with, and to say he was charismatic is an understatement. A contemporary called him physically and spiritually irresistible.[7] Another man who met Bernard commented that he was something superhuman, that his face had a divine majesty and grace poured out of his lips. It was also said that

5 McGuire, *Bernard of Clairvaux*, 13.

6 McGuire, *Bernard of Clairvaux*, 15–18.

7 McGuire, *Bernard of Clairvaux*, 23.

mothers hid their sons and wives hid their husbands when he was near lest he tempt them to run off to be a monk.[8] Bernard learned of the monastery at Cîteaux around 1100, though he did not go right away. First he ran a practice monastery of sorts on his family's property, where he convinced his male family members, including an already-married brother, and friends to join.[9] So when Bernard finally arrived at the New Monastery at Cîteaux, he brought with him around thirty companions.[10] It should perhaps come as little surprise then that the young Bernard, only in his mid-twenties, became the abbot of one of Cîteaux's daughter houses, Clairvaux. The appointment was controversial—he was young, he had health problems, and there is evidence that he did struggle, at least in the early years, with leading a community that included members of his own family, and the stress undoubtedly took a toll on his health.[11] He persevered and continued in his role as abbot throughout his life, though over time he increasingly spent more time away from Clairvaux as he was pulled into more political controversies.

Bernard was a talented and capable individual, which inevitably meant that he was sought after to assist the Catholic Church in public roles. In 1128 he was involved in the Council of Troyes, where the first rule for the Order of Templars was established. His involvement brought further notice in both monastic and political circles. However, it was with the papal schism in 1130 that Bernard truly emerged as a diplomat. The scope of the papal schism is far beyond our interest here, and it is sufficient to say that two popes were elected and consecrated: Innocent II, whom Bernard supported, and Anacletus, who is known

---

8 Michael Casey, "Reading Saint Bernard," in *A Companion to Bernard of Clairvaux*, ed. Brian Patrick McGuire (Leiden: Brill, 2011), 81–82.

9 Brian Patrick McGuire, "Bernard's Life and Works: A Review," in McGuire, *Companion to Bernard of Clairvaux*, 26–27.

10 G. R. Evans, *Bernard of Clairvaux* (Oxford: Oxford University Press, 2000), 8.

11 Evans, *Bernard of Clairvaux*, 9–10.

to history as an antipope.[12] Throughout the 1130s, Bernard continued to exert influence and backed Cistercian candidates for episcopal positions, though he refused a position of archbishop himself. It is also likely that he composed his moving text, *On Loving God*, discussed further below, during the 1130s as well.[13]

In 1140, after a request from his friend and biographer, William of Thierry, Bernard attacked the theology of theologian Peter Abelard, which resulted in Abelard's excommunication (the excommunication was lifted after Abelard's death).[14] Also in the 1140s came his enthusiastic participation in promoting the Second Crusade, which was called in 1146 by Pope Eugenius III. Bernard put his preaching skills to work and rallied French soldiers to head to the Holy Land. The Second Crusade was both a moral and military disaster. Since this is one of the most criticized actions of the saint, it is also worth mentioning one of his more admirable actions, his fervent condemnation of Jewish persecution at a time when Christian violence toward Europeans Jews was high.[15] Bernard continued to be active until his death in August 1153. It was reported that even after his death, he kept himself busy granting miracles to the faithful.[16]

Bernard had an active life, much more so than one might expect of a monk, but his heart was in the monastery. As a twelfth-century Cistercian, he was committed to the contemplative goal of experiential union with God.[17] His writings are overwhelmingly concerned with love. While the idea of courtly love was a strong cultural force in the High Middle Ages, Bernard was concerned with divine love. His text *On Loving God*, which is both readable and relatable to the modern

---

12 Evans, *Bernard of Clairvaux*, 11–13.

13 McGuire, "Bernard's Life and Works," 46–47.

14 McGuire, "Bernard's Life and Works," 49.

15 McGuire, "Bernard's Life and Works," 53; David Berger, "The Attitude of St. Bernard of Clairvaux toward the Jews," *PAAJR* 40 (1972): 89–108.

16 McGuire, "Bernard's Life and Works," 60.

17 Casey, "Reading Saint Bernard," 94.

reader, is not a mystical guide or an instruction manual. It is a treatise on love. He begins his text rather humorously: "You wish me to tell you why and how God should be loved. My answer is that God himself is the reason why he is to be loved. As for how he is to be loved, there is to be no limit to that love. Is this a sufficient answer? Perhaps, but only for a wise man."[18] Luckily for us, Bernard does not stop there. He continues:

> *As I am indebted, however, to the unwise also, it is customary to add something for them after saying enough for the wise. . . . Hence I insist that there are two reasons why God should be loved for his own sake: no one can be loved more righteously and no one can be loved with greater benefit. Indeed, when it is asked why God should be loved, there are two meanings possible to the question. For it can be questioned which is rather the question: whether for what merit of his or for what advantage to us is God to be loved. My answer to both questions is assuredly the same, for I can see no other reason for loving him than himself. So let us see first how he deserves our love.*[19]

The rest of the treatise does just as the title and opening paragraph promise. Various sections cover topics such as how God should be loved and how God is not loved without reward. One particular section that often gets attention in this text is the degrees to which people should love themselves and God. The first degree of love is how humans love themselves for their own sake. The second degree is how people love God their own benefit. The third is how people love God for God's sake, and finally is how people love themselves for God's sake. The final stage, which is likely the most difficult to understand, Bernard

18 Bernard of Clairvaux, *On Loving God* (Kalamazoo, MI: Cistercian Publications, 1995), 1.1.

19 Bernard, *On Loving God*, 1.1.

describes as such: "Happy the man who has attained the fourth degree of love, he no longer even loves himself except for God."[20] This is not any sort of annihilation of self, though Bernard does speak of losing oneself in God as a divine experience. Losing oneself in God cannot be gained by human efforts, and he believed it was unlikely one could truly reach this stage in this life. As he explains, "For it is impossible to assemble all these and turn them toward God's face as long as the care of this weak and wretched body keeps one busy to the point of distraction." However, "He will easily reach the highest degree of love when he will no longer be held back by any desire of the flesh or upset by troubles as he hastens with the greatest speed and desire toward the joy of the Lord."[21]

At this point, one may be wondering whether Bernard, who wrote so beautifully on love, was able to incorporate this love into his life and his political engagement. This is a complex question and one that eludes easy answers. On the one hand, Bernard cared deeply for his brothers in the monastery. In a letter he wrote to the monks at Clairvaux in 1135, he "claimed that if the brothers missed him, then for him it was all the more the case. They experienced the absence of one person, while he had to cope with the absence of many."[22] Beyond that one can see his love and attachment for others in his insistence that so many of his friends and family come with him to the New Monastery. On the other hand, he did not seem to extend this love toward those he disagreed with or those he believed were doing harm to the church. As Brian Patrick McGuire states in his helpful biography on Bernard: "Sometimes Bernard could express himself in so direct a manner that he was close to being insulting."[23] This is not to mention his treatment of individuals such as Abelard or Gilbert de

20 Bernard, *On Loving God*, 10.27.

21 Bernard, *On Loving God*, 10.29.

22 McGuire, "Bernard's Life and Works," 81.

23 McGuire, "Bernard's Life and Works," 231.

la Porrée.[24] Yet, these activities should not negate the genuine love he demonstrated for God, the monastery, and his monastic brothers.

Gender and Politics in the Middle Ages

Bernard had to balance his vocation as a monk with the demands the church made of him. Being a capable leader and politician, he was sought after and dragged into political situations of all kinds. Such was the lot of a talented churchman of the Middle Ages. The situation was different for women. There were exceptions, of course, but most religious women of the Middle Ages were cloistered in a convent. Abbesses, like abbots, had a degree of interaction with the outside world, but by and large they were not being sought out to engage in church and worldly affairs. This makes the political engagement of two women, Birgitta of Sweden and Catherine of Siena, who were roughly contemporaries, all the more surprising.

There are similarities between Bernard, Birgitta, and Catherine. All three were involved in papal politics; they all supported crusades. Catherine in particular seems to have had some of the charisma Bernard possessed. Birgitta and Catherine, who both lived during the harrowing years of the plague, however, lived in a darker and harsher world than Bernard. Birgitta was an adult when the plague arrived in Europe—a recent widow, to be exact. She began her public career around the time the plague hit. Catherine was born in the year the plague arrived, so she knew nothing else.

GENDER AND MYSTICISM

There has been much written about the role of gender in Christian mysticism. Mysticism is one area of Christian

24 Gilbert de la Porrée was a theologian and bishop of Poitiers. Bernard was convinced his theology was heretical, and even after the Council of Reims exonerated Gilbert in 1148, Bernard continued to argue his case against Gilbert.

thought that has consistently been inclusive of women, at least from the High Middle Ages on. There are various reasons for this, and a full analysis could take up an entire book, but I will highlight a few items here. Throughout most of history, women were largely denied access to both formalized church leadership roles and more formal educational opportunities. There are exceptions to this, though. Women had leadership opportunities within monastic communities, and they were often more educated in monastic communities too. However, women were denied leadership within the church hierarchies, and even wealthy women were limited in educational opportunities. Therefore, theology was written by men, largely for other men. Mystics, on the other hand, did not necessarily gain their authority from earthy institutions; often they claimed their authority came directly from God. When a woman wrote about her own mystical experience, she was speaking from her own experience. Yet, serious theology was being done in these mystical texts.

Not only were there contextual differences between Bernard in the twelfth century and Birgitta and Catherine in the fourteenth, but one cannot seriously examine their engagement in the world without dealing with the issue of gender. With Bernard, there is a sense that he may have preferred to stay at Clairvaux more often, but he kept being pulled into worldly affairs. He expressed discomfort with his choices. He writes: "It is time that I cease being forgetful of myself. My monstrous life cries out, and my bitter conscience. I am like a chimera of my age, neither a cleric nor a layman, for I have for some time thrown off the monk's way of life, but not the habit."[25] He felt

25 Quoted in Casey, "Reading Saint Bernard," 68.

the tension between the contemplative life he chose and the active life he lived. This tension existed for Birgitta and Catherine as well, but it was profoundly different. Whereas Bernard seemed to see politics as a hindrance to contemplation, it was mystical experiences that both propelled and justified Birgitta and Catherine's place in the public realm.

Birgitta of Sweden (1303–1373)

Despite all the similarities between Birgitta and Catherine, their beginnings were remarkably different. Birgitta was born to an aristocratic family in Sweden, which was a relatively small and underdeveloped country during the High Middle Ages. Her father, who held a powerful political position, oversaw codification of laws and the election of the Swedish king, Magnus Eriksson.[26] She married a man named Ulf Gudmarsson, who was also from a prominent Swedish family, when she was fourteen years old. The couple even served in the Swedish court. When the king married, Birgitta became the adviser to Queen Blanche, likely instructing her on the language and customs of the queen's newly adopted home.

Until the death of her husband in the mid-1340s, Birgitta lived a life fairly typical of a pious aristocratic woman of her era. She served both her country and those in need, offering works of Christian charity. By all accounts she had a good and loving marriage, which produced eight children, six of whom survived to adulthood, including a daughter named Catherine, who too would be canonized as a saint. There was very little to indicate the wild direction Birgitta's life would take—except, of course, Birgitta's tendency to experience religious visions.

Her hagiography reports a number of visions that she experienced as a child. These visions are typical for this particular genre of writing. For example, she reportedly had a vision of the Virgin Mary giving her a crown at the age of six; she had a vision of Christ being

---

26 Claire L. Sahlin, *Birgitta of Sweden and the Voice of Prophecy* (Rochester, NY: Boydell, 2001), 14.

crucified at the age of ten, and sometime later she had a vision of the devil. There are also accounts of miraculous events, thus demonstrating that she had God's favor since childhood.[27] Despite these stories, Birgitta's mission truly began after the death of her husband.

Birgitta was in her early forties when she was widowed. Only a few days after her husband's death, she had a vision in which she was called to the religious life:

> *Do not be afraid. For I am the creator of all and am not a deceiver. You should know that I do not speak to you for your sake alone, but for the sake of the salvation of all Christians: Therefore, hear what I say. For you shall be my bride and channel, and you shall hear and see spiritual things and heavenly secrets, and my Spirit shall remain with you until your death. Therefore, believe firmly that I am he who was born from a pure virgin, who suffered and died for the salvation of all souls, who rose from the dead and ascended into heaven, and who now with my spirit speaks with you.*[28]

Critical to understand in this vision is that she was specifically called to be God's conduit. This is different from other types of mystical experiences throughout this book. In fact, *prophet* may indeed be a better term for how she functioned within society, and indeed her hagiography refers to her true spirit of prophecy and intellectual vision.[29] She functioned as a mouthpiece, a position not everyone appreciated.

Because of the nature of her particular call, she did not retire to a convent, which may have been the more expected route for a wealthy widow. She did, however, move to the grounds of a men's Cistercian monastery, but did not join the order and probably had limited

---

27 Bridget Morris, *St. Birgitta of Sweden* (Woodbridge, UK: Boydell, 1999), 37–38.

28 Claire L. Sahlin, "Extrav. 47," in Sahlin, *Birgitta of Sweden*, 45.

29 Morris, *St. Birgitta of Sweden*, 66.

access to the buildings on the grounds. Her presence was not welcomed by the monks at first. Then a monk had a mystical experience himself in which he was told that through her presence, the monastery would experience a renewal of spiritual life—and thus her presence was sanctified.[30] Birgitta continued to have visions, and many of them concerned public affairs, issues of the state, and religious abuses. For example, she had a vision and then sent a message to Pope Clement VI to arrange peace between France and England, who were in the throes of the Hundred Years' War. This was unsuccessful, and the war continued for another century. When her own king led a Crusade against the Russians, she had visions justifying the action. However, when the Crusade proved unsuccessful and the Swedish nobility rose up against the king, she sided with the nobility and wrote a condemnation of the king.[31]

THE AVIGNON PAPACY

The Avignon papacy refers to the period running from 1309 to 1376, in which seven successive popes, beginning with Clement V, resided in Avignon rather than in Rome. This was an era that is remembered for both corruption and the willingness of the popes to act in the interest of the French Crown. This era coincided with the arrival of the plague in Europe, and there were many who believed that the storm of pestilence was indeed divine punishment for the popes' absence from Rome. In addition, the Hundred Years' War was also playing out, and France's enemies increasingly resented the papacy, which they believed had France's interests at heart. In 1377, Gregory XI returned the papacy to Rome; however, the victory was short-lived,

30 Morris, *St. Birgitta of Sweden*, 75.

31 Morris, *St. Birgitta of Sweden*, 79–86.

as an even worse situation, later known as the Great Papal Schism, spanned from 1378 to 1417. Without question, the chaos of the Avignon papacy and the Great Papal Schism created an atmosphere in which people were looking for reform within the Catholic Church.

In 1349, while Europe was suffering from the plague, Birgitta felt called to go to Rome. Over the next two decades, many of her visions had to do with church reform, and many of her messages were directed at members of the church hierarchy. She had two major goals in mind: to get papal approval for her religious order, which resulted in the establishment of the Order of the Most Holy Savior, more commonly known as the Bridgettine Order, and to persuade the pope to return to Rome, which did not happen within her lifetime. In Rome, she lived a quasi-monastic life, ran a center for Scandinavian pilgrims, and cared for the sick and needy.

She died in 1373 and was canonized in 1391; however, that was hardly the end of her story. Her canonization caused great controversy for a variety of reasons, including that she had been a married laywoman. In fact, due to continued tensions, her canonization had to be confirmed three times by three different popes, yet there was still disapproval within the church. Regardless of canonization controversies, Birgitta occupied an usual place in medieval life, and when she died some church officials were looking for someone else to fill the role.

Catherine of Siena (1347–1380)

Catherine of Siena took up Birgitta's quest to bring the pope back to Rome after her death. Whereas Birgitta lived a long and full life, Catherine's time on earth was fleeting, a mere thirty-three years. Like Birgitta, she did not fit the mold of a typical religious woman of the era. She rejected both marriage and the monastery, became a highly influential woman, and left an impressive legacy within the Catholic Church.

It is genuinely difficult to surmise exactly what Catherine of Siena's motivations were in life, especially regarding her very public persona. The most important source of information about Catherine comes from a hagiography written after her death by her confessor, Raymond of Capua, who promoted her cause for sainthood extensively after he became the head of the Dominican Order. There are always problems when trying to reconstruct a life using hagiographic material. These texts were not meant to be histories as history is understood today—they were meant to promote a person for sainthood. There are tropes that are used frequently, and by their very nature they tend to smooth over a person's faults, perceived faults, or activities that the church or public may not view as holy. For someone such as Catherine, a woman who exerted political influence to a degree that was unusual in fourteenth-century Europe, there is some massaging of facts and motivations, especially regarding her political ambitions.[32] That being said, this text does provide a general outline of her life, and Catherine also wrote (or dictated) letters and other writings, including her famous mystical text, *The Dialogue*.

Catherine is often described as the daughter of a tradesman, a dyer of wool, to be exact. This is true but not the full story. Her family was upwardly mobile, and her father and brothers more than likely were wool masters and shop owners, not just simple tradesmen. They were not members of Siena's elite, but they had a degree of wealth and influence.[33] Catherine was one of twenty-five children, and she had a twin who died shortly after birth. As is typical in hagiographic accounts, Catherine is reported as having received visions as a child. At the age of six, she saw Jesus on a throne with saints Peter, Paul, and John the Evangelist by his side. Raymond of Capua highlights this moment as a turning point in her life—a transformative experience

32 For a deep dive into the politics of Catherine's life and how her real-life situation likely deviated from her hagiographic account, see F. Thomas Luongo, *The Saintly Politics of Catherine of Siena* (Ithaca, NY: Cornell University Press, 2006).

33 Luongo, *Saintly Politics of Catherine*, 30.

that influenced her future religious vocation. After this time, he reports, she withdrew to her home and began practicing serious prayer, meditation, and extreme asceticism.[34]

Another typical aspect in a hagiography of a woman is the battle over an unwanted marriage, and this plays in a role in Catherine's story. Despite her parents wanting to arrange a marriage for her, Catherine was determined to devote her life to God. While Catherine certainly desired a religious life, it seems that the death of her older sister in childbirth, when Catherine was fifteen, also soured the prospect of marriage for her. According to her hagiography, she was drawn to the religious life, but she did not enter a monastery, as would have been the expectation of the time. Instead, she became associated with a group of women called the *mantellate*, who were financially stable widows that loosely associated with the Dominicans. This group was fairly unstructured and living out in the world.[35] They were different from Beguines, religious laywomen who ended up facing persecution due to their lack of association with the Catholic Church (who will be discussed in more detail in chs. 6 and 8), but realistically the groups likely functioned similarly in that they consisted of unenclosed religious women doing good works in the world. Therefore, Catherine occupied an unusual space for the time. She was a young, unmarried women who was out in the world, and this proved pivotal for her future influence and fame.

Catherine was undoubtedly charismatic, and she began to attract a group of followers that included both men and women, laypeople and clergy. Three years after joining the *mantellate*, her biographer tells us, she heard a voice urging her into the world against her own protests. While this is entirely possible, and there are many, many miracles associated with Catherine, this statement also has the feel of a

---

34 Raymond of Capua, *The Life of St. Catherine of Siena* (Dublin: James Duffy, n.d.), 8.

35 Maria H. Oen and Unn Falkeid, eds., *Sanctity and Female Authorship: Birgitta of Sweden and Catherine of Siena* (New York: Routledge, 2020), 4.

hagiographic embellishment that could justify Catherine's entrance into political life, which she undertook in the early 1370s. Her letters demonstrate that she forged relationships with local senators, and by 1374, it appears that she was someone to whom the elite members of Sienese society would turn for spiritual matters. That same year Raymond of Capua, her future biographer, became her confessor. He was already a prominent friar who would end up climbing the ranks of the Dominican Order. Evidence suggests that by this time, Catherine had already established much ecclesiastical support, and by 1374 the Catholic Church was fully intending to draw her into church politics.[36]

When Birgitta died in 1373, Catherine's reputation was already well-known. While it seems somewhat counterintuitive, there was power in Catherine's position as a well-connected, holy laywoman. Like Birgitta, she acted as a mouthpiece for God, gaining authority from her unusual position in society. Catherine engaged in large-scale political events, and likely the most important was her involvement in bringing the Avignon papacy to a close. In the spring of 1376, she was called to Avignon to meet with Pope Gregory XI. Catherine urged the pope to return to Rome. In the same year, she negotiated a peace between the pope and the city of Florence, which was critical in creating the circumstances in which the pope would return to Rome. The return of the pope was short-lived. Soon after he returned to Rome, he died. The election of the next pope resulted in a church schism, but Catherine was at least briefly able to accomplish what Birgitta had long fought for. Gregory's successor requested her support in his claim to the papacy against the schismatic pope, Clement VII.[37] Catherine died in 1380 at the age of thirty-three, and it is likely that her extreme lifestyle led to her early death. She was canonized a century later and declared a doctor of the church in 1970.

---

36 Luongo, *Saintly Politics of Catherine*, 64–65, 69–71.

37 Julia Barrett and A. A. Lukowski, "Wedded to Light: The Life, Letters, and Legend of St. Catherine of Siena," *The Journal of the Midwest Modern Language Association* 41, no. 1 (2008): 1–2.

The obvious question around this political involvement is *why*? Why did church officials seek out someone such as Catherine for political engagement? Scholars have suggested that it was the death of Birgitta of Sweden that prompted Catherine's drawing in, but this only pushes back the question further. Why engage these atypical figures at all? They were both, though Catherine more so because she was not even a member of the nobility, outsiders in a highly political system. Perhaps this is obvious, but it is essential to understand: People, including members of the church hierarchy, *must* have believed that both Birgitta and Catherine were genuine mystics. People must have accepted, at least to a degree, that each woman had a close and unusual connection to God, that their visions were authentic, and that what they said mattered because it was divinely inspired.

Three Modern Political Mystics

We leave the messy church politics of the Middle Ages behind for an examination of how three modern mystics engaged in social reform and politics in modern America. The contexts were vastly different, as were the goals of the mystics involved. Yet, there are undeniable similarities in how all these figures were drawn to engage in the world through both a powerful mystical faith and political and societal factors. In the Middle Ages, it was largely church crises and wars that drew the mystics in. The modern mystics were more concerned with societal change, particularly around the issue of human rights. Roughly one hundred years separates Truth from Thurman and Day, so there are contextual differences between these figures. Yet, they were all American and largely engaged with social issues. Truth and Thurman identified as preachers and public speakers, but their methods and styles were different. Day, on the other hand, was not a preacher at all; she was a writer and activist. All three carried a deep faith, a profound mysticism that affected those around them.

Sojourner Truth (1797–1883)

Sojourner Truth is a well-known American historical figure, not only in Christian history but in American history, and she is best known for being a social reformer. She was a leader in the abolitionist movement, a women's right's activist, and advocate of temperance. Her dedication to bettering the lives of others, her bravery, and her perseverance stand out in American history. She was also a deeply religious woman, and her Christian faith guided her throughout her life.

Truth was born Isabella Baumfree in New York state around 1797. At the time of her birth, slavery was still legal in New York, and while the state was in the long process of emancipation, ending in 1827, Truth spent her childhood and her childbearing years enslaved. Of the northern states, New York had the largest number of slaves, and in the 1790 census it was reported that more than a third of households in the area where Truth lived owned slaves.[38]

Truth lived during a strange time in which slavery was still legal, but everyone knew it was coming to end soon. The man who owned her had promised to free her in 1826 but then refused when the time came and sold her son Peter. It was illegal to sell slaves outside the state at this time, because of the impending emancipation, so he sold Peter to nearby family, but of course it was still a terrible hardship for Truth. Soon after, she took her youngest child, Sophia, who was still a baby, and walked to freedom in the early morning. An abolitionist family purchased her freedom and that of her youngest daughter, but she had to leave her two older daughters enslaved.[39] Meanwhile, Peter had been sold to a slave owner in Alabama, which *was* illegal. To reclaim her son, Truth took the man who had sold him to court. She became the first Black woman to successfully sue a white man in US history.

---

38 Nancy Koester, *We Will Be Free: The Life and Faith of Sojourner Truth* (Grand Rapids: Eerdmans, 2023), 1.

39 Koester, *We Will Be Free*, 18–19.

AMERICAN REVIVALISM

The United States has a rich history of Christian revivals. The First Great Awakening was a series of religious revivals that took place on the Eastern Seaboard in the 1730s and 1740s. Key figures of this awakening include preacher George Whitefield and theologian Jonathan Edwards. While this awakening did not result in massive conversions, it did help establish general patterns of American revival, which included calls to conversion, itinerant outdoor preaching, use of modern media, and an ecumenical emphasis.

The Second Great Awakening lasted longer than the first and reached far more people. It ran from roughly 1795 to the 1830s. Key leaders of this awakening included Methodist Francis Asbury and Presbyterian Charles Finney. The Methodists and the Baptists in general were heavily involved, and preachers tended to emphasize free will and holy living. Also important was the fusion of social reform efforts with religious revival. Women played a much larger role than in the First Great Awakening, as both preachers and reformers.

Shortly after she gained her freedom, Truth had a mystical vision. What is so remarkable about Truth's account of her vision is its similarity to other mystical visions from previous centuries. Truth, an illiterate, enslaved American woman, influenced by American revivalism rather than classic mystical texts, writes of a sudden event that was brought on by a sense of guilt for sin (reminiscent of purgation) and then a sudden understanding of the incredible love of God through this encounter (similar to illumination).

Prior to the vision, Truth wrote that she wanted to talk to God, but she believed herself to be so vile that she could not approach him.

She desired someone else who could speak to God for her. Then it seemed that a space opened, and a friend appeared to stand between her and God. Then a vision came upon her, and she recognized Christ:

> *"Who are you?" she exclaimed, as the vision brightened into a form distinct, beaming with the beauty of holiness, and radiant with love. She then said, audibly addressing the mysterious visitant—"I know you, and I don't know you." . . . At length, after bending both soul and body with the intensity of this desire, till breath and strength seemed failing, and she could maintain her position no longer, an answer came to her, saying distinctly, "It is Jesus." "Yes," she responded, "it is Jesus."*[40]

Through this vision, she came to see and know Christ. She recognized him as the friend who stood between sinful humanity and the First Person of the Trinity. This vision was not the result of a lengthy spiritual journey in a monastery but was a moment when Truth came to intimately know who Christ was and that Christ was with her. This suddenness is not unheard of in other mystical literature; there are other instances of mystics experiencing a vision that completely changed their lives (Catherine of Genoa, discussed in ch. 7, is a good comparison), but it is not the norm. Also remarkable are the similarities of the vision to older Catholic mystical visions and experiences, though Truth was not Catholic, and her context and religious influences were incredibly different.

This was not the only time that Truth had a profound interaction with God. On Pentecost Sunday 1843, Isabella Baumfree changed her name to Sojourner Truth. She believed that it was the name God was giving her, and accepting the name was acceptance of a divine call. It

---

40 Sojourner Truth, *The Narrative of Sojourner Truth* (Battle Creek, MI: Review and Herald Office, 1884), 66–67.

was also a rejection of slavery and her old life. In her autobiography she explains: "My name was Isabella; but when I left the house of bondage, I left everything behind. . . . I went to the Lord an' asked him to give me a new name. And the Lord gave me Sojourner, because I was to travel up an' down the land, showin' the people their sins, an' bein' a sign upon them."[41]

The exact nature of Truth's religiosity is complex. She is generally described as a Methodist, and she was associated with the African Methodist Episcopal Church. She was also associated with a self-proclaimed holy man who styled himself the Prophet Matthias in the 1830s.[42] This religious community fell apart within a few years, embroiled in numerous scandals, including adultery and even suspected murder, though Truth was not involved in the more unsavory aspects of the story. She also had some associations with the Millerites, the spiritualists, and the Seventh-day Adventists.[43] Her association with the nineteenth-century holiness movement was the most important influence regarding her spiritual development. Indeed, she was a skilled itinerant preacher who preached both at Christian revivals and for social causes.

Her involvement in the abolitionist movement is a primary example of her faith and politics intertwining. This was not a casual engagement; she joined an abolitionist commune called the Northampton Association of Education and Industry. The association was coed and multiracial. It hoped to promote free labor (as opposed to labor dependent on slavery) and the abolition of slavery. The community's industry was silk production, which would be produced entirely through

---

41 Truth, *Narrative of Sojourner Truth*, 164.

42 The Prophet Matthias has been the subject of some interest, particularly related to nineteenth-century fringe religious movements. The rather thrilling story of this dubious holy man is detailed in Paul E. Johnson and Sean Wilentz, *The Kingdom of Matthias: A Story of Sex and Salvation in 19th Century America* (Oxford: Oxford University Press, 1994). For a full account of Truth's participation in the religious community, see Koester, *We Will Be Free*, ch. 4.

43 Koester, *We Will Be Free*, 124–26.

free labor. Through this association Truth because connected to some of the more famous abolitionists of the era, including William Lloyd Garrison and Frederick Douglass.[44] Truth became an important abolitionist leader, traveling around the country and speaking out on the issue even though to do so could be quite dangerous.

She was also involved in the fight for women's rights and temperance—in this era, a time when women had few legal protections and were vulnerable when their husbands drank excessively, the two movements were largely connected. A line from her famous "Ain't I a Woman?" speech highlights her commitment to women's rights and how it was intertwined with her strong religious faith: "And how came Jesus into the world? Through God who created him and woman who bore him. Man, where is your part?"[45] While it is easy to imagine a crowd of people chuckling at this line of hers because it is quite funny and surely meant to be, it also demonstrates that her activism was theologically informed.

Truth had an active faith. She experienced mystical visions and a strong relationship with God. She was also incredibly active in the world, fighting for the causes she held dear. There is no disentangling her preaching from her engagement with social reform—those aspects of her call were fused together.

Howard Thurman (1899–1981)

Howard Thurman was a scholar who cared about social engagement, and his influence on other social activists was immense. He was undoubtedly a mystic, though he spoke very little about his own mystical experiences (unlike Truth). He did, however, speak and write about other

---

44 Koester, *We Will Be Free*, 74–75.

45 Sojourner Truth, "Ain't I a Woman?" (speech delivered at Woman's Rights Convention, Akron, Ohio, May 29, 1851). This line is from the 1851 version transcribed by Marius Robinson, who was in attendance at the convention and published the speech on June 21, 1851, in the *Anti-slavery Bugle*. For more information, see The Sojourner Truth Project, https://tinyurl.com/3enfc655.

mystics and mysticism in general. He wrote about what mysticism is and how it affects a believer's life. In an introductory sermon to a series about mystics that Thurman gave in 1953, he provided a succinct and helpful definition of mysticism for his audience, which is a good place to start an examination of his mystical thought. He writes, "There is an all-pervasive Spirit, time-transcendent, space-transcendent, that gathers up into itself the total gamut of human experience."[46]

As a person living in modernity, he had a different understanding of mysticism from those who lived in antiquity or the Middle Ages, though there are echoes of earlier mystical thought. He explains that God surrounds people and dwells within them. As he writes later in that same sermon:

> *I am not only created by this Spirit—this all-pervasive Spirit of God—but that within me is not a manifestation of the Spirit of God, but* the Spirit of God. *And when, therefore, I seek within myself to commune with the Spirit of God, there is available to me, without any "go-betweener," primary, immediate, direct living contact with this living Spirit. Those are the two pillars about which the whole mystical insights rest, that we are surrounded by an all-pervasive Spirit of God, which Spirit is the Creator of life and the world, and which Spirit is in* me.[47]

This quote provides an introduction to Thurman and his mystical thought, but his theology, especially as related to his role in social activism, must be understood within his life and his social context.

Thurman was born in Daytona Beach, Florida, at the very end of the nineteenth century. His grandmother, Nancy Ambrose, was

---

46 Howard Thurman, "Men Who Have Walked with God: The Mystics," in *The Way of the Mystics*, ed. Peter Eisenstadt and Walter Early Fluker (Maryknoll, NY: Orbis Books, 2021), 4.

47 Thurman, "Men Who Have Walked," 5–6 (emphasis original).

formative in the development of Thurman's Christian faith. As he once said in an interview, "I learned more, for instance, about the genius of the religion of Jesus from my grandmother than from all the men who taught me."[48] Thurman was a bright child, and his mother and grandmother encouraged his educational endeavors despite racist policies in Daytona that barred many Black students from attending high school. He attended Florida Baptist Academy in Jacksonville, Florida, and then headed to Morehouse College in Atlanta. From there he went to Rochester Theological Seminary in Rochester, New York, where he trained for the ministry. Following seminary, he took a call at Mount Zion Baptist Church in Oberlin, Ohio,[49] where he spent a semester studying with Quaker scholar of mysticism Rufus Jones (discussed further in ch. 8). Prior to this experience, Thurman's mysticism was more intuitive, but Jones gave him history and language regarding mysticism that would stay with him.[50] Thurman's study under Jones was not just academic; his own mystical theology was especially affected by Quaker spirituality.

In 1935, Thurman, his wife, and another couple served as the delegation for a six-month "pilgrimage of friendship" to India, Burma, and Ceylon. Among the most transformative moments on the trip was Thurman's meeting with Mohandas Gandhi. After his return to the United States, Thurman traveled through the country speaking about nonviolence as a resistance method for addressing racial injustice. In turn, he inspired others to meet with Gandhi and to learn more about nonviolent resistance, which of course became an important tool in the civil rights movement in the United States.[51]

---

48 Roberta Byrd Barr, interview with Howard Thurman, January 1969, quoted in Luther E. Smith Jr., "Introduction: The Call to Prophetic Spirituality," in *Howard Thurman, Essential Writings*, ed. Luther E. Smith Jr. (Maryknoll, NY: Orbis Books, 2006), 15.

49 Smith, "Introduction," 14–17.

50 See Howard Thurman, "Mysticism and Social Change: Rufus Jones," in Eisenstadt and Fluker, *Way of the Mystics*, 141–60.

51 Smith, "Introduction," 17–20.

In 1944, Thurman joined a small group of people to form an interracial and intercultural church fellowship in San Francisco called the Church for the Fellowship of All People, or the Fellowship Church. When Boston University offered him the position of dean of Marsh Chapel and professor of spiritual resources and disciplines, he took the opportunity to replicate the Fellowship Church model in Boston. He stayed in this position from 1953 to 1963. After he retired, he moved back to San Francisco, where he continued to write, speak, and direct the Howard Thurman Educational Trust, which he founded in 1965, until his death in 1981.[52]

Thurman wrote over twenty books plus many articles, though he saw himself primarily as a speaker and was sought after as such throughout his career. Thurman's inclusion in this chapter may seem surprising since he was not as directly involved in political dealings as others discussed here. He was private man and an intellectual—he was not an activist. Yet, he served as a mentor for those involved in the civil rights movement. His ideas were profoundly important to those who did feel the call to fight directly for social justice. Thurman's mysticism was an active one that manifested in the world, and it propelled him to write the books and sermons that inspired others.[53]

From Thurman's autobiography comes a beautiful reflection on the oneness of life despite the trials and tribulations that all people face:

> *My testimony is that life is against all dualism. Life is one. Therefore, a way of life that is worth living must be a way worthy of life itself. Nothing less than that can abide. Always, against all that fragments and shatters and against all things that separate and divide within and without, life laborers to melt together into a single harmony.*

---

52 Smith, "Introduction," 20–25.

53 Paul Harvey, *Howard Thurman and the Disinherited: A Religious Biography* (Grand Rapids: Eerdmans, 2020), 6–7.

> *Therefore, failure may remain failure in the context of all our strivings, hatred may continue to be hatred in the social and political arena of the common life, tragedy may continue to yield as anguish and its pain, spreading havoc in the tight circle of our private lives, the dead weight of guilt may not shift its position to make life even for a brief moment more comfortable and endurable, for any of us—all this may be true. Nevertheless, in all these things there is a secret door which leads into the central place, where the creator of life and the God of the human heart are one and the same. I take my stand for the future and for generations who follow over the bridges we have already crossed. It is here that the meaning of the hunger of the heart is unified. The Head and the Heart at last inseparable; they are lost in wonder in the One.*[54]

The failures and hatred of the world will continue, yet, according to Thurman, humans have access to the Creator of the universe and can dwell in wonder. While the above quote demonstrates obvious mysticism, the relationship with God and neighbor is particularly strong in his theology; this is a mysticism that is quite different from older forms of medieval or even early modern mystical thought. It is a type of inner mysticism deeply influenced by Quaker theology. It is also less explicitly Christian, though Thurman was a Christian pastor. He had powerful experiences with others of different faiths; his experiences in India were of particular relevance.

In *The Way of the Mystics*, Thurman writes of classic Christian mystics such as Francis of Assisi and Meister Eckhart, but also of mystics who belonged to other faiths such as ancient Chinese philosopher Lao Tzu, the Buddha, and Gandhi. This ecumenism became more common in modernity, and Thurman is quite explicit about

54 Howard Thurman, *With Head and Heart: The Autobiography of Howard Thurman* (San Diego: Harcourt, Brace, 1979), 269.

ecumenism in his writings. He essentially argues that all mystics are saying the same thing; regardless of faith tradition, mystics reject intermediaries and institutions, and they find God through renunciation and detachment. As he writes in his sermon on Lao Tzu, "Therefore he who seeks God may find him within; there is a door that no man can shut, and that door is deep within the human spirit."[55] Thurman then states that intermediates are not necessary.

In the final analysis, while he was not necessarily an activist himself, Thurman's mystical thought and political teachings were influential on the American civil rights movement and nonviolent resistance. He demonstrated an openness to the mystical streams in other faiths and taught those to others, bringing greater understanding of these traditions to Americans.

Dorothy Day (1897–1980)

Perhaps no person embodied a fusion of faith and activism better than Dorothy Day. While she was one of the more public and well-known activists, it is worth asking: To what degree should Day be considered a mystic? There are no visions or miracles associated with her life, unless one considers the radical love she modeled, which was so strong that one wonders whether it was perhaps divine. However, if she is judged on her deep and experiential relationship with God and her neighbors, then she most certainly should be considered a mystic. Unlike the medieval mystics, she did not experience mystical union. Yet, her spiritual journey, which is described in detail in her memoir, *The Long Loneliness*, demonstrates a radical conversion experience, a growing relationship with God, and a deep love of humanity. She also took the concept of the mystical body of Christ very seriously, and it inspired both her conversion and her active faith. Her friend and cofounder of the Catholic Worker Movement, Peter Maurin, believed her to be a modern-day Catherine of Siena. To a degree, he was right, especially

55 Howard Thurman, "Loa-Tse," in Eisenstadt and Fluker, *Way of the Mystics*, 20.

when looking at her willingness to engage in political action to address a wrong, though perhaps she more closely falls within the mold of Francis of Assisi. Like Francis, she was committed to voluntary poverty and helping those who had the least.

Day had a radical conversion experience to the Catholic faith, which resulted in a commitment to a quasi-monastic lifestyle and devoting her life to others. Yet, in a sense, Day stayed who she always had been. She always had a heart for the poor. She always spoke up for those who were oppressed. What changed with her conversion was how and why she addressed these issues. Like the mystics of old, she had a moment in childhood where she showed signs of her future vocation. It was not a religious vision of Christ or the Blessed Virgin but a vision of what humanity *could* be.

Day was born in Brooklyn, New York, at the end of the nineteenth century. When she was seven her family moved to San Francisco, and then after the 1906 earthquake the family moved to Chicago, where they had to live in a poor rowhouse, and there Day was first exposed to true poverty. Her family was not religious, but Day felt a pull toward Christianity. As a child she went to an Episcopal church and learned the catechism so she could be baptized. Yet, by college she had rejected Christianity and scorned the religious students. She was drawn to Marxism. Christians, to Day, seemed too comfortable in the face of societal injustice.

When pregnant with her first and only child, she felt increasingly drawn to the Catholic faith. She decided she was going to have her child baptized, no matter the personal cost. There was no question that it would be the Catholic faith into which she would baptize her child. For Day, Catholicism was the faith of the proletariat, the immigrant, and the oppressed. Considering immigration patterns in the early twentieth century, she was not wrong in this assessment. Her child's father, a committed anarchist and atheist, was against his child being baptized into the Catholic Church or any church. After the birth of their daughter, Tamar Teresa, who was named after the great mystic Teresa of Ávila, Day took steps to ensure her child's baptism. She sought help from a nun named Sister Aloysia, who trained her in the faith, all the while telling Day she too needed to convert so she could raise her Catholic daughter. Finally, "in the Church of Our Lady, Help of Christians, the seed of life was implanted in [Tamar Teresa] and she was made a child of God."[56]

Afterward Day made the decision to be baptized herself. Her baptism, First Communion, and confirmation, which she received at the same time, did not bring her particular joy. It came at a great personal price, but she could not deny the pull of God any longer. In phrasing that reflects the essence of more typical Catholic mysticism, particularly mystical bridal imagery, she describes her state after the baptism:

> *I wanted to be poor, chaste, and obedient. I wanted to die in order to live, to put off the old man and put on Christ. I loved, in other words, and like all women in love, I wanted to be united to my love. Why would not Forster [the father of her child] be jealous? Any man who did not participate in this love would, of course, realize my infidelity, my adultery. In the eyes of God, any turning toward creatures to the exclusion of Him is adultery and so it is termed over and over in Scripture.*[57]

Interestingly in the above quote, Day employs language that would not have been entirely out of place in the Middle Ages. She compares God to a lover, and instead of continuing in a romantic relationship with her human lover, she took on a semimonastic life.

Despite believing she did the right thing by joining the mystical body of Christ, she struggled in her initial years after baptism. A life-changing moment occurred five years later when she was

---

56 Dorothy Day, *The Long Loneliness: The Autobiography of the Legendary Catholic Social Activist* (San Francisco: HarperSanFrancisco, 1997), 144.

57 Day, *Long Loneliness*, 151.

covering a hunger march organized by communists. Discouraged that the Catholics were not there fighting for justice, she went to a nearby church to pray that God would use her to serve the poor. When she returned home, a man named Peter Maurin was waiting for her. The two would work together to establish the *Catholic Worker* newspaper in 1933, and later they would start the Catholic Worker Movement. Today, her impact is still felt in the 187 Catholic Worker communities that remain. These communities embrace "nonviolence, voluntary poverty, prayer, and radical hospitality for the homeless, exiled, hungry, and forsaken."[58] As Day writes in her autobiography, "Community—that was the social answer to the long loneliness. That was one of the attractions of religious life and why couldn't lay people share in it?"[59]

One final and amusing anecdote demonstrates that Day was not a medieval mystic of old but a modern laywoman practicing her faith out in the world, dealing with all the trials and tribulations that come with following a divine call. In her autobiography, Day tells of a time a reader of her paper came to Day's door with an unexpected question:

> *The first time she came down she stood at the door dramatically and said to me abruptly, "Do you have ecstasies and visions?" Poor dear, so hungry for mystical experience, even if secondhand, after a long life of faith.*
>
> *I was taken aback. "Visions of unpaid bills," I said abruptly. Her warmth, her effusiveness, were embarrassing but I soon learned to take them for what they were, an overflowing of an ardent soul, ready to pour itself out in love.*[60]

---

58 "About the Catholic Worker Movement," Catholic Worker Movement, accessed August 9, 2023, https://catholicworker.org/about-the-catholic-worker-movement/.

59 Day, *Long Loneliness*, 224.

60 Day, *Long Loneliness*, 188.

Day did have a vision. It was not a vision of angels or Jesus or any of the other heavenly beings that the mystics of old wrote about. It was a vision of justice and love, a vision of humanity truly living like Christ. She had a vision of people living together in community and striving for a New Testament ideal. She loved God deeply, and she loved humanity in the way Jesus commanded us all to.

Politics for a Modern World

There seems to be widespread discontentment about the general state of our nation. Of course, there are those who fight for social justice, for the poor, the forgotten, and the downtrodden, though increasingly there seems to be a divide between the faithful and those who support social reform, despite the very long history of intertwining the two.[61] Yet things are not actually that much different from in the past.[62] As demonstrated throughout this chapter, social injustices, corruption, and dysfunctional systems have always existed.

This chapter examined mystics who engaged in both church and societal politics, working for change on a large scale. The need for reform, both in institutions and in larger society, has not lessened with time. Perhaps this seems pessimistic, but institutions will always contend with corruption, and societies will always contend with problems of inequality. Perfection will always be impossible on this side of eternity, but the mystics can show us a way in which to engage with our institutions and our society that can be both life giving and beneficial

---

61 There is an interesting article written by Christopher Evans, a scholar of the social gospel, about the Christian left and activism that digs deeper into this issue. See Evans, "How the Social Gospel Movement Explains the Roots of Today's Religious Left," The Conversation, July 17, 2017, https://theconversation.com/how-the-social-gospel-movement-explains-the-roots-of-todays-religious-left-78895.

62 There is evidence that people have stayed relatively consistent in believing the US is morally bankrupt. This speaks only to perception, not actual decline. See A. M. Mastroianni and D. T. Gilbert, "The Illusion of Moral Decline," *Nature* 618 (2023): 782–89.

to others. Their faithfulness and action can be a model for how to navigate complex situations as faithful people.

Suggested Reading List

Bernard of Clairvaux. *On Loving God.* Kalamazoo, MI: Cistercian Publications, 1995.

———. *Sermons on the Song of Songs.* 4 vols. Translated by Kilian Walsh and Irene M. Edmonds. Spencer, MA: Cistercian Press, 1971–1980.

Birgitta of Sweden. *The Revelations of Birgitta of Sweden.* 4 vols. Translated by Denis Michael Searby. Oxford: Oxford University Press, 2006–2012.

Catherine of Siena. *The Dialogue.* Translated by Suzanne Noffke. New York: Paulist Press, 1980.

Day, Dorothy. *The Long Loneliness: The Autobiography of the Legendary Catholic Social Activist.* San Francisco: HarperSanFransisco, 1997.

Eisenstadt, Peter, and Walter Early Fluker, eds. *The Way of the Mystics.* Maryknoll, NY: Orbis, 2021.

Truth, Sojourner. *The Narrative of Sojourner Truth.* Battle Creek, MI: Review and Herald Office, 1884.

5

INTELLECT

Immediately before, and for a good while after my conversion, I was of the opinion that to lead a religious life meant one had to give up all that was secular and to live totally immersed in the Divine. But gradually I realized that something else is asked of us in this world and that, even in the contemplative life, one may not sever the connection with the world. I even believe that the deeper one is drawn into God, the more one must "go out of oneself" that is, one must go to the world in order to carry the divine life into it.

—Edith Stein, *Essential Writings*

THERE IS A fanciful legend about Augustine of Hippo, likely dating from the Middle Ages, that addresses his quest to understand the Trinity. The story goes like this: Augustine was walking along the seashore when he met a child who was using a shell to try to pour the sea into a small hole in the sand. Augustine told the child that this task was impossible—the small hole could not contain the sea. The child responded that it was no more impossible than a human trying to comprehend the mystery of the Holy Trinity. Augustine turned in amazement, and when he looked back, the child was gone. Some have interpreted the child as an angel or the Christ child. Regardless, Augustine left the encounter understanding that the Trinity was a mystery, one the human mind can never truly comprehend.[1]

---

1 Augustine did write extensively on the Trinity. See his important book on the subject, *On the Trinity*, ed. D. P. Curtin, trans. Arthur West Hadden (Philadelphia: Dalcassian, 2018).

While this delightful little tale is only a legend and was likely written many centuries after Augustine's death, it helps illuminate the complexity of mystical scholars. On the one hand, scholarship tends to make a subject of God, and it must engage the knowable aspects of God. Just as the child does pour *some* of the seawater into the hole, there are things Christians can profess to know about God. Christian theology provides a vital backbone to a believer's relationship with God, and the most important mystics in history have had a firm intellectual understanding of God. Yet, just as a small hole cannot contain the entirety of the sea, no one, at least in this life, will understand the fullness of God's nature. In this legend Augustine learns this lesson through an encounter with either the divine or a heavenly being. This understanding emerged from experience, not scholarly endeavor.

The beauty of Christian mysticism, especially relating to academic scholarship, is that it tempers the tendency to make a subject of God. The mystics emphasized relationship and experience. They were not content to make a thought project out of the Triune God. There is often a false dichotomy presented when talking about the head and the heart. One can either think about God *or* one can experience the love of God. This is an unhelpful way to think about both mysticism and theology. Studying the mystics provides a more balanced approach, and combating this false binary is precisely the intention of this chapter.

Evagrius of Pontus, a gifted theologian, wrote in his text *On Prayer*: "One who prays truly will be a theologian, and one who is a theologian will truly pray."[2] There is a bit of nuance that is lost in both the linguistic and cultural translation, but this is still a useful quote for thinking about the relationship between mysticism, its foundation of prayer, and the more academic study of theology. The truth is, there are theologians who have profound mystical experiences. For example, there are few theologians who have left a greater mark on the Christian faith than Thomas Aquinas, and he wrote poetry inspired by mystical

---

2 Evagrius, "On Prayer," 192, point 61.

experiences. There are also people classified as mystics who engaged in profound theological reflection. Julian of Norwich's longer text of *Revelations of Divine Love* was the product of over a decade of theological reflection on her own mystical experience. These are just two examples of many to emphasize the intertwined nature of intellectual and experiential encounters with God. Mysticism and theology can and should balance each other and our faith; there are risks involved in neglecting either the head or the heart. At best, neglecting the intellect can run the risk of establishing a feel-good faith that has little substance; at worst, it can result in harmful theologies that ignore centuries of theological reflection. To neglect the heart and lived experience can result in a harsh and unapproachable faith.

The Christian mystics who had the most impact in history used both their intellect and their experiences with God in their theology. As Mark McIntire astutely notes, separating spirituality from theology can have negative results:

> *The problem with this separation from theology is that it tends to disorientate spirituality, to deprive it of some of the stable communal goal and reference, and hence render it susceptible to the idols, compulsions, or fears of the individual. There is another danger as well: the intensity of the mystical experience can easily lead to a kind of absolutism that oppresses the lives of the mystics themselves or of cultures receptive to them. Theology reminds spirituality that "interpretation is intrinsic to experience."*[3]

This chapter is filled with men and women who took theology seriously, and they were all intellectuals who shaped Christian thought. They also understood that God was more than a subject. They longed to know God intimately. While these individuals are remembered

3 Mark A. McIntosh, *Mystical Theology: The Integrity of Spirituality and Theology* (Malden, MA: Blackwell, 1998), 14.

as great theologians, they are not outliers in having fusing faith and intellect. Their stories represent a larger trend in Christian mystical thought. They may be exemplars, but they are not uncommon.

These scholars are a varied group, living in different places and during different time periods. Some of them claimed miraculous occurrences and events; others did not. Some wrote about achieving mystical union with God; others did not. The first two figures are, without exaggeration, some of the most influential Christian theologians in history. This short chapter can only scratch the surface of their theology and accomplishments. The first, Origen of Alexandria, admittedly has a mixed legacy. Many of his writings were declared heretical after his death, yet his influence on Christianity, including Christian mysticism, is unquestionable. The second, Augustine of Hippo, is often seen as *the* theologian of the Latin West; it is doubtful whether anyone has had more impact on the shape of Western Christian history and theology. Then the chapter moves to Gertrude the Great, the only woman in the Catholic Church to hold the title "the great." Her writings, full of marriage imagery and evincing a dependence on the monastic life, epitomize the medieval mystical experience. Francis de Sales, a man of many talents, was a well-educated and intellectual mind but also a profoundly gentle presence in the early modern era. The chapter ends with Edith Stein, a philosopher turned Carmelite nun, whose theological contributions were significant before she was murdered in a Nazi death camp. Each of these individuals provides a model of what the fusion of mysticism and intellectualism can look like.

Origen (ca. 185–253)

Origen of Alexandria had one of the great minds of the early church; he was not only brilliant but creative and prolific, and his influence on Christianity has been immense. Accusations and condemnations of heresy after his death have long marred his legacy, but it is important to understand that he wrote in a time when Christianity was still illegal in the Roman Empire and therefore before the great ecumenical church councils formally established doctrine and creeds.

Origen was born around 185, probably in Alexandria, Egypt, which at the time was a cosmopolitan city known for its intellectualism. He was the son of pious Christians, but he studied under a well-respected Platonist. This Platonic influence is important both for his mystical leanings and in relation to his later condemnation. While in his teens, his father was martyred during the persecution under Emperor Septimius Severus in 202. Origen was eager to die for the faith as well, but his mother hid his clothes so he could not offer himself up. Shortly after this, the bishop of Alexandria, Demetrius, appointed Origen to the task of training catechumens. In the early church, the process of becoming a Christian took about three years and involved much education about the Christian life. Origen's position was both important and quite respected.[4]

Origen is a model of the classical philosopher and Christian ascetic.[5] Though he lived before the blossoming of the monastic movement, his lifestyle and thought can certainly be seen as a precursor to desert spirituality. In fact, he had a tremendous influence on a number of desert mystics, including Evagrius (examined in ch. 2). Origen lived a strict life of asceticism, devotion, prayer, and study. His scholarship brought him fame, which led to conflict with Demetrius. In 233, Origen left Alexandria for Caesarea, where he continued to write and teach for the rest of his life. Origen's literary output was incredible, though many of his writings have been lost.

Like other early mystics, Origen's mysticism cannot be defined by the later medieval ideas around mystical union. However, there are a number of important mystical aspects of his theology, including the idea of an ascent to God, his approach to biblical interpretation, and the role of martyrdom. Origen had an idea of an upward journey or ascension to God, which continues to be an important aspect of

4 McGinn, *Foundations of Mysticism*, 108–9.

5 McGinn, *Foundations of Mysticism*, 109.

mystical thought. While this was certainly influenced by Plato, Origen associated this ascension with Christ.[6] Hans Urs von Balthasar explains and clears up a common misconception about this ascent beautifully in an introduction to Origen's works. He writes, "This ascension model has often been confused with Pelagianism and a self-empowered works. Falsely, we believe, for according to Origen (as later according to Augustine) every step upwards entails being lifted and drawn. . . . All that he is, he is solely by the grace of Christ."[7] This emphasis on grace and God's actions in the mystic's ascent to God is of utmost importance because it is such a common theme throughout mystical literature in the history of Christianity. It is not a sort of works-righteousness or some individualist quest to reach God.

Also important to Origen's mystical thought is the role of martyrdom, which he believed to be the apex of Christian life and the perfect imitation of Christ. Considering how much this ideal changed later in Christian history (though martyrdom, of course, continues to the present day in certain places in the world), it is worth dwelling on it for a moment. For Origen, being a Christian came with inherent risk. As the son of a martyr and as someone who suffered profoundly for his faith, he lived with a deeply personal understanding of this fact. For Origen, the perfect imitation of Christ was to literally take up one's cross and die just as Christ had done.

One last point must be made on Origen's mysticism, and that is his introduction of erotic symbolism to mystical thought. This continued to be a major theme of Christian mysticism for centuries and was employed by both men and women mystics, though Bernard of Clairvaux is one of the best known to do so. This is one aspect of Christian mysticism that has been wildly misinterpreted and misunderstood by modern readers. A short excerpt from Origen's *Commentary on the*

---

6 McGinn, *Foundations of Mysticism*, 115.

7 Origen, *Spirit and Fire: A Thematic Anthology of His Writings*, ed. Hans Urs von Balthasar, trans. Robert J. Daly, SJ (Washington, DC: Catholic University of America Press, 1984), 9.

Song of Songs provides a foundational example of both bridal imagery and the inclusion of eroticism to describe the relationship between the creature and Creator:

> *This book [the Song of Songs] seems to me an epithalamium, that is, a wedding song, written by Solomon in the form of a play, when he recited in the character of a bride who was being married and burned with a heavenly love for her bridegroom, who is the Word of God. For whether she is the soul made after His image or the Church, she has fallen deeply in love with him. Moreover, this book of Scripture instructs us in the words this marvelous and perfect bridegroom uses toward the soul or the Church that has been united with Him.*[8]

The Song of Songs became a central text in mystical writing—often being interpreted with the bride as the soul and the bridegroom as God, as Origen demonstrates. While this association with erotic love may be uncomfortable for modern readers, many mystics would have argued that this is the most appropriate use of erotic language and a purer form of it than eroticism between two human beings.

Toward the end of Origen's life, between 249 and 250, yet another Christian persecution began, this one under the reign of Emperor Decius. Origen, who had avoided the persecution that took his father (though considering the length to which his mother went to keep him safe, *avoided* might not be the best word), fell victim to this round. He was arrested and tortured. Because of his status as a well-respected Christian, Roman authorities wanted him to recant his beliefs, and his torment was significant. He did not submit to the will of the empire, and he was eventually released after the emperor died.

---

8 Origen, "Commentary on the Song of Songs," in *An Anthology of Christian Mysticism*, ed. Harvey Egan, SJ (Collegeville, MN: Liturgical Press, 1991), 25.

Origen died within a few years, spending the rest of his life suffering from the effects of the state's cruelty.

Following Origen's death, church leaders and theologians denounced him for his ideas and for how some of his followers interpreted his teachings. He was condemned at the Second Council of Constantinople in 553. Two of his most controversial ideas were that all, even the devil, would be saved, and that souls preexisted. In the Eastern church, he was given the title "heretic of heretics." Regardless, by the time of the Renaissance, theologians were starting to reassess Origen, and modern scholars have come to appreciate both his genius and his theological contributions to Christianity. He led the way for many foundational aspects of mysticism for centuries to come.

Augustine (354–430)

While Origen lived during an era of Christian persecution, Augustine was born into a world where Christianity was legal and flourishing. Both men were intellectual giants of their day, but their political situations were drastically different, and that affected both their scholarship and their faith, including their mystical tendencies. Augustine is arguably the most influential theologian in Christian history, particularly for Catholics and Protestants; his influence has been more limited in the Eastern Orthodox tradition. His life included a dramatic conversion event, and in some ways it became *the* model for conversion. His theology was foundational to the Latin church. Monastic orders, most notably the Dominicans (properly, Ordo Praedictorum or the Order of Preachers), follow his monastic rule. His writings not only deal with theology but also with politics and how a Christian should live in the world. While Augustine is not primarily thought of as a mystic, he did affect Christian mysticism, and he lived in a way that should be interpreted as mystical.

Augustine was born in 354 in Thagaste, which is today in Algeria. His father was a minor Roman official, and his mother, Monica, was a devout Christian. Monica is a constant presence in

Augustine's *Confessions*, and her influence on Augustine is unquestionable. From a young age, Augustine demonstrated a sharp intellect, and his parents, though not wealthy, sought to provide him the best education possible. At the age of seventeen, he went to Carthage, a great and cosmopolitan city, where he studied rhetoric, which would have been the proper course of study for a future in politics or law. Also in Carthage, he took a lover, a woman usually referred to as his "concubine." They were a monogamous couple for many years, even having a child together (a boy named Adeodatus), but due to differences in social class and societal expectations, they could not marry. There is no question that he loved her, though she remains entirely anonymous because he never recorded her name in any of his writings.

ROMAN NORTH AFRICA

The Romans held sway in North Africa for approximately five hundred years (146 BCE–439 CE). Following the Third Punic War (149–146 BCE), the Romans destroyed Carthage and created a new province called Africa out of the rest of the Carthaginian territory. By the second century CE, most of the province was urbanized and Romanized, enjoying a time of relative prosperity. At the beginning of the fifth century, the Vandals, a Germanic people, invaded and migrated en masse to North Africa. The independence of the Vandal kingdom in North Africa was recognized by the Western Roman Emperor, Valentinian III, in 442. The Vandals were laying siege to Hippo as Augustine lay dying in 430.

Augustine moved to Milan to teach rhetoric (he had also taught rhetoric in Carthage, but his students were an unruly bunch, and he was hoping for better students). After years of being a Manichaean,[9] in Milan he became a Neoplatonist, which was a philosophy with heavy religious overtones that has had a profound impact on Christian mysticism in particular. Neoplatonism indeed proved a gateway to Christianity. While in Milan Augustine felt called to convert, in a mystical moment in a garden, but he was not a man to do things halfway, and he hesitated to devote his life to the religion his mother had so long prayed that he would embrace.

Augustine was baptized by Ambrose of Milan shortly after Easter in 387. Not long after, he decided to return home to North Africa. As he and his fellow travelers were waiting to leave, a military blockade left them stuck at the Roman port of Ostia.[10] There Augustine and his mother, Monica, had a conversation that led to a mystical vision of the divine Wisdom that transcends all things:

> *Our minds were lifted up by an ardent affection towards eternal being itself. Step by step we climbed beyond all corporeal objects and the heaven itself, where sun, moon, and stars shed light on the earth. We ascended even further by internal reflection and dialogue and wonder at your works, and we entered into our own minds. We moved up beyond them so as to attain to the region of inexhaustible abundance where you feed Israel eternally with truth for food. There life is the wisdom by which all creatures coming to being, both things which were and which will be. But wisdom itself in not brought into being but is as it was and always will be.*

---

9 Manichaeism started with the Persian prophet Mani in the third century. Mani's desire was to gather the religions of the world into one, and he was influenced by Judaism, Christianity, Buddhism, and most notably Zoroastrianism, the religion of the Persian Empire. At its core, Manichaeism is a dualist faith, with an eternal light and an eternal darkness.

10 Peter Brown, *Augustine of Hippo: A Biography* (Berkeley: University of California Press, 2000), 121.

> *Furthermore, in this wisdom there is no past and future, but only being, since it is eternal.*[11]

A particularly notable aspect of this vision is that Augustine and Monica experienced it together, which is not common throughout mystical literature, though perhaps it is fitting. Augustine's mother was so influential in her son's conversion and faith that they were able to have a miraculous moment together. A more common element of the vision is its theme of ascent, first through the physical heavens and then through their minds.

After his mother's death and then the death of his son, Augustine took up monastic living, but Bishop Valerius of Hippo forced him to accept ordination *and* to become his assistant. While forced ordination seems odd today, it happened more often than we might think in those days. For example, Gregory of Nazianzus was ordained *and* made bishop against his will, and Ambrose of Milan, the bishop who baptized Augustine, was pressured into becoming bishop—before he was even a baptized Christian. After Valerius's death, Augustine became sole bishop of Hippo, a post he held for thirty-five years. During his time as bishop, Augustine wrote much of what would become foundational to Christianity. He was involved with both theological and political debates of the era (most notable were conflicts with the Manichaeans, the Donatists, and Pelagius and his followers), and as a priest and a bishop he was concerned with the well-being of his flock.

THE PELAGIAN CONTROVERSY

Pelagianism is an understanding of how human beings are able to merit their salvation. It places a strong emphasis on human works and downplays grace.

11 Augustine, *Confessions*, trans. Henry Chadwick (Oxford: Oxford University Press, 2008), 171.

The term is derived from Pelagius, a theologian and possibly a monk, who was a native of the British Isles. It is not known when he was born, but he encountered Augustine of Hippo's theology in Rome at the beginning of the fifth century. The subsequent Pelagian controversy, which primarily involved Pelagius and Augustine of Hippo, is complex, but the main issues revolved around the understanding of free will, sin, grace, and the basis of salvation.

Augustine held to humanity's fallen nature without falling into fatalism. For him, human beings were dependent on God's grace for salvation. While human being do possess free will, it has been weakened and is biased toward doing evil. Human beings are universally affected by sin as a result of the fall, and humanity does not have control over its sinful nature. Augustine places tremendous importance on God's grace, which is given freely.

However, for Pelagius and his followers, humanity had total free will. Pelagius argued that humans were born sinless (rejecting the concept of original sin). He downplayed the necessity of God's grace since he thought human beings were indeed capable of choosing to do good and avoiding sin. In his thought, because human beings are capable of good, any failure to do so is their own.

Augustine's relationship with God is critical to interpreting him. While a full examination is entirely beyond the scope of this chapter, a few aspects are worth mention. His *Confessions* is of primary importance since it traces his conversion experience and his relationship with God. His *Homilies on the Psalms*, *The Trinity*, and *Homilies on the First Epistle of John* are all important in establishing his mystical thought.[12]

12 Bernard McGinn, *The Beginnings of Western Mysticism* (New York: Crossroad, 1991), 229.

Bernard McGinn, who refers to Augustine as the "prince of mystics," helpfully lays out three building blocks of Augustine's mystical thought and his contributions to later Western mysticism: "First, [Augustine's] account of the soul's ascension to contemplative and ecstatic experience of the divine presence; second, the ground for the possibility of this experience in the nature of the human person as the image of the triune God; and third, the necessary role of Christ and the church in attaining this experience."[13]

Augustine was the last of the great theologians of the imperial church. During his life, Rome, that eternal city, was crumbling. The motivation for him to write his great opus, *City of God*, was the sacking of Rome in 410. As he lay dying in 430, the Germanic tribe the Vandals were at the gates of Hippo, ready to take North Africa. Even though he was the last great theologian of the age, no one was quoted more often than he was in the Middle Ages, and one cannot seriously study the Christian tradition without dealing with the North African bishop. But it was not just the brilliance of his theology that made him so influential. Christianity was not an abstract subject for him. He was a true and genuine believer who loved God and did his best to live accordingly.

Gertrude of Helfta, the Great (1256–1302)

Nine hundred years and a continent away from Augustine of Hippo was Gertrude of Helfta. Augustine wrote as his political order fell apart, and Christianity was being criticized for that decline; Gertrude wrote in a relatively stable political situation and a blossoming Christian atmosphere. As a man, Augustine had freedoms Gertrude could never have imagined, while she spent almost her entire life enclosed in a convent. Despite these differences, Gertrude, like Augustine, possessed a brilliant mind and left a lasting impact on mystical theology.

---

13 McGinn, *Beginnings of Western Mysticism*, 231.

Gertrude the Great spent her life in the vibrant intellectual atmosphere of the convent of Helfta in the Holy Roman Empire. The convent was Benedictine but heavily influenced by the Cistercians, although the priests who tended to the sisters' spiritual needs were Dominicans. Among her companions were Mechthild of Magdeburg and Gertrude of Hackeborn, both respected mystics. Even among this illustrious company, Gertrude's writings stand out.

While Gertrude is careful to give accurate dates for important mystical visions, she gives little other information about her life. Historians know she born in 1256 but do not know where or who her parents were. She entered Helfta at the age of four. This may sound shocking to modern readers, but children entering monasteries was not uncommon. What is surprising is that there is no indication of who her family was—the name is missing from the otherwise careful records. She seems to have been born far from Helfta, with no family whatsoever near her, nor any contact with family after entering the convent. In other words, she never knew any life other than the convent.[14]

Gertrude received an excellent education—far better than most medieval women could hope for. When she was a child, the nuns at Helfta recognized her intellectual gifts. She may have made the decision to become a nun in her teenage years so she could continue with her education. She was described as excessively attached to her secular studies, though she became more interested in theology as an adult.[15] She was well read in Scripture, the church fathers, and contemporary theologians (Bernard of Clairvaux was a particularly important influence on her). She was well versed in rhetoric, and, most notably, she knew and wrote in Latin. While Latin was commonly taught to boys, it was less common for women to write in Latin during the time; many

---

14 Margaret Winkworth, "Introduction," in *The Herald of Divine Love*, by Gertrude of Helfta, ed. and trans. Margaret Winkworth (New York: Paulist Press, 1993), 5–6.

15 Gertrude, *Herald of Divine Love*, 53.

of the extant mystical texts we have from women were written in the vernacular, or the language of the people.

Gertrude had a transformative mystical experience at age twenty-five. Years later she wrote about it in her text *The Herald of Divine Love*:

> *I looked up and saw before me a youth of about sixteen years of age, handsome and gracious. Young as I then was, the beauty of his form was all that I could have desired, entirely pleasing to the outward eye. Courteously and in a gentle voice he said to me: "Soon will come your salvation; why are you so sad? It is because you have no one to confide that you are sorrowful?"*

She continues: "I heard these words: 'I will save you, I will deliver you. Do not fear.' With this, I saw his hand, tender and fine, holding mine, as though to plight a troth, and he added: 'With my enemies you have licked the dust (cf. Ps. 71:9) and sucked honey among thorns. Come back to me now, and I will inebriate you with the torrent of my divine pleasure' (Ps. 35:9)."[16] Of particular note is the use of bridal imagery. This was common among mystics of this era, especially women mystics, and this quote provides a rather typical example. Like Origen and Bernard, she uses erotic language, not to sexualize her relationship with God but to demonstrate a deep intimacy. Gertrude continued to have other visions throughout her life, but it was this one in particular that she believed marked a break with her previous life, and it was significant enough that she referred to it as a conversion event. She wrote that she constantly felt Christ's presence within her soul from that day forward.[17]

Gertrude's day-to-day life changed little as a result of her conversion of heart. She continued to live in her monastery; her days

---

16 Gertrude, *Herald of Divine Love*, 95.

17 Gertrude, *Herald of Divine Love*, 99.

were filled with the Divine Office, which is a theme in her writing, especially her *Spiritual Exercises.* She was an assistant chantress and a teacher. Living in a Benedictine monastery, Gertrude likely helped with the manual labor. Historians know that she was a sought-after spiritual adviser to both sisters living within the convent and people from the outside world. She was also a writer, completing spiritual works and explanations of the Scriptures.[18] There are two extant works from Gertrude, *The Herald of Divine Love* and her *Spiritual Exercises.*

The Herald of Divine Love is the book of her revelations. It is divided into five books, though book 2, titled "The Memorial of the Abundance of Divine Sweetness," is the only section written by Gertrude. The first book was written after Gertrude's death and is an introduction to the rest of the work. Books 3–5 were written by another nun (or more than one) during Gertrude's lifetime, likely with Gertrude dictating some of the language. It is possible these sections were written toward the end of her life when she was too sick to write herself.

Gertrude's *Spiritual Exercises* is the more popular and more enjoyable to read of her extant works. It is a collection of meditations, prayers, chants, hymns, and litanies. As one scholar notes, "In short, [it is] ruminations of a medieval mystic on various themes based on Scripture and liturgy."[19] The text is composed of seven chapters, which focus on subjects such as rebirth, mystical union, and death. The first four chapters are based on liturgical rites, and the last three use the Divine Office. While there is an obvious monastic tone to this work, it is perfectly readable and helpful to anyone.[20] The prayers and meditations in particular can be used by laypeople in a variety of settings. A short excerpt will demonstrate the poetic feel of this text:

---

18 Winkworth, "Introduction," 9.

19 Gertrud Jaron Lewis and Jack Lewis, "Introduction," in *Spiritual Exercises,* by Gertrud the Great of Helfta, ed. and trans. Gertrud Jaron Lewis and Jack Lewis (Kalamazoo, MI: Cistercian Publications, 1989), 1.

20 Lewis and Lewis, "Introduction," 11.

> *Ah! O God, love, you alone are my entire and true love. You are my dearest salvation, all my hope and joy and my supreme and best good. My God, my dearest love, in the morning I will stand before you and will see that you yourself are everlasting pleasantness and gentleness. You are what my heart thirsts for. You are the entire sufficiency of my spirit. The more I taste you, the more I hunger; the more I drink, the more I thirst.*[21]

Love and longing are at the heart of this excerpt, and indeed within her writing in general.

When reading Gertrude, it is easy to imagine her in solitude contemplating divine mysteries, writing about her experiences alone in her cell. However, it is important to remember that she lived in community with other women, many of whom were accomplished intellectuals themselves. Her writings were communal texts, especially *The Herald of Divine Love.* That Helfta was a robust intellectual community specifically for women in the medieval era rightly pushes people today to appreciate the long and robust history of women's intellectual accomplishments in Christianity, even if those accomplishments have too often been diminished and overlooked in favor of highlighting the more public discourse of male theologians. As she was a woman writing in the Middle Ages, it is difficult to compare her works to the scholastic theologians who were her contemporaries. Even though her education was far more than an average woman received, she was not trained as a theologian. Yet, history has remembered her as a scholar. Her designation as "the great" indeed acknowledges the importance of her theological work. Perhaps most important, Gertrude grew up and lived among highly educated women, and her writings represent not only her intellectual gifts but those of her community in general.

Gertrude died in November of either 1301 or 1302, and for a time she disappeared into obscurity. A Latin edition of her work

---

21 Gertrud, *Spiritual Exercises*, 73–74.

was published in 1536, in the midst of the tumultuous years of the Protestant Reformation, which brought renewed fame to the medieval mystic.[22] She was never formally canonized, but she was given a feast day in the early seventeenth century, still celebrated on November 16.[23]

Francis de Sales (1567–1622)

Francis de Sales was a man of many talents and is difficult to categorize. He is included in this chapter highlighting intellect because he was a scholar and popular writer of devotional books. He was also a bishop, gifted preacher, effective evangelist, and cofounder of a monastic order (Visitation). His gentle and reconciling attitude toward Protestants stands out in an era of hostilities. De Sales was part of a seventeenth-century French reform movement (along with others such as Pierre de la Bérulle, St. Vincent de Paul, and Jeanne de Chantal) that long affected Catholic spirituality.

As the eldest of thirteen children born to a noble family in Savoy, France, he was never meant for the church. His intellectual gifts were apparent when he was a child, and he received an excellent education with the intention of pursuing a secular career. He was educated at a Jesuit institution, where he followed a humanist curriculum typical of a young gentleman. Because of personal interest, he studied theology in addition to his other subjects. Around age twenty, he had a spiritual crisis of sorts about the issue of predestination, which was being hotly debated in both Catholic and Reformed circles. He fell into a state of despair, but after giving himself over to God's mercy, he decided he would live in the moment and not fear the future.

---

22 Caroline W. Bynum, "Vita: Gertrude of Helfta," *Harvard Magazine*, May–June 2012, https://www.harvardmagazine.com/2012/03/vita-gertrude-of-helfta.

23 Benedict XIV, *Novembris in Festo S. Gertrudis Virginis, et Abbatissoe Ordinis S. Benedicti* (Rome: Typis Joseph Francesci Ferri Impress. Episc, 1739). The Latin text can be found at https://archive.org/details/wotb_6743650/page/n1/mode/2up.

He continued his education in Padua, where he officially studied law but continued to pursue theological studies on his own time. Augustine and Aquinas were of particular help regarding his questions around the issue of predestination, and he finally accepted the theological position that God wanted to save all of humanity, not an elect few. In 1592, he returned home a changed man and told his parents he wanted to become a priest. His family reluctantly agreed. He never attended a seminary, but his extensive private studies qualified him for the priesthood. He accepted a prestigious position as provost of the Church of St. Peter in Geneva and was an assistant to the bishop. The bishop died quickly after de Sales's appointment, and de Sales became bishop himself. Geneva, the location of the John Calvin's reforming activities in the sixteenth century, was a Calvinist stronghold, but de Sales vowed to win the city back for Catholicism. He believed it was his duty to build up a community of pious Catholic believers, which is apparent in his devotional writings for the laity.

CALVIN AND PREDESTINATION

Francis de Sales was the bishop of Geneva, which was the location of John Calvin's reformation activities. Calvin can hardly be considered a mystic by any definition, but he did leave a long theological legacy in Geneva and beyond. Calvin, born in 1509 in France, became a Protestant sometime in the 1530s and first published his massively influential book, *The Institutes of the Christian Religion*, in 1536. Forced to leave France due to his Protestant commitments, he ended up the leader of the church in Geneva in 1541. Central to Calvin's theology is God's sovereignty. Calvin believed in predestination, though it was not a central doctrine of his own theology. Later Reformed theologians developed the idea of "five-point Calvinism," which emphasizes total depravity, unconditional election, limited atonement, irresistible grace, and perseverance of the saints, which was laid down definitively at the Synod of Dort (1618–1619).

De Sales wrote two books that have had particular impact on Catholic spirituality. First is *Introduction to the Devout Life*, which was first published in 1608. The book is a structured reworking of pastoral letters he had written over the years to people who sought him out for spiritual guidance. De Sales is modest in what he sets out to accomplish in the book. In his preface, he states, "I neither can nor will, nor indeed should I, write in this Introduction anything but what has already been published by our predecessors on the same subject." He acknowledges that most devotional books are written to those who have withdrawn from the world (meaning a monastic life). His "purpose is to instruct those who live in town, with families, or at court, and by their state of life are obliged to live an ordinary life as to outward appearances."[24] He succeeded in providing a systematic overview of the holy life directed at lay believers, and people responded well to his work. The book was enthusiastically received all over France, going through multiple editions and eventually being translated into other languages. The tone of the book is highly pastoral and readable, even all these centuries later. It is not an exaggeration to say that modern readers could pick up this text and find themselves immersed in de Sales's pastoral guidance. Topics range from aspects of holy life, such as prayer, how to attend Mass, and invoking the saints, to more practical daily issues, such as contending with anxiety and spiritual dryness.

The second book, which is of particular relevance for the study of Christian mysticism, *On the Love of God*, was first published in 1616. It functions as a summary of mystical teaching. When describing the

24 Francis de Sales, *Introduction to the Devout Life*, ed. and trans. John K. Ryan (New York: Image Books, 1989), 33.

work in his preface, de Sales explains its purpose: "I have merely sought to set the origin, growth, slackening, and working, the particularities and blessings, of God's Love simply and plainly before my readers."[25] The book is addressed to a fictional "advanced soul" by the name of Theotimus. It is broken into twelve sections that deal with topics such a divine love, progress and perfection, and union. De Sales includes beautiful and intriguing imagery, including a memorable comparison of mystical union and a child breastfeeding. He writes:

> *See that lovely babe as its mother offers it the breast, how it throws itself with all the energy of its tiny frame into her lap, nestling up to her tender bosom, while the mother presses it closely to her, kissing and fondling it. Mother and babe seem to have but one existence between them, so fondly does he co-operate in that clinging embrace. . . . And so this union is perfect, it is equal as regards both mother and child; and yet it originates actually with the mother.*[26]

The gentleness of the image is very much in line with his sincere and generous personality. In an age that was not known for compassion or love (one of the more notorious wars in history, the Thirty Years' War, began toward the end of his lifetime), de Sales won converts through holiness, effective preaching, popular writing, and his charming personality. The concept of God as a gentle and loving mother, helping her children, is one that stands out among mystical writings on union as particularly relatable, especially when considering his audience of laypeople, who often would have been parents themselves.

De Sales died in 1622 and was canonized in 1665. He left his mark in a variety of ways on Christianity, specifically modern Catholicism. While it is critical to note his influence through both his work as

---

25 Francis de Sales, *On the Love of God*, trans. H. L. Sidney Lear (London: Rivingtons, 1888), vii.

26 De Sales, *On the Love of God*, 217–18.

a bishop and as the cofounder of the Sisters of the Visitation, his ability to make both Catholic spirituality and mysticism accessible to regular people is perhaps his greatest legacy. He was not writing to other monastics or theologians, and his ability to make these concepts relatable to nonspecialists is of note. He represents an important change in this time. Mysticism was leaving the monasteries and heading out into the world. This continued to be the trend in modern Catholicism.

Edith Stein (1891–1942)

In August 1942, a Carmelite nun by the name of Teresa Benedicta of the Cross, born Edith Stein, was passing through a series of Nazi transit camps. She found herself at Westerbork, where many women and children were being held. In the short time she was there, she tended to the suffering children, washing them, combing their hair, and trying, despite the impossibility of their situation, to make sure they were fed and cared for. Those who were there remembered her kindness and resolve, though she did not stay long. One week after her arrest by the SS, she was murdered at Auschwitz because of her Jewish ancestry. The world lost not only a compassionate and loving Christian that day but also a talented scholar.

Stein was born to Orthodox Jewish parents in Breslau, Germany (now Wroclaw, Poland), in 1891. She was the youngest of seven surviving children, and her father died when she was only two years old. Despite the religiosity of her upbringing, by her teenage years, Stein was an atheist. Yet even after her conversion to Catholicism, Stein had a very positive feeling for her Jewish upbringing, and she wrote a memoir called *Life in a Jewish Family* to fight against the growing tide of anti-Semitism, the bulk of which was written in 1933. The opening line of her foreword explains, "Recent months have catapulted the German Jews out of the peaceful existence they had come to take for granted."[27]

---

27 Edith Stein, *Life in a Jewish Family: An Autobiography 1891–1916*, ed. L. Gelber and Romaus Leuven, trans. Josephine Koeppel (Washington, DC: Institute of Carmelite Studies, ICS Publications, 1986), 23.

From a young age, Stein demonstrated intellectual prowess, which allowed her to pursue university studies. In 1917, she was one of the first women in Germany to earn a doctorate, studying under Edmund Husserl. She earned the degree in the field of philosophy; her dissertation was titled "The Problem of Empathy." Stein should have been considered one of the great academics of the era. If she had been a man, that likely would have been the case, but her career suffered because she was a woman, and she was unable to find a university appointment.[28] Husserl, her dissertation adviser, for whom she worked as a research assistant, wrote the following recommendation: "Should academic careers be opened up to ladies, then I can recommend her whole-heartedly and as my first choice for admission to a professorship."[29] This is a sad commentary on the limitations that women faced as late as the twentieth century. Later her career was affected by anti-Semitism as well.

During her studies, Stein began a spiritual search. She studied the Gospels and read Danish religious philosopher Søren Kierkegaard. But it was a chance encounter with one of the great mystics, Teresa of Ávila, that brought Stein to the Catholic faith. In 1921 she was staying with friends, and she looked through their bookshelves wanting something to read one night while her friends were away from home. There she found Teresa's autobiography. Once she picked it up, she stayed up all night reading the book. When she finally finished the next morning, she said to herself, "This is the truth." The scholar Stein was profoundly drawn to Teresa's understanding that God was not understood through deductive intelligence but through hearts that surrender to him.[30]

---

28 John Sullivan, OCD, "Introduction," in *Essential Writings*, by Edith Stein, ed. John Sullivan, OCD (Maryknoll, NY: Orbis Books, 2002), 18.

29 "Teresa Benedict of the Cross, Edith Stein (1891–1942)," The Holy See, accessed January 21, 2024, https://www.vatican.va/news_services/liturgy/saints/ns_lit_doc_19981011_edith_stein_en.html.

30 Waltraud Herbstrith, *Edith Stein: A Biography*, trans. Father Bernard Bonowitz, OCSO (San Francisco: Harper & Row, 1985), 31.

Stein's conversion was a bit unusual. She bought herself a catechism and a missal and studied them on her own. Later she attended Mass, which would have been in Latin, and found she could easily follow along. After it was over, she approached the priest, Monsignor Breitling, and asked him to baptize her. He was surprised and explained that usually there was a period of preparation before baptism. In response, Stein asked her to examine her instead, which went so well that the priest scheduled her baptism.[31] Her baptism shocked her family; her mother in particular was upset by the conversion. Yet, her mother, seeing the transformation in her daughter, did believe the conversion was God's action. Even after becoming Catholic, Stein continued to attend synagogue with her mother, and her mother remarked that she had never seen anyone pray like her daughter did.[32]

Following her conversion, Stein taught at a girls' school run by Dominican nuns. Throughout this time, she translated writings by Thomas Aquinas and John Henry Newman. She obtained a position at the German Institute for Scientific Pedagogy in Münster in 1931, but she lost it in 1933 due to Nazi laws forbidding Jews from holding public positions. No longer able to work in any sort of public position or ministry, she entered the Cologne Carmel and took the name Sister Teresa Benedicta of the Cross. After the events of Kristallnacht, she was moved to Carmel in Echt, Netherlands, where she was joined by her sister Rosa, who had also converted and became a Carmelite nun. After the Germans took the Netherlands, Catholic leadership attempted to have the sisters moved to Switzerland for their safety, but they needed permission from government authorities to leave the country. Before they could be moved, in retaliation for a protest letter against the Nazi pogroms and deportations of the Jews written by Dutch Roman Catholic bishops, the Nazis ordered all Catholics of Jewish descent to be

---

31 Herbstrith, *Edith Stein*, 32.

32 Herbstrith, *Edith Stein*, 32.

deported. On August 2, 1942, Stein and her sister were among three hundred people arrested.

Stein was highly influenced by the mystics. As noted, her conversion was inspired by Teresa of Ávila, and when she was killed she was writing a book titled *The Science of the Cross* about John of the Cross, in honor of the four hundredth anniversary of his birth. Her theology is steeped in contemplation that manifests itself in the world. For Stein, being drawn into God results in a movement away from the self to be a service to others. Through relationship with God, one brings the light of God into a broken world. An excerpt from her essay "Mystery of Christmas" provides an explanation of what this is supposed to look like. While lengthy, the quote is profoundly relevant to the Christian life, especially a modern understanding of mystical Christian life:

> *One with God: that is number one. However, a second proceeds from this. If Christ is the Head and we the members in the Mystical Body, then we relate to each other as member to member and we are all one in God, a divine life. If God is in us and if he is Love, then it cannot be otherwise but to love one another. Therefore, our love for our brothers and sisters is the measure of our love for God. But it is different from a natural, human love which affects this one or that one who may be related to us, or who may be close to us because of the bonds of temperament or common interests. The rest are "strangers" who don't concern us, perhaps even by their presence annoy us, so that love is kept as far away as possible. For the Christian there is no "strange human being." He is in every instance the "neighbor" whom we have with us and who is most in need of us. It makes no difference whether he is related or not, whether we "like" him or not, whether he is "morally worthy" of help or not. The love of Christ knows no bounds, it never ceases, it never withdraws in the face of hatred or foul play. He came for the sake of sinners and not*

> *for the righteous. If the love of Christ lives in us, then we do as he did and seek after the lost sheep.*[33]

Both the theology of the mystical body of Christ and the importance of love permeate this excerpt. While she is a modern mystic, she incorporates these classic themes of mystical thought (love being likely the most important theme of all). Most remarkable about her reflections on this theological command to love is the hardships she endured throughout her life relating to deep-seated hate, culminating in her death in a Nazi death camp. Yet, she did not show bitterness or hatred in return—she taught love.

Stein represents an important model of modern mysticism. She was influenced by the classic mystics of old, particularly the great Spanish mystics Teresa of Ávila and John of the Cross, yet her own theology was oriented toward her own modern world. Her faith in God sustained her as the world around her descended into the chaos of war. She became a nun, but she did not reject the world. In fact, as is evident, she understood engagement with the neighbor and the world as a critical aspect of loving God. Stein was beatified in 1987 and canonized in 1998. One year later, she was named copatroness of Europe, along with two other great mystics, Birgitta of Sweden and Catherine of Siena.[34]

Intellectual Mysticism for a Modern World

Through the lives of these varied individuals, the connection between faith and understanding comes center stage. While their intellectual gifts were obvious, they did not hide in ivory towers writing to an elite minority. They used their gifts to serve both the neighbor and the

---

33 Edith Stein, "The Mystery of Christmas," *Plough*, December 25, 2022, https://www.plough.com/en/topics/culture/holidays/christmas-readings/the-mystery-of-christmas#.

34 Stein, *Selected Writings*, 8.

church. Origen trained new Christians, wrote an astounding number of foundational Christian texts, and demonstrated his faith by persevering against torture from a hostile government. Augustine, always concerned for his flock, engaged in the theological debates of his day and provided a vigorous defense of the Christian faith. Gertrude of Helfta used her gifts within her community of women, producing beautiful writings that have inspired generations. De Sales and his pastoral heart wrote to and for everyday people while living a life of compassion. Stein, both scholar and religious sister, taught that to be drawn into God meant a life of service to the world.

Intellectualism and the academy are often insular. Scholars too often write for each other, even within the various Christian academic disciplines. Ego and arrogance plague these fields, just as they do other academic disciplines. Yet these individuals show a different path, a path in which faithful Christians use their gifts for the service of others. They did not write to glorify themselves but to glorify God and to serve others. This is the gift that Christian mysticism brings to the intellect.

Suggested Reading List

Augustine of Hippo. *Confessions.* Translated by Henry Chadwick. Oxford: Oxford University Press, 2008.

———. *On the Trinity.* Edited by D. P. Curtin. Translated by Arthur West Hadden. Philadelphia: Dalcassian, 2018.

Gertrude of Helfta. *The Herald of Divine Love.* Edited and translated by Margaret Winkworth. New York: Paulist Press, 1993.

———. *Spiritual Exercises.* Edited and translated by Gertrud Jaron Lewis and Jack Lewis. Kalamazoo, MI: Cistercian Publications, 1989.

Origen. *Spirit and Fire: A Thematic Anthology of His Writings.* Edited by Hans Urs von Balthasar. Translated by Robert J. Daly, SJ. Washington, DC: Catholic University of America Press, 1984.

Sales, Francis de. *Introduction to the Devout Life.* Edited and translated by John K. Ryan. New York: Image Books, 1989.

———. *On the Love of God.* Translated by H. L. Sidney Lear. London: Rivingtons, 1888.

Stein, Edith. *Life in a Jewish Family: An Autobiography 1891–1916.* Edited by L. Gelber and Romaus Leuven. Translated by Josephine Koeppel. Washington, DC: Institute of Carmelite Studies, ICS Publications, 1986.

———. "The Mystery of Christmas." *Plough*, December 25, 2022. https://www.plough.com/en/topics/culture/holidays/christmas-readings/the-mystery-of-christmas#.

———. *The Science of the Cross.* Translated by Josephine Koeppel, OCD. Washington, DC: ICS, 2002.

6

LITERATURE

Rejoice always, pray continually, give thanks in all circumstances; for this is God's will for you in Christ Jesus.

—1 Thessalonians 5:16–18

SOMETIMES THERE ARE truths that can only be expressed in poetic language, a love or a longing that is simply too powerful to write about plainly or analytically. There is a reason that the great works of literature have endured. While novels and poems may in one sense be fictional, they are also true. The story of Romeo and Juliet, to take one of the most well-known stories from the history of English literature, has endured not because they were real lovers who met a tragic end in fair Verona but because as humans we deeply feel their young and reckless love, and then we grieve their tragic loss. The play holds truths that transcend the story and speak to our basic longing as human beings.

Many of the mystics wrote in ways that defy academic expectation. There is a sense to many mystical texts that the author believed their words to be inadequate in describing their visions, their union, and their love for God. Therefore, often these texts can be difficult to categorize. Yet, for other mystics, their works firmly fall into the category of literature. There are mystics who wrote poems and novels. It does not make their encounters or their feelings any less true, but their work is decidedly different from something like a mystical guide of spiritual progress or a theological treatise. Because many mystical writings are to a degree abstract, it can be difficult to identify a clear boundary between the poetic and the theological, and many authors engaged in both. For example, John of the Cross, one of the more talented and influential Spanish poets, also wrote in-depth theological commentary to accompany his poems.

This chapter focuses on mystics and mystical texts that firmly fall into the category of literature. The chapter begins with two beguines who wrote poetry, Mechthild of Magdeburg and Hadewijch of Antwerp. Without knowing that their poems were about God, one could be forgiven for assuming they were writing about a human lover. Then, in Spain, John of the Cross wrote astoundingly beautiful lines about the intimate love with God while suffering from imprisonment and physical torture. In Russia, an Orthodox spiritual classic, *The Pilgrim's Tale*, follows an unnamed pilgrim through his quest to pray ceaselessly. Last, two modern writers, both Anglican, one English, one American, searched for and found a sort of mysticism that inspired their faith and their works. Evelyn Underhill did much to bring mysticism back to the modern consciousness, and T. S. Eliot, a poet, essayist, and playwright, wrestled with Christian mystical themes throughout his literary career.

Two Beguine Poets

Two poets, Mechthild of Magdeburg and Hadewijch, were both beguines, though eventually Mechthild did enter the convent at Helfta, the same one where Gertrude the Great lived. The beguines have been capturing the imagination of scholars of women's history for decades. This group—or, more accurately, many groups—of women constructed a quasi-monastic lifestyle outside official church structures. They were dispersed around Europe, though there was a high concentration in the Low Countries. There were numerous beguines who wrote mystical texts, some of which have been accepted by the Catholic Church at large, while others have been condemned, but both provide a glimpse into the mystical mindset of this medieval lay movement.

MEDIEVAL MONASTICISM AND BEGUINES

One of the more important religious developments of the High Middle Ages were the monastic reforms and the establishment of the mendicant ("wandering" or "begging") orders, the two most influential being the Order of Preachers (the Dominicans) and the Franciscans. Essential to their mission was being out in the world, oftentimes preaching. A combination of revival, influence of the mendicants, and general cultural and economic trends inspired many Christians to join monastic orders. Unfortunately, there were several factors that made access to the monastic life difficult for women, though the most problematic was that several orders came to see care for women's monastic houses as a burden, and many severely limited the number of women's houses they would allow. The situation was untenable. The established church could not provide for the multitude of women seeking a holy life. Out of necessity grew a creative solution: the rise of beguines. These communities were unregulated and did not follow any established monastic rule.

Responding to a lack of monastic options, women throughout Europe began to come together to participate in religious life in communities that were not regulated by the Catholic Church and did not follow any established monastic rule.[1] The women simply pledged to live celibate lives in community and survive off their own labor, which is in stark contrast to some of the wealthier monasteries, in which monks and nuns were able to live a comfortable existence off

1 For a full explanation, see Wojciechowksi, *Women and the Christian Story*, 81–85.

the income of their lands. There was a mixed reaction to the beguines. Early in the movement, there seemed to be general support for them, but during the middle of the thirteenth century there was a shift of public opinion against these religious communities, and over time the church sought greater control over the beguines. Beguines were charged with heresy even from the earliest days, though there was never widespread persecution.[2] Marguerite Porete, who may have been a beguine, was executed and will be discussed further in chapter 8. However, it appears that neither Mechthild or Hadewijch faced serious persecution from church officials for their writings, and their literary work demonstrates that important theology came from this particular tradition.

Mechthild of Magdeburg (ca. 1207–1282/84)

Mechthild of Magdeburg is one of the more famous of the German beguines and the writer of *The Flowering Light of the Godhead*, which has the distinction of being the first collection of mystical writings composed in the Middle Low German.[3] The outline of Mechthild's life is fuzzy. She was likely born sometime after 1200, perhaps in 1208, to a noble family. Little is known of her early life, but she experienced her first mystical revelation at the age of twelve. She calls herself unlearned, though this claim should not be taken too seriously. Such assertions were common for women writers of the time, especially since they were rarely trained in Latin or theology. She was, however, literate and demonstrates an understanding of contemporary literature. She joined a beguine community at Magdeburg in 1230. Around 1250, when she was in her forties, she told her confessor about her spiritual experiences, events that would now be classify as mystical, and he encouraged her to write about them. Over the course of the next decade she

2 R. W. Southern, *Western Society and the Church in the Middle Ages* (Baltimore: Penguin Books, 1979), 321.

3 Sara S. Poor, *Mechthild of Magdeburg and Her Book: Gender and the Making of Textual Authority* (Philadelphia: University of Pennsylvania Press, 2004), 1–16.

wrote the first five books of *Flowering Light*, then sometime in the next twenty years she wrote books 6 and 7.[4]

While *Flowering Light* was written in the vernacular, the text was translated into Latin before the turn of the fourteenth century. Margot Schmidt writes, "In essence Mechthild of Magdeburg's book . . . is nothing other than the moving story of God's heart and the human heart, and of Lucifer's cunning attempts to interfere with the ties that join then."[5] Mechthild uses a variety of literary genres throughout *Flowering Light*, and it is not easily classified as a whole work. The book is a collection of different types of writing, including "poems, prose, songs of divine love, allegories, moral reflections, admonitions, and practical advice on daily conduct." There are also visions, revelations, and mystical experiences. Her confessor acted as her editor.[6] Within this collection of writings the role of love and longing for God is the most important aspect. The human heart yearns for God, so much so that it is all-consuming. The following excerpt demonstrates this deep desire for God that runs throughout her writing:

> *I have such a hunger for the heavenly Father that I forget all cares. And I so thirst for his Son that it removes from me all earthly desires. And I have such a need for the Spirit of them both that it goes beyond the wisdom of the Father, which I cannot grasp; and beyond the Son's suffering, which I cannot bear; and beyond the consolation of the Holy Spirit, which I cannot receive.*[7]

From the text, one can see a person utterly enthralled with God. This except is highly Trinitarian, with attention paid to each person of the

---

4 Frank Tobin, "Introduction," in *The Flowering Light of the Godhead*, by Mechthild of Magdeburg, trans. Frank Tobin (New York: Paulist Press, 1998), 4–5.

5 Margot Schmidt, "Preface," in Magdeburg, *Flowering Light of the Godhead*, xxvi.

6 Egan, *Anthology of Christian Mysticism*, 247–48.

7 Mechthild, *Flowering Light of the Godhead*, 110.

Godhead. Mechthild's writing is poetic, and the text is reminiscent of courtly love poems, though of course the divine is the object of her love.

Sampling one of her poems clarifies that she was not just a mystical thinker with a skill for language but an adept poet. Her poem "The Most Lowly Praises God in Ten Things" once again highlights this all-encompassing love. God is presented as everything, and she as lowly and unworthy:

O you burning Mountain
O you chosen Sun
O you full Moon.
O you bottomless Well.
O you unscalable Height.
O you Brightness without measure.
O Wisdom without ground.
O Mercy without opposition.
O Crown of all honors!
The most lowly person you ever created praises you.[8]

The juxtaposition of God as the mountain, sun, moon, and so on compared to Mechthild, who identifies as the lowliest person ever created, is jarring yet a powerful image and speaks to her enthrallment with God.

Around 1270, she joined the intellectually and spiritually active convent at Helfta.[9] Many of the women were well educated, especially in terms of both theology and Latin. There are indications that Mechthild was a well-respected member within the community, though she was plagued by ill heath toward the end of her life. She likely died sometime around either 1282 or 1294.[10] One wonders how the elderly

8 Mechthild, *Flowering Light of the Godhead*, 45–46.

9 Poor, *Mechthild of Magdeburg*, 1-2.

10 Tobin, "Introduction," 5.

Mechthild, after living in a beguine community, adjusted to living in the highly intellectual atmosphere of Helfta. There is little indication as to how she came to live there, but one can imagine her interacting with her younger monastic sister Gertrude.

Hadewijch (ca. 1200–ca. 1260)

Mechthild was not the only beguine to leave her mark on the mystical literature of the era. Mechthild's younger contemporary Hadewijch too wrote mystical texts in the vernacular that affected medieval spirituality. Like Mechthild, Hadewijch was a thirteenth-century mystic and beguine. Her work is one of the most important examples of medieval love in mysticism. This phenomenon, which was mostly written about by women, is essentially that "union with God is lived here on earth as a love relationship: God lets himself be experienced as Love (Minne) by the person who goes out to meet him with love (minne)."[11] The term *minne*, which means "love," was often used in the German courtly love tradition to describe human love. Yet there is nothing human about this love that Hadewijch describes. The love is highly emotional and ecstatic, and descriptions of her visions and experiences show a person completely enraptured by love for her God.

Through Hadewijch's life she wrote letters, poems, and prose about her mystical visions. Like Mechthild, there are certain facts about Hadewijch that can be gleaned from her writings, though there is very little available information about her life. She never wrote any sort of autobiography, nor did anyone write a work about her life, for the sake of canonization. Therefore there is a level of guesswork in her admittedly meager biography. Historians do not know exactly when she was born or when she died, but she likely lived during the thirteenth century. Her family name is also not known, but due to her education level, it seems likely she was upper class. Her writing shows that she was familiar with Latin, the rules of rhetoric, medieval

---

11 Hadewijch, *The Complete Works*, trans. Mother Columba Hart, OSB (New York: Paulist Press, 1980), xiii.

numerology, Ptolemaic astronomy, and musical theory, and she was proficient in French. She was familiar with Scripture and several Christian theologians, both ancient and contemporary. Historians are fairly certain that Hadewijch was the head of a community of beguines for a while, but due to some sort of conflict, she was kicked out of that community. After that, there is no record of what happened to her.

Her works were known in the fourteenth century, but by the sixteenth she and her writings seem to have disappeared into obscurity. She was rediscovered in Brussels in 1838 by three medieval scholars who found a collection of her works in the Royal Library in the manuscript collection—four works total, two prose and two poetry—written in medieval Dutch. This discovery led to publication and then later a significant amount of scholarship on this elusive mystic.[12] So what was so intriguing about her? Beyond the fact that it is always exciting to find such a robust collection of writings from a historical figure, especially a woman, who wrote during this time period, her writings are engaging and beautiful. She is an adept theologian, and it seems that she did have at least some influence on mystical thought during her era. A brief quote from one of her letters demonstrates both the depth of her mystical thought and her literary skill:

> *If [the soul] maintains this worthy state, the soul is a bottomless abyss in which God suffices to himself; and his own self-sufficiency ever finds fruition to the full in this soul, as the soul, for its part, ever does in him. Soul is a way for the passage of God from his depths into his liberty; and God is a way for the passage of the soul into its liberty, that is, into his inmost depth, which cannot be touched except by the soul's abyss. And as long as God does not belong to the soul in his totality, he does not truly satisfy it.*[13]

---

12 Hadewijch, *Complete Works*, 1–7.

13 Hadewijch, "Letter 18: Greatness of the Soul," in Hadewijch, *Complete Works*, 86.

The language is abstract, but she is describing an intimate union between the soul and God. It is important to note that she understands God as unfathomable and wholly other even as she is describing the possibility of relationship. Through this deep relationship with God, she can be more open to the world and better serve others.

Likely Hadewijch's most famous vision was a reception of Christ in the form of the Eucharist. Hadewijch describes the union in language that is bridal and highly erotic. Another significant aspect is that this union comes through the sacraments. Often beguines are viewed as being opposed to the Catholic Church because they chose to live in a community that did not have an official monastic rule, but that was often not the case. Many beguine communities had close ties with the church and/or relationships with priests from different religious orders. This vision of union with Christ was only possible through the reception of the Eucharist, which was administered through the church. Hadewijch writes that she received the vision while she was in church on a Sunday during Pentecost. During the service, she saw a great eagle, who told her that if she wanted to attain oneness, she needed to make herself ready. Then Christ came to the altar, and in his right hand he had the ciborium—a container that holds the Eucharist—with the bread, and in the left he had the chalice with the wine.

> *With that he came in the form and clothing of a Man, as he was on that day when he gave us his Body for the first time; looking like a Human Being and a Man, wonderful, and beautiful, and with glorious face, he came to me as humbly as anyone who wholly belongs to another. Then he gave himself to me in the shape of the Sacrament, in its outward form, as the custom is; and then gave me the drink from the chalice, in form and taste, as the custom is. After that he came himself to me, took me entirely in his arms, and pressed me to him; and all my members felt his in full felicity, in accordance*

> *with the desire of my heart and my humanity. So I was outwardly satisfied and fully transported.*[14]

Modern students of mystical theology are often taken aback by the erotic nature of this vision. Yet, *erotic* does not mean "sexual" in this instance, and Hadewijch is using this type of language to describe an intimate moment between her and Christ. It also must be remembered that Hadewijch did not invent this type of erotic language for her writings. This had been a component of mystical writings since the very earliest days of Christianity. Hadewijch was staying firmly within the tradition while also using a Christianized version of contemporary love images (especially the courtly love tradition). Love and intimacy are present not only in her visions but also in her poetry, of which there are two collections, one in stanzas and one in couplets. An excerpt from one poem will have to suffice to demonstrate her skills as a poet and her ability to weave her theology throughout her words:

> *To be reduced to nothingness in Love*
> *Is the most desirable thing I know*
> *Among all the word I have experience of,*
> *Although I know it is beyond my reach.*
> *And if anyone then dares to fight Love with longing,*
> *Wholly without heart and without mind,*
> *And Love counters this longing with her longing:*
> *That is the force by which we conquer Love.*
>
> *Thenceforward, whether with joy or pain,*
> *If anyone can dare to fight Love with ardor;*
> *Love cannot resist the violence of the assault;*
> *But he shall abide firm in the story, conformed to Love.*[15]

---

14 Hadewijch, "Vision 7: Oneness in the Eucharist," in Hadewijch, *Complete Works*, 281.

15 Hadewijch, "Nothingness in Love," in Hadewijch, *Complete Works*, 239.

Love is the subject of this poem, and it would not feel out of place in a volume of secular love poetry. Yet, the longing and desire explicit in this poem are between the author and God, not between two human beings. This is just one small example of Hadewijch's skill with verse but also a demonstration of why she is so associated with love mysticism.

John of the Cross (1542–1591)

Like Mechthild and Hadewijch, John of the Cross used erotic imagery to describe a relationship between a soul and God in his poetry, though his poetry is more expansive and touches on a variety of theological themes. With the possible exclusion of Eliot, who was truly a masterful poet, John is the most skilled of the writers in this chapter. John is respected and read outside religious circles because he is considered one of Spain's most influential poets. Through his life, he knew poverty, suffering, and persecution. He also understood love, and it jumps off the page.

John of the Cross was born as Juan de Yepes in 1542 in a small town named Fontiveros, about twenty-four miles from Ávila, Spain. The story of his parents is one of a tragic romance. His father, Gonzalo, was disowned by his wealthy family when he married a poor woman, Catalina Alvarez, who was a weaver by trade. The couple had three sons before Gonzalo died young, leaving Catalina to raise their children alone. John was put into a school for poor children, and he was given a job as a nurse at a local hospital. While working at the hospital, he took classes at a nearby Jesuit school, where he was encouraged to write his own literary compositions. After turning down an opportunity for ordination and a post as a chaplain at the hospital where he had been working, he decided to enter a Carmelite monastery in Medina. From 1564 to 1568, he went to the University of Salamanca and the College of San Andrés, where he studied philosophy and theology, and he was appointed prefect of studies at the College of San Andrés. Despite his skill as a theologian, by the time he was ordained into the priesthood he was considering transferring to the Carthusian Order, likely so he could engage in a contemplative life.[16]

This was when he met Teresa of Ávila. Teresa, now in her early fifties, was well into her reforming efforts for the women of the Carmelite Order, and she was looking for friars to help open men's monastic houses. Teresa taught John about the contemplative life and the reforms she was enacting. In November 1568, John and two other friars promised to follow the primitive Carmelite rule, and he changed his name to Juan de la Cruz, or in English John of the Cross.[17]

Even though John was quite a bit younger than Teresa and she had acted as his teacher, he became her spiritual director. This happened after she became the head of the Convent of the Incarnation in Ávila, and he was assigned to be the priest who served the community as its spiritual director. Despite difficulties with various spiritual directors in the past (which she mentions in her various writings), Teresa seemed to appreciate his faithfulness and intelligence, and the two worked closely together. In addition to his role as spiritual director for the sisters, he also engaged in public ministry in the community, including teaching poor children to read and write.[18]

There was a lot of tension during this time among the Carmelites regarding the reforms that Teresa and others were enacting. A full examination of the conflicts is beyond the scope of this investigation; it is enough to know that the tension escalated between the factions of Carmelites. After Teresa left the Convent of the Incarnation in 1574, John too requested a transfer, but he was denied. Three years later, in 1577, members of the Carmelite Order from Tostado, who opposed the Teresian reforms, kidnapped John, and declared him a rebel. When John refused to renounce the Teresian reforms, they imprisoned him in a small room (six feet wide by ten feet long). Despite Teresa's efforts to

---

16 John of the Cross, *John of the Cross, Selected Writings*, ed. Kieran Kavanaugh (New York: Paulist Press, 1987), 8–10.

17 John of the Cross, *John of the Cross*, 14.

18 John of the Cross, *John of the Cross*, 16–17.

have him freed, including writing to the king of Spain, he was held for nine months, getting nothing to eat but bread and water and suffering from frequent floggings.[19]

There in his miserable imprisonment, John wrote poetry in his mind. One of the poems composed during his suffering was the "Spiritual Canticle," which is based on the Song of Songs, an ever-popular mystical text. The opening stanza seems to recall the desolation of John's condition:

Where have you hidden away?
You left me whimpering, my love.
Wounding me you vanished
like a stag. I rushed out
shouting for you—but you were gone.[20]

The poem is a dialogue between lovers, a bride and bridegroom. The progress of the poem, told through the voices of lovers, parallels the mystical journey to union. First the bride is longing for her lover and tries to come closer to him. She wants to know why he is hiding from her. After she finally finds her lover, she realizes that her "initial longings for union were the work of her beloved and [she] begins to interpret her search in a new light." Indeed, the lover has been desiring her and "rejoices in the bride's triumph even more than she."[21]

One night in August 1578, John escaped from his imprisonment and sought refuge at one of Teresa's convents in Toledo, where he was cared for.[22] Later he was placed in a variety of leadership positions within the discalced Carmelite Order. He was briefly a superior in El Calvario, a rector in Baeza, a prior in Granada, and a vicar provincial

19 John of the Cross, *John of the Cross*, 18–19.

20 John of the Cross, *The Poems of Saint John of the Cross*, trans. Willie Barnstone (Bloomington: Indiana University Press, 1968), 43.

21 John of the Cross, *John of the Cross*, 213–14.

22 John of the Cross, *John of the Cross*, 19.

of Andalusia and then again a prior there. During his time in Andalusia, between 1585 and 1588, he wrote a number of literary works. He spent the last years of his life living in relative isolation, which suited the old contemplative fine, and he died in December 1591.[23]

John's life was full of burdens, but deep love and longing for God sit at the center of his theology. As one scholar explains, "It is this longing for encounter, this delight and comfort in one another's presence, that permeates John's works and constitutes the core of his theological contribution."[24] For John, like so many other mystics, humans were made for relationship with God. In addition to his poetry, John wrote commentaries about his poetry at the request of others who, after reading his work, wanted to understand it better. For example, he wrote a commentary for his poem "The Living Flame of Love" for a woman named Dona Ana de Penalosa, a layperson to whom John was giving spiritual direction while serving as vicar provincial in Granada.[25] In this particular case, he expresses hesitation at having taken on this commentary because the stanzas of his poem deal with matters so "interior and spiritual."[26]

John of the Cross is in some ways a rather atypical figure in the history of Christian mysticism. Unlike so many other mystics who came from affluent families, John grew up poor and gained an education only after others recognized his intellectual skill. He certainly had the ability to be a great theologian; indeed, his poetry demonstrates adept theological understanding, but he was first and foremost a poet and a contemplative at heart, and he sought a quiet reflective life. External conflict and his commitment to the Teresian reforms cost him dearly, but they may have made him the poet he became. The image of him fleeing in the night, escaping his persecutors, with the poetry he

---

23 John of the Cross, *John of the Cross*, 20–21, 24.

24 Gillian T. W. Ahlgren, *Enkindling Love: The Legacy of Teresa of Avila and John of the Cross* (Minneapolis: Fortress, 2016), 71–128.

25 John of the Cross, *John of the Cross*, 288.

26 John of the Cross, *John of the Cross*, 292.

had written in his suffering and solitude is poignant. John was canonized in 1726 and made a doctor of the church in 1926.[27]

The Pilgrim's Tale

The Pilgrim's Tale, also translated as the *Way of the Pilgrim*, is like nothing else discussed in this chapter or even this book. It is a work of fiction about a man, the pilgrim, who learns to pray unceasingly. The story follows the pilgrim through a series of adventures as he wanders through Siberia. Despite the rather unusual premise, particularly for a work of mystical literature, the book is edifying, instructional, and genuinely interesting.

THE RUSSIAN ORTHODOX CHURCH

Both the Russian and Ukrainian Orthodox Churches trace their existence back to a fanciful tale from the tenth century. As the story goes, Prince Vladimir of Kievan Rus sent emissaries out to the Bulgars, who were Muslim, the Germans, who were Catholic, and the Greeks, who were Orthodox, to examine their faith. The emissaries were reportedly unimpressed with both Islam and Catholicism, but they were exceedingly impressed with the faith they found in Constantinople. The *Russian Primary Chronicle* reports them as saying, "Then we went to Greece and the Greeks led us to the edifices where they worship their God, and we knew not whether we were in heaven or on earth."[28] Prince Vladimir converted and had his subjects baptized in the Dnieper River (lest they face the prince's displeasure) in 988.

27 John of the Cross, *John of the Cross*, 24.

28 *The Russian Primary Chronicle Laurentian Text*, trans. and ed. Samuel Hazzard Cross and Olgerd P. Sherbowitz-Wetzor, Mediaeval Academy of America (Cambridge: Crimson, 1953), 111.

The story takes place in Russia during the nineteenth century, likely midcentury. It consists of various tales or short stories about the pilgrim. The first four tales were first published at Saint Michael the Archangel Monastery in Kazan in 1881, and the next year the Russian monastery of St. Panteleimon published the text under the title "The Remarkable Tale about the Grace-Giving Effects of the Jesus Prayer." In 1884, Saint Michael the Archangel published a revised edition of the text, and this version received large distribution.[29] "Repeatedly reissued in Russian and in numerous translations, the tales of the unknown pilgrim became not only one of the most famous works of Russian spiritual literature but also one of the fundamental sources for the study of Russian spirituality."[30]

The book is told from the first-person perspective of the pilgrim, who identifies himself by saying, "By the mercy of God I am a Christian; by my deeds, a great sinner; and by vocation a homeless pilgrim, a man of mean estate who wanders from place to place."[31] From on the onset of the story, the reader is aware that the story is about a layperson. In some of the later tales, the reader learns that the pilgrim had once been married, but his wife died, and he took up this life of wandering after her death. He takes on odd jobs occasionally and has some adventures, but he has a simple life of living on little and filling his days with prayer.

In the first tale, indeed, on the first page, the pilgrim tells that reader that on the twenty-fourth Sunday after Trinity Sunday, he was at church and heard 1 Thessalonians 5:17 ("Pray without ceasing").[32] He then went to check the Bible and found the passage there as well.

---

29 The full story of the history and authorship of this text is complex and far beyond the scope of what we can do in this short chapter. For an excellent analysis, see Aleksei Pentikovsky, "Introduction," in *The Pilgrim's Tale*, ed. Aleksei Pentikovsky, trans. T. Allan Smith (New York: Paulist Press, 1999), 1–36.

30 *Pilgrim's Tale*, 1–2.

31 *Pilgrim's Tale*, 49.

32 *Pilgrim's Tale*, 49.

He wonders how anyone can pray unceasingly, and this sends him on a quest to learn how to accomplish this command. He goes to various holy men but finds their answers lacking, and he then wanders from place to place trying to find a spiritual guide, which eventually he does. The spiritual father teaches him the Jesus Prayer (which has various forms, as discussed in ch. 1, but in this text it is "Lord Jesus Christ, Son of God, have mercy on me"). The spiritual guide explains, "The unceasing interior Jesus prayer is an uninterrupted, never dying, invocation of the divine name Jesus Christ with the mind and the heart, all the while imagining his ongoing presence and asking for pardon."[33] The pilgrim then spends the entire week saying the Jesus Prayer daily six thousand times; then he recites it twelve thousand times; then his spiritual father permits him to say the prayer as many times as he can in a day. By this point, with his frequent repetitions, the prayer has settled into the pilgrim's inner being. When he is awake, he recites it continually, and in his sleep he dreams it.[34]

The book is representative of a particular type of Russian Orthodox mysticism. The text also deals with some specifically Russian religious issues, such as the conflict between the Russian Orthodox Church and the Old Believers.[35] It also references a number of influential Orthodox mystical texts, such as John Climacus's *The Ladder of Divine Ascent* and most importantly the *Philokalia*, a collection of religious texts written in the fifth and sixth centuries but put together by two Greek monks in the eighteenth century at Mount Athos. The *Philokalia* is very much steeped in the wisdom of desert monasticism—which was overwhelmingly concerned with stillness

33 *Pilgrim's Tale*, 60.

34 *Pilgrim's Tale*, 64–66.

35 The Old Believers, or the Old Ritualists, were Russian Christians who maintained the old liturgical practices when the Moscow patriarch Nikon, encouraged by Czar Alexei Mikhailovich, reformed church practices to bring them more in line with the Greek Orthodox Church in the middle of the seventeenth century. The schism led to a brutal persecution of the Old Believers.

and union with God—and the pilgrim starts reading that as well. At one point in *The Pilgrim's Tale*, the pilgrim asks whether the *Philokalia* is more sublime and holy than the Bible. The response both demonstrates the poetic nature of this text and shows its reliance on ancient forms of desert mysticism.

> *No, it is not more sublime nor is it holier than the Bible, but it does contain lucid explanations of what the Bible holds mystically and what cannot be easily grasped by our short sighted mind. I will give you an example of this. The sun is the greatest, most brilliant, and most excellent luminary of the heavens, but you cannot contemplate it and examine it with the naked eye. You need a piece of treated artificial glass and although it is a million times smaller and duller than the sun, with the glass you can examine this magnificent emperor of the heavenly luminaries, admire it and attract its fiery rays. In the same way Sacred Scripture is a brilliant sun and the* Philokalia *is the necessary piece of glass which facilitates our access to that most sublime luminary.*[36]

This is rather remarkable claim: the *Philokalia* facilitates human access to the Bible because the Bible is so brilliant and difficult. Likely this response lands flat in terms of Western sensibilities, but is an important perspective to read regarding this particular Christian tradition.

What *The Pilgrim's Tale* does so well is show the reader a deep mystical spirituality that is difficult to convey in more conventional terms. The concept of unceasing prayer can seem bizarre and unrelatable to most modern readers. Yet, through literature, one can encounter a character who is so sincere and so desirous to follow God that he takes on this seemingly impossible spiritual quest. One sees the process, albeit a fictional process, by which a person becomes so reliant on prayer that his relationship with God becomes the most important

---

36 *Pilgrim's Tale*, 61.

thing in his life. The quest seems far more relatable with each page. Readers grow fond of the pilgrim and want him to succeed. Over time, he becomes a personification of wandering faith.

Evelyn Underhill (1875–1941)

About twenty years before *The Way of the Pilgrim* was translated into English, an Englishwoman published a particularly important book on Christian mysticism called *Mysticism: A Study in the Nature and Development of Spiritual Consciousness*. She begins the text with a generalization: "The most highly developed branches of the human family have in common one peculiar characteristic. They tend to produce . . . a curious and definite type of personality; a type which refuses to be satisfied with that which other man call experience, and is inclined, in the words of its enemies, to 'deny the world in order that it may find reality.'"[37] She is, of course, referring to the mystic. From the outset, it is clear this is a very different type of book, a different look at mysticism from the medieval or even the early modern view. This is a type of mystical examination that looks beyond a Christian framework, although Underhill was a committed Christian.

Underhill, who did much to popularize Christian mysticism within her life, was concerned with making the topic accessible to the everyday believer who was not inclined toward an overly experiential faith. In her book *Practical Mysticism*, which was published during the first few months of the First World War, Underhill tackles the thorny question *What is mysticism?* She has a rather poetic answer that speaks to the confusion of the term. She explains that a genuine inquirer will find several answers, but those answers will only help to obscure the question, not to provide any true answers. She explains that the inquirer will learn that "mysticism is a philosophy, an illusion, a kind of religion, a disease; that it means having visions, performing

37 Evelyn Underhill, *Mysticism: A Study in the Nature and Development of Spiritual Consciousness* (Grand Rapids: Christian Classics Ethereal Library, 1911), 4.

conjuring tricks, leading an idle, dreamy, and selfish life, neglecting one's business, wallowing in vague spiritual emotions, and being 'in tune with the infinite.'"[38] She goes on to argue that others will say that mysticism means Catholic piety or that it comes from the East. In the end, the genuine inquirer will be exasperated and still have no idea what mysticism is.

Underhill then does something unexpected. She argues that the object of her essay is to convince inquirers to discover the answer for themselves.[39] Then she immediately provides her own definition of mysticism, which admittedly undercuts her previous assertion. She argues that mysticism is the art of union with reality. The mystic is a person who has attained that union in greater or lesser degree, or who aims at and believes in such an attainment.[40] She admits that this definition likely will not be satisfactory to the inquirer at first. It is clear in her writings that Underhill was inspired not only by the Christian mystics of old but also by poets and mystics of other faiths, such as Sufis. Underhill is a mystic for the modern era. When she published her first book, *Mysticism*, in 1911, mystical thought was largely considered suspect, especially in more intellectual circles.[41]

Underhill seems an unlikely candidate to bring a popular mysticism back into English society. She was born in London in 1875. The daughter of a barrister, she had a comfortable childhood. She was raised in the Church of England, but her family was not particularly religious. Intellectually curious, she attended King's College for Women in London, where she studied history and botany.[42] After college she took to writing novels. Her first three books, *The Grey World* (1902), *The Lost World* (1907), and *The Column of Dust* (1908), all deal

---

38 Evelyn Underhill, *Practical Mysticism* (Columbus, OH: Ariel, 1914), 22.

39 Underhill, *Practical Mysticism*, 22–23.

40 Underhill, *Practical Mysticism*, 23.

41 Emilie Griffin, "Introduction," in *Evelyn Underhill: Essential Writings*, by Evelyn Underhill, ed. Emilie Griffin (Maryknoll, NY: Orbis Books, 2003), 1.

42 Griffin, "Introduction," 8–9.

with spiritual questions. During this time, she became interested in Roman Catholicism and even expressed interest in converting but did not do so due to a variety of factors including her genuine hesitation, particularly around the church's opposition to modernism, general prejudice against Catholics among the upper-class English, and her fiancé's (and eventual husband's) opposition to it.[43] While she maintained close ties with Catholics, she became an active member in the Church of England in 1921.[44]

Underhill wrote thirty-nine books. She led religious retreats and frequently gave lectures. In 1921 she became the first woman invited to give a series of theological lectures at Oxford, and she was made a fellow at King's College in 1928. Ten years later, she received a doctor of divinity from Aberdeen University.[45] She apparently did not think too much of the honor. In a letter, she writes, "Not so much of the Frau Doctor stuff, please. I do not wish to be addressed as Dr. E.U. I think it is swanky and revolting, and quite against Matt. 23.8. A discreet D.D. is as far as I care to go. Rather sad not to be at the graduation. The present Lord Rector used to pull my hair when I was small."[46]

One of the things that made Underhill's mystical thought so influential is the approachability of it. Underhill was a laywoman, a wife, and novelist. She did not cloister herself away but was an active member in London society. She took historic mystical figures seriously and introduced them to modern people. Her own mystical thought was both active and practical. It was no abstract negation; God was the Beloved, and union with God resulted in an authentic transformation

43 Griffin, "Introduction," 10–11.

44 Griffin, "Introduction," 16.

45 Griffin, "Introduction," 19.

46 Margaret Cropper, *The Life of Evelyn Underhill: An Intimate Portrait of the Groundbreaking Author of Mysticism* (Woodstock, VT: Skylight Paths, 2003), 219. Matt 23:8 reads, "But you are not to be called rabbi, for you have one teacher, and you are all brothers and sisters."

in which the mystic became selfless.[47] This understanding of her thought makes her comment about becoming real all the more intriguing: "Living in this atmosphere of Reality, you will, in fact, yourself become more real."[48] Underhill died in 1941 as Europe was once again plunged into war.

In the quote below, Underhill is responding to the question of how and why mysticism is useful. What does someone gain from engaging in mysticism? This is a perennially important question, and her answer, while it would not nor could satisfy everyone, is worth dwelling on:

> *But now, because you have achieved a certain power of gathering yourself together, perceiving yourself as a person, a spirit, and observing your relation with these other individual lives—because too, hearing now and again the mysterious piping of the Shepherd, you realise your own perpetual forward movement and that of the flock, in its relation to that living guide—you have a far deeper, truer knowledge than ever before both of the general and the individual existence; and so are able to handle life with a surer hand.*[49]

She says that by turning to God, one understands oneself, one understands others, one gains knowledge of existence. Indeed, one can "handle life with a surer hand."

T. S. Eliot (1888–1965)

In T. S. Eliot's most famous poem, "The Waste Land," largely considered his best, he writes,

---

47 Underhill, *Evelyn Underhill: Essential Writings*, 13.

48 Underhill, *Practical Mysticism*, 175.

49 Underhill, *Practical Mysticism*, 177.

Who is the third who walks always beside you?
When I count, there are only you and I together?[50]

The lines recall two other writings. The first is from Sir Ernest Shackleton, who led the British Imperial Trans-Antarctic Expedition (1914–1916). The expedition went poorly, and their ship first got trapped in ice for five months and then sank, which led Shackleton and two of his crew to row in an open-air boat looking for help. He later wrote, "When I look back at those days I have no doubt that Providence guided us. . . . It seemed to me often that we were four, not three."[51] The second writing this passage recalls is the biblical story of the road to Emmaus, when the resurrected Christ walks next to two men, though they do not recognize him at first (Luke 24:13–32). This is by no means the only Christian reference to grace this poem. Earlier in the text, he writes:

To Carthage then I came
Burning burning burning burning[52]

This is a clear reference to Augustine of Hippo when he arrived in Carthage as a young man. These are just two of the many religious allusions that run throughout Eliot's work, though when he wrote "The Waste Land" he was still wrestling with the Christian faith.

Few would think of T. S. Eliot as a primarily Christian figure, though he was highly concerned with faith. He was never a priest or monk, and few if any would consider him a saint. His preoccupation with the mystics and mystical writings, though, ran throughout his life, and elements worked their way into his writing both before and after his conversion to Christianity. He was a product of modernity. He was an American expatriate living in England through the war

---

50 T. S. Eliot, *The Waste Land*, ed. Michael North (New York: Norton, 2001), 17.

51 Sir Ernest Shackleton, "The Extra Man," in Eliot, *Waste Land*, 60.

52 Eliot, *Waste Land*, 15.

years; his mysticism long carried the mark of purgation and penance, but with little hope or salvation.

Eliot was born in St. Louis, Missouri, in 1888. His mother was a New England schoolteacher, and his father, who died still thinking Eliot a failure, was a successful merchant. His family's faith was Boston Unitarianism, which Eliot rejected by the time he had headed off to Harvard as a young man.[53] He was not a particularly good student, though he did publish several poems in the *Harvard Advocate*. At Harvard, then as a graduate student studying philosophy, he completed his first professionally published poem, "The Love Song of J. Alfred Prufrock."[54] In 1914 he received a fellowship to study at Merton College, Oxford. There he met American poet Ezra Pound and an Englishwoman named Vivienne Haight-Wood, whom he later married. The marriage was an utter failure. Vivienne was certified insane, committed to an asylum in 1938, and died nine years later. Eliot never visited her.[55]

Eliot's faith during his early life was complicated. There was a time of intense interest in Christianity for the young Eliot, around 1914. He wrote four religious poems that year, including one called "I Am the Resurrection."[56] In his last years at Harvard, he studied the lives of a number of noted mystics, including Teresa of Ávila, Julian of Norwich, Madame Guyon, Walter Hilton, John of the Cross, Jakob Boehme, and Bernard of Clairvaux.[57] He read mystical texts between 1908 and 1914, including Rufus Jones's *Studies in Mystical Religion* and Henry Suso's *Life of Henry Suso, by Himself*.[58] As one scholar says, "St.

53 Lyndall Gordon, *T. S. Eliot: An Imperfect Life* (New York: Norton, 1998), 18.

54 For the poem, see T. S. Eliot, "The Love Song of J. Alfred Prufrock," The Poetry Foundation, https://www.poetryfoundation.org/poetrymagazine/poems/44212/the-love-song-of-j-alfred-prufrock.

55 Gordon, *T. S. Eliot*, 310; Eliot, *Waste Land*, 281–82.

56 Gordon, *T. S. Eliot*, 87.

57 Gordon, *T. S. Eliot*, 89.

58 Gordon, *T. S. Eliot*, 538.

John was for Eliot the 'only mystic who was a great poet.'"[59] Underhill, who was only about a decade older than Eliot, was a particular influence on his thought as well. He read and took copious notes in Underhill's 1911 book, *Mysticism*. He may have also experienced some sort of mystical moment while still living in Boston. In 1910, seventeen years before his conversion, he wrote about it in a poem called "Silence," which he never published. Later he described this mystical moment as a "communion with the Divine" or a "crystallization of the mind,"[60] though considering those two descriptors are hardly the same, it seems Eliot struggled to interpret this moment himself. Yet, for all his interactions with mystical thinkers and texts, and perhaps even having a mystical experience himself, he did not devote himself to the religious life at this time.

When he was finally baptized into the Church of England in 1927, it came as a tremendous surprise to his friends and family, though perhaps it should not have. An interest in religion was not new for Eliot, and in the previous year he had started attending early morning Communion services. In 1926 he had asked to be confirmed, which he was, but since he had been raised a Unitarian, he wanted to be baptized in the name of the Father, Son, and Holy Spirit, as is customary for Trinitarian Christians.[61] This was no lukewarm religiosity. His biographer, Lyndall Gordon, writes, "Eliot's temperament raved an exacting moral code. Chastity, austerity, humility, and sanctity, he said he must have—or perish."[62]

She also paints a stark picture of his life after his conversion and before his marriage to his second wife. In 1946, he moved in with his friend John Hayward, and Gordon describes his life like this: "There

---

59 Nicoletta Asciuto, "Light and Mystical Writing: T. S. Eliot's Poetic Practice in Four Quartets," *Religion & Literature* 52/53, no. 3 (2020): 47–69.

60 Gordon, *T. S. Eliot*, 23.

61 Gordon, *T. S. Eliot*, 223.

62 Gordon, *T. S. Eliot*, 226.

he lived, I imagine, like Jeremiah in the pit, or St. John of the Cross in the dark prison. There, under the crucifix, he observed religious rules, some given, some of his own devising. He memorized passages from the Bible, said the rosary every night, and kept fasts. During Lent he denied himself gin."[63] Of course, some factors complicate this image of an ascetic mystic. The first is the fact that his idea of detachment seemed to hold a level of selfishness that other mystics rarely had. He pushed people away, hurting them in the process. Then there was his second marriage. At age sixty-eight he married his thirty-year-old secretary, Valerie Fletcher.[64] From then on, he seemed to exhibit an uncharacteristic happiness.

A full analysis of mystical themes in his poetry is a topic is far beyond the scope of this chapter, though it is the subject of various scholarly works.[65] However, his poetry shows that he was interested in the "stages of the mystical way," in other words, purgation, illumination, and union.[66] Whether he was interpreting these stages as more traditional Christian mystics did is another question. Regardless, Christian themes run throughout his work, though poems such as "Ash Wednesday," written after his conversion, are particularly Christian in nature. His *Four Quartets*, a collection of four poems, "Burnt Norton," "East Coker," "The Dry Salvages," and the "Little Gidding," deals with time, eternity, and God. "Little Gidding," the last of the four, ends with a powerful allusion to Julian of Norwich:

> *And all shall be well and*

---

63 Gordon, *T. S. Eliot*, 461–62.

64 Gordon, *T. S. Eliot*, 496.

65 A few of particular interest include Susan McCaslin, "Vision and Revision in Four Quartets: T. S. Eliot and Julian of Norwich," *Mystics Quarterly* 12, no. 4 (1986): 171–78; Donald J. Childs, "T. S. Eliot: From Varieties of Mysticism to Pragmatic Poesis," *Mosaic: A Journal for the Interdisciplinary Study of Literature* 22, no. 4 (1989): 99–116; Asciuto, "Light and Mystical Writing."

66 Childs, "T. S. Eliot," 102.

All manner of thing shall be well
When the tongues of flames are in-folded
Into the crowned knot of fire
And the fire and the rose are one.[67]

As one scholar puts it, "Certainly for Eliot, who echoes her crucially at the end of 'Little Gidding,' she is an exemplar of the English mystic."[68]

Eliot was not a perfect man or an exemplar of the religious life. He did, however, wrestle with Christianity and exhibit a genuine faith that carried him through difficult times. His faith and allusions to Christianity run through his work, creating some of the most powerful literature written in the twentieth century. Including someone as difficult as Eliot in this chapter is a reminder that one does not need to be perfect to engage in mysticism.

Mystical Literature for a Modern World

Mystical literature can make the sometimes-difficult content of Christian mystical theology more approachable. History books can sometimes be dry, as can works of theology. But literature is meant to draw a reader in. Most of the people in this chapter were poets whose skill with language helped them articulate feelings and longings in a way that more typical theology may not be able to express. Therefore, literary representations of Christian mysticism can be a more approachable way to interact with this stream of Christian thought than others. A poet's skill with language helps the reader truly appreciate the beauty of their relationship with God. To sit down with, say, John of the Cross's poetry is breathtaking. His ability to articulate a feeling of love and longing surpasses that of most others. Similarly, the author of *The Pilgrim's Tale* is able to express a longing to follow God in a way that would have been difficult, if not impossible, without using

67 T. S. Eliot, *Four Quartets* (Orlando: Harcourt Books, 1943).

68 McCaslin, "Vision and Revision," 171.

that particular genre of writing. While some do not enjoy poetry or other more artistic renderings, literature can appeal to a wide variety of people, especially those who would not necessarily want to read a theological treatise.

Suggested Reading List

Hadewijch. *The Complete Works.* Translated by Mother Columba Hart, OSB. New York: Paulist Press, 1980.

John of the Cross. *John of the Cross, Selected Writings.* Edited by Kieran Kavanaugh. New York: Paulist Press, 1987.

———. *The Poems of Saint John of the Cross.* Translated by Willie Barnstone. Bloomington: Indiana University Press, 1968.

Mechthild of Magdeburg. *The Flowering Light of the Godhead.* Translated by Frank Tobin. New York: Paulist Press, 1998.

The Pilgrim's Tale. Edited by Aleksei Pentikovsky. Translated by T. Allan Smith. New York: Paulist Press, 1999.

Underhill, Evelyn. *Mysticism: A Study in the Nature and Development of Spiritual Consciousness.* Grand Rapids: Christian Classics Ethereal Library, 1911.

———. *Practical Mysticism.* Columbus, OH: Ariel, 1914.

A selection of poems by T. S. Eliot that deal with Christianity and Christian mysticism: "The Waste Land," "Ash Wednesday," "Burnt Norton," "East Coaker," "The Dry Salvages," "Little Gidding," "Silence."

7

A CHANGED LIFE

This soul witnessed many other signs of God's love that are beyond telling. A ray of God's love wounded her heart, making her soul experience a flaming love arising from the divine fount. At that instant, she was outside of herself, beyond intellect, tongue, or feeling. Fixed in that pure and divine love, henceforth she never ceased to dwell in it.

—Catherine of Genoa, *Purgation and Purgatory: The Spiritual Dialogue*

DURING A LENTEN confession in 1473, Catherine of Genoa (1447–1510) had a sudden and overwhelming experience of God as pure love and a crushing feeling of sorrow for her past sins. This moment was especially surprising considering Catherine had not been particularly religious up until this point in her life. At age thirteen she had tried to enter a convent but was turned away because she was too young, and her parents arranged a marriage for her to a young nobleman. Her husband was unfaithful, and the marriage was a failure. Catherine was lonely and unhappy, and she reportedly turned to a life of immorality and frivolity. However, from the moment of her mystical experience, her life was changed. After her moment of transformation during confession, she went from a life of aristocratic luxury to nursing the poor in the slums of Genoa. Eventually her husband joined her in her work, as he too had a conversion of the heart. Catherine lived the rest of her life serving others, taking Communion daily, and, during Lent and Advent, surviving on only water and Communion wafers.[1] Catherine's

1 Egan, *Anthology of Christian Mysticism*, 405.

experience is unusual but not unheard of in Christian history; there are many recorded incidents of people having dramatic conversion experiences that transformed their lives. Propelled by religious vision, Catherine, a married laywoman, followed a call and eventually became a canonized saint.

Like Catherine of Genoa, the people featured in this chapter were radically transformed by either an event or a mystical experience (or both). It is true that all mystics are affected by their experiences with the divine, and the process of becoming more holy and growing closer to God is indeed a form of change. When mystics speak of purgation, illumination, and general progress in the holy life, they are speaking of change. The mystics featured in this chapter, however, had intense and sudden conversion experiences at a mature age. These were not people who found their religious callings as children or teenagers, as many other mystics did. They were wives, husbands, soldiers, aristocrats, and workers engaged in business and trade. In other words, they all lived in a way that would be considered typical for a layperson. Some were churchgoers prior to their conversion experiences, but none were exceptionally religious; before their conversion experiences, no one would have assumed these individuals would become saints or religious leaders (even if some later hagiographic embellishments might imply so). This is what marks their transformation as particularly drastic.

Through this chapter the reader will meet Angela of Foligno, an aristocrat turned mystical teacher and leader; Ignatius of Loyola, a solider who founded the Society of Jesus; Jakob Boehme, a Lutheran cobbler who became a prolific mystical writer; Marie of the Incarnation, a mother with a penchant for business who became a missionary nun; and Phoebe Palmer, a wife and mother who became a revival preacher. These are not necessarily people who have much in common besides a dramatic conversion later in life and then a profound Christian witness to the world through their writings and actions. Yet, they each demonstrate how a moment (or moments) can transform a life. This group also tended to be exceptionally outwardly focused, their spiritual life highly influencing their public life. In other words, their conversions did not lead to a quiet, private faith—quite the opposite.

Except for Angela, these mystics all lived in the modern era. This is not because people in antiquity and the Middle Ages did not have dramatic conversion experiences. They did. For example, Augustine of Hippo could have been placed in this chapter. He had a rather dramatic conversion event, described in detail in his *Confessions*, one of the best-known conversions in history (though his prowess as a theologian placed him in ch. 5). That said, it was in the modern world that spiritual autobiographies became more prominent, literacy rates climbed, and people became more able to share their experiences. The modern world, especially since the Enlightenment, is also more accepting of atheism and religious apathy, which tends to lead to more outwardly dramatic stories of conversion.

Angela of Foligno (ca. 1248–1309)

Angela of Foligno has finally been formally recognized for her contributions to Christian theology, but this conclusion to her story was anything but assured. Over seven hundred years after her death, in October 2013, she was canonized by Pope Francis, and she is one of a few married laywomen to gain real recognition for her mystical theology. She experienced a dramatic transformation from worldly aristocrat to holy woman. She was a member of the Third Order of St. Francis, created for laymen and -women who continued their lives in the world, and she was a founder of a monastic house. She can also be difficult to relate to. Her words can be off-putting, and her actions sometimes seem bizarre, even compared to other mystics, who as a group can tend towards eccentricity. Despite these difficulties, she left a significant mark on medieval mysticism, including influencing other important religious figures.

Angela was born around 1248 in Foligno, Italy, within twenty-five years of Francis of Assisi's death. Foligno is only a few miles away from Assisi, and during Angela's lifetime, Francis's legacy was very strongly felt. Angela therefore was affected by this pervasive Franciscan spirituality. In her youth, she married, though historians do not know to whom. She apparently enjoyed luxury and the comforts of the world, something she would come to feel great shame over. Judging from the quality of her works, which she dictated, she received a good education. She certainly could read, though it is unknown whether she could write. Her book was transcribed and translated into Latin by her confessor. Her text demonstrates sound theological reflection, and she is articulate in her descriptions. She comes across as a profound spiritual teacher guiding others to a life of union with God.

Angela experienced a dramatic conversion, perhaps in her thirties. Angela was ashamed of her sins and feared going to hell. She petitioned Francis of Assisi in prayer to help her find a confessor, and the next day she gave a full confession to a priest, thus starting her life devoted to Christ.[2] Sometime after this conversion event, Angela's mother, husband, and sons all died. She does not explain how, but considering the rapid succession of their deaths, it may have been some sort of epidemic. She describes these deaths as a consolation and something she had been praying for because her family was an obstacle to her faith.[3] This is a tremendously difficult line to interpret. To pray for the death of one's mother, husband, and children seems far beyond typical behavior for mystics. As a comparison, Birgitta of Sweden, who was also a parent, maintained strong relationships with her children despite her religious life. Though we cannot know Angela's mental state when she wrote these lines, it may have been a coping mechanism to

---

2 Margaret Gallyon, ed., *The Visions, Revelations and Teachings of Angela of Foligno: A Member of the Third Order of St Francis* (Liverpool: Liverpool University Press, 2012), 2–3; Paul Lachance, OFM, "Introduction," in *Angela of Foligno: Complete Works*, by Angela of Foligno, ed. and trans. Paul Lachance, OFM (New York: Paulist Press, 1993), 16–18.

3 Angela of Foligno, *The Book of Blessed Angela*, in Foligno, *Angela of Foligno: Complete Works*, 126.

deal with such a horrific event. Or perhaps she may have been embracing an ideal of detachment. In other places, she does say that she experienced great grief at their passing, so it is possible her comment is an exaggeration of the original situation written later in life.

Around ten years after her initial conversion, she had another important mystical experience. In 1290–1291, when Angela was around forty years old, she went on pilgrimage to first Rome and then Assisi. In Rome, Angela believed God had blessed her with a state of perfect poverty, and on the road to Assisi, she had an encounter with the Holy Spirit.[4] This encounter with the Holy Spirit is rather unusual in mystical literature. As she relates the experience, she tested the Spirit to deduce whether it was indeed God. After considerable back-and-forth, she states:

> *There is no way that I could possibly render a just account of how great was the joy and sweetness I was feeling, especially when I heard God tell me: "I am the Holy Spirit who enters into your deepest self." Likewise, all the other words he told me were so very sweet. In my eagerness, I then said: "I will be able to discern if you are the Holy Spirit if you indeed accompany me on this pilgrimage just as you have promised." To this, he replied: "I will not leave you as far as this consolation is concerned until the second time you enter St. Francis's church; but from now on I will never leave you if you love me."*[5]

Whereas mystics often write of a profound moment of mystical encounter, this was more of a conversation, and Angela seems to have questioned whether the spirit was genuinely God. She was not a passive recipient. After she came back home to Foligno, she had more

4 Angela, *Book of Blessed Angela*, 139–40.

5 Angela, *Book of Blessed Angela*, 139–40.

conversations with God and received what might best be described as a mystical engagement to God.

After her pilgrimage to Assisi, Angela and her confessor, Brother Arnaldo, worked on her book, *The Book of Blessed Angela*, which is broken into two major parts, "Memorial" and "Instructions." The book is a collaboration between the two; it is a prime example of a phenomenon of the time in which a woman who reported highly mystical visions worked with a well-educated member of the clergy to compose a mystical text. Interestingly, some scholars have questioned whether Angela was a historical person. It has been suggested that she was merely a construct to demonstrate ideal Franciscan believer.[6] It seems unlikely she was entirely made up, but one does need to recognize the influence of Brother Arnaldo on the book and her story. As one scholar states, "There are three narrators [of the book]: God speaks and reveals himself to Angela, and she in turn speaks to Arnaldo, who, as the prologue to the *Memorial* affirms, then narrates what he hears."[7]

The Book of Blessed Angela is considered one of the more important mystical texts of the thirteenth century. While her confessor plays an important role in the text, he admits that there are times when even he lacks the ability to truly understand what she is dictating. The text also went through an approval process by a cardinal and a group of Franciscan theologians, so there was another level of oversight.[8] Like other mystics, Angela describes a process or "steps of penance" that begin with confession and end with visions, revelations, illuminations, and greater theological understanding. Her work can roughly fit into the purgation-illumination-union framework that is so common within medieval mysticism.

There is little known about her life after about 1296. Historians know that she took up a semimonastic lifestyle and gathered a group of followers, which included mostly men, and became their spiritual

---

6 McGinn, *Flowering of Mysticism*, 143.

7 Angela, *Book of Blessed Angela*, 47.

8 Angela, *Book of Blessed Angela*, 50.

teacher. She died in January 1309, following a brief illness that began around Christmas. She warned her followers ahead of time that she would soon be passing away. She was laid to rest in the church of San Francesco in Foligno, and it soon became a site of veneration.[9] Her book became popular in Europe in the centuries after her death, and there were multiple printings of it in the sixteenth century.[10] Her writings affected a number of other mystics, most notably Francis de Sales.[11] Her conversion from aristocratic lady to a spiritual leader of a semimonastic group of primarily men is a fascinating transformation. For whatever reason, she did not desire to join a women's monastic house, though there were options associated with the Franciscans, such as the Poor Clares. Perhaps her life in the world made a more restrictive enclosure unappealing. Regardless, she emerged as an important mystical voice in the thirteenth century, an example of Franciscan spirituality and women's mystical thought in medieval Italy.

Ignatius of Loyola and Jesuit Spirituality (1491–1556)

The sixteenth century was a time of great change in Europe, and Ignatius of Loyola lived through some of the most significant moments in the Protestant Reformation (he was roughly eight years younger than Martin Luther and outlived him by a decade). Due to Ignatius's lifespan and his founding of a mission-focused monastic order, he is often viewed as a Catholic counter-Reformer. This designation is oversimplistic, and neither does it appreciate the motivations and the accomplishments of this Spanish saint. He was not just reactionary—he was spiritually minded and forward thinking, and he was one of the more influential leaders in Catholic history. He was not only a church reformer and a monastic founder and leader but an initiator in global missions, a spiritual director, and

9 Angela, *Book of Blessed Angela*, 22.

10 Gallyon, *Visions, Revelations, and Teachings*, 5.

11 Gallyon, *Visions, Revelations, and Teachings*, 6.

the genius behind the *Spiritual Exercises*, which has helped shape Catholic spirituality from the sixteenth century to the present day. He was unquestionably a mystic, though his other accomplishments often overshadow his importance as a mystical thinker. He also has one of the most dramatic conversion stories in Christian history. Transforming from a soldier to a founder of a monastic order is a rather abrupt change of lifestyle, but that is precisely what Ignatius did. Remarkably, the Order of Jesus, better known as the Jesuits, can likely credit its existence to a military battle between France and Spain at Pamplona in 1521.

MARTIN LUTHER AND THE NINETY-FIVE THESES

In 1517, Martin Luther, a monk and professor at the University of Wittenberg, posted his Ninety-Five Theses, which attacked the sale of indulgences. It is safe to say that in 1517 he had no idea that this act would set off a series of events that would result in the fracturing of Western Christendom. Luther was an adept theologian and a master of rhetoric. He penned works of theology in German so laypeople could read them, and he led a popular reformation. Core theological beliefs for Luther included justification by faith alone, the centrality of the cross, and the dialectic of law and gospel. Soon the spirit of reformation spread throughout Europe.

In May 1521, French troops stormed the city of Pamplona in the former kingdom of Navarra. The French faced little opposition from the vastly outnumbered Spanish, except at the citadel. This is where the thirty-year-old Ignatius (or Iñigo Lopez de Oñaz de Loyola, his name in Spanish) was making a last stand. Apparently, he was the one who initiated the defense, and the Spanish did offer a heroic, if perhaps unwise, stand against the French. During the battle, a cannonball hit Ignatius's legs, injuring him terribly, but he survived. The French, impressed by his bravery, tended to his wounds once they took the citadel, and a few days after the battle he was taken home to his family's castle in Loyola. His experiences, not surprisingly, made him reassess his life.

Prior to his injuries, Ignatius showed little interest in the religious life. The youngest of thirteen children, he was born to a Spanish aristocratic family, known for their military service one year before the Spanish completed the Reconquista, the centuries-long campaign of the Spanish Christian kingdoms to reclaim the Iberian Peninsula from the Muslim kingdoms following the Umayyad conquests in the eighth century. Loyola was drawn to the adventurous life of a soldier. As a teenager, he was sent to live with a relative who was the treasurer of the royal court, and he became familiar with the life of a courtier. Even after his conversion, his skill at cultivating relationships with the rich and powerful served him well. As was typical of the nobility in this time and place, Ignatius was influenced by the culture of chivalry. His education was typical for a noble of his station, but one would not call it extensive—which became apparent when he began to train for a life in the church. As for lifestyle, he had the somewhat lax morals that again were typical for someone in his station, enjoying gambling, dueling, and women.

Following the battle for Pamplona, Ignatius had multiple surgeries on his shattered leg. It was a miserable recovery that lasted about a year, and he would always walk with a limp. Regarding his conversion, as the story goes, as he was in bed recovering, he requested something to read—preferably some romances (also a favorite genre of Teresa of Ávila when she was young), but he was brought only religious books. He read a four-volume translation of the *Life of Christ* by the Carthusian Ludoph of Saxony and a collection of lives of the saints. He came to see St. Dominic and St. Francis as models to be followed. Once his recovery was over, he had devoted his life to Christ.[12]

Much later, he wrote about the transformation he experienced following his injuries.[13] In it, he describes a rather typical mystical vision. He saw an image of the Virgin Mary and the Christ child, gained an understanding and revulsion for past sins (in a moment of purgation), and demonstrated an outward change from that point forward:

> *One night, as he lay sleepless, he clearly saw the likeness of Our Lady with the holy child Jesus, and because of this vision he enjoyed an excess of consolation for a remarkably long time. He felt so great a revulsion for his past life, especially for his sins of the flesh, that it seemed to him that all the images that had been previously imprinted on his mind were now erased. Thus, from that hour until August 1553, when this is being written, he never again consented, not even in the least manner, to the motions of the flesh. Because of this effect on him, he concluded that this had been God's doing, though he did not dare to specify it any further, nor say anything more than to affirm what he had said above. His brother interpreted his external change, as did other members of the household, to mean that an interior change had taken place in his soul.*[14]

What is interesting about this account and his conversion story in general is both the suddenness of the conversion and the lengthy process that went on both before and after this vision. His injuries, his

---

12 Markus Friedrich, *The Jesuits*, trans. John Noël Dillon (Princeton: Princeton University Press, 2022), 1–3.

13 Technically this was an oral account that was transcribed and worked on by a scribe.

14 Ignatius of Loyola, *A Pilgrim's Journey: The Autobiography of Ignatius of Loyola*, ed. and trans. Joseph N. Tylenda, SJ (San Francisco: Ignatius, 2001), 49.

surgeries, and his contemplation of religious things while recovering all led to this moment of sudden change, prompted by a mystical vision of the Virgin Mary and the Christ child. By the time he recovered, he was a changed man, but he still had more learning to do. He left Loyola in 1522 and traveled first to a Marian shrine north of Barcelona, and then settled in a nearby town called Manresa, where he stayed for nearly a year, living as a hermit in a cave. He then headed to Jerusalem and on his return went to school. He spent the next three years learning Latin and studying philosophy and theology in Spain, which did not go particularly well. His prior education had not prepared him for theological studies. He then went to study at the University of Paris, where he stayed from 1528 to 1535. In Paris he became part of a group of seven students, and the men took a vow of poverty, chastity, and obedience together in 1534. They were not yet Jesuits, but this was certainly laying the foundation for the Society of Jesus.[15]

Later the group of friends met in Venice, with plans to head to the Holy Land, but if the trip fell through, the group decided they would instead go to Rome and offer their services to the pope. The trip fell through, and off to Rome they went. The College of Cardinals was wary of this group, but the pope at the time, Paul III, issued a papal bull that transformed the group into a proper order—the Society of Jesus—in September 1540.[16] The growth the Jesuit order saw is astounding. In 1540, the order had ten members. By 1556, the order had a thousand members. By 1600, the order had 8,519 members. By 1679, the order had 17,655 members. In 1750, the order reached peak membership, with 22,589 members.[17]

One cannot examine Ignatius and his impact on spirituality without briefly looking at his masterpiece, *The Spiritual Exercises*. Ignatius developed it over the course of about twenty years, and it was and

15 Avery Dulles, "Preface," in *The Spiritual Exercises of St. Ignatius*, by Ignatius of Loyola, trans. Louis J. Puhl (New York: Vintage Spiritual Classics, 2000), xvi.

16 For a full history of the Society of Jesus, see Friedrich, *Jesuits*.

17 Friedrich, *Jesuits*, 22–24.

continues to be a critical aspect of Jesuit spirituality. *The Spiritual Exercises* roughly follow the medieval mystical journey of purgation, illumination, and union. The text is both mystical and practical. It is meant as a handbook for retreat directors, not a book for personal reading and edification. In fact, to read the text through is a bit tedious. Ideally the retreatant is supposed to take about four weeks, spending four to five hours per day in intense prayer, to go through the entire course of *The Spiritual Exercises.* [18] However, the *Exercises* are meant to be adaptable. Ignatius was realistic about the fact that not everyone would be able or willing to devote that amount of time to prayer over a full month. The text acknowledges some people will be more diligent than others in this process, and factors such as health, education, and circumstances will affect how the retreatant experiences the *Exercises.* For example, the text notes that one who is engaged in public affairs or business (in other words, a layperson) should take an hour and half for spiritual exercises rather than the four to five hours.[19] Like Francis de Sales writing in the next century, Ignatius was concerned with the laity.

It is remarkable that so much good could stem from such a violent battle and gruesome injury. Over the course of recovering from his injuries, Ignatius of Loyola became a changed man. Able to dwell for the first time on the life of Christ, and then experiencing that transformative love, he changed his life from that of a solider to that of a religious leader. A commitment to holy living, spiritual direction, and missionary activity came to define Ignatius's legacy. While he lived during a complex time in history and the Jesuits did become one of the most important missionary groups in history, Ignatius's activities were not merely reactionary. He followed a call resulting from his mystical conversion event. His commitment to spiritual direction, for both members of his order and laypeople, contributed to the lasting success of the *Exercises.* This is not to mention the adaptability of the *Exercises*

---

18 Dulles, "Preface," xv.

19 Ignatius, *Spiritual Exercises of St. Ignatius*, 6–10.

and that they can be done anywhere (critical for a monastic order committed to missionary activity all around the world).

More than any other figure featured in this chapter, Ignatius seems to be a result of wild circumstances and divine intervention.

THE COUNCIL OF TRENT

For years, Charles V, the Catholic Holy Roman Emperor, pushed for an ecumenical council to deal with the Luther affair. The council was slow to happen for various reasons, but eventually the Council of Trent, held in three different phases, was called by Pope Paul III to contended with Protestantism. The first phase, which was plagued with poor attendance, began in 1545, the year before Luther died. The second phase of Trent ran from 1551–1552. The third phase came over ten years later, from 1562–1563, and there the Jesuits, now a significant force in the church, played a role.

The council affirmed much of Catholic doctrine and cleared up some ambiguities. The council rejected theological assertions such as justification by faith alone. It affirmed the importance of Scripture and tradition, and the church's authority in interpreting Scripture as opposed to the idea of *sola Scriptura*. Also important was the issue of original sin. Catholics reaffirmed that Adam's sin had affected human nature, but baptism removed the stain of corruption—so the only sin that remained was "potential sin."

Jakob Boehme (1575–1624)

While the Protestant Reformation made few inroads in sixteenth-century Spain, where Ignatius began his life and career, Germany, where Jakob Boehme lived, is another story. By the time Boehme was born, Protestantism had firmly taken root, and Boehme grew up in a thoroughly Lutheran atmosphere. There are undoubtedly fewer Protestant mystics than Catholic, but the life and experience of Boehme demonstrate that even in the earlier days of Protestantism there was a distinct and important stream of Lutheran mystical thought. Boehme is one of the more unusual figures in the history of Christian mysticism, and his theology is unique. His primary religious influence was Lutheranism, particularly its more pietistic forms, but his thought also seems to have been affected by the Schwenkfeldians, the Paracelsians, humanism, and even the kabbalah.[20] Also evident are more classic elements of medieval Christian mysticism, such as mystical union, but Catholic mysticism was not his primary influence. He was an unlikely mystic, and he paid a heavy price for his writings, though he did gain followers and his writings left an impressive, though divisive, legacy.

Boehme was born in the Upper Lusatian village of Old Seidenberg in 1575. His parents were farmers, though Boehme was not to inherit their land, so he was apprenticed to a shoemaker after he received an elementary education. There is not much else known about his early life until 1599. That year, he became a professional cobbler, became a citizen of the city of Görlitz, and married a woman named Catharina Kuntzschmann, who was a baker's daughter. In August of that year, he purchased a house. Over the next twelve years, the couple had four sons.[21] During this time he was an active guild member, and there are plenty of records of his dealings in the city.

In 1600, a new Lutheran pastor came to Görlitz by the name of Martin Moller. Moller's theology was of a more pietistic thread of Lutheranism, and he had read and appreciated medieval mystical

---

20 Schwenkfeldians were followers of Caspar Schwenkfeld von Ossig, who was a Protestant Reformer and spiritualist. The Paracelsians were an early modern medical movement based on Swiss physician and lay theologian Paracelsus.

21 John Joseph Stoudt, *Jacob Boehme: His Life and Thought* (New York: Seabury, 1968), 49.

literature. Upon his arrival in Görlitz, Moller organized a Christian small group called the "Conventicle of God's Real Servants," which Boehme joined.[22] Around this time, Boehme was suffering from a case of melancholy, a state that may be roughly compared to the modern concept of depression. Boehme stated that in this state no Scripture could comfort him, and the devil was often beating into him "heathenish thoughts." Then something remarkable happened. He had a mystical experience that changed his life. Writing about it later, he describes it like this:

> *But when in this* affliction *and trouble I elevated my spirit (for I then understood very little or not at all what is was), and I* earnestly *raised it up into God, as with a great storm or onset, wrapping up my whole heart and mind, as also all my thoughts and whole will and resolution,* incessantly *to wrestle with the love and mercy of God, and not to give over, until he blessed me, that is, until he* enlightened *me with his holy spirit, whereby I might* understand *his will, and be rid of my sadness.* And then the spirit did break through.[23]

This vision marks a change from typical medieval Catholic visions. There is more personal action, and the imagery is situated in a Protestant theological framework. Common aspects of medieval visions steeped in Catholic spirituality, such as the Virgin Mary, eucharistic imagery, saints, and the dead, are absent. Even Christ is lacking in this description, with a focus on God the Father and the Holy Spirit. Yet, Boehme still describes a moment of transformation followed by an inbreaking into his life by the Holy Spirit.

---

22 Peter Erb, "Introduction," in *The Way to Christ*, by Jacob Boehme (New York: Paulist Press, 1978), 5–6.

23 Jacob Boehme, *The Aurora*, trans. John Sparrow (London: John M. Watkins, 1914), 487 (emphasis original).

Boehme spent the next twelve years developing this insight. He published his first book, *The Aurora*, in 1612, though it is not entirely clear what he intended to do with his book—perhaps he meant it for just a few close friends. By 1613, a copy of the book had fallen into the hands of Görlitz's new pastor. Moller had died in 1606 and had been replaced with the decidedly less mystically inclined Gregory Richter, who had the book confiscated and Boehme banned from writing anything else.[24] Boehme did cease writing for a while, though by 1619 he began to write once again. Propelled by holy visions, he wrote *Three Principles of Divine Being* in that year, and then in 1620 he wrote an astounding five works, which include *The Threefold Life of Man*, *Forty Questions on the Soul*, *The Human Genesis of Christ*, *Six Theosophical Points*, and *Six Theosophical Letters*. He wrote *Birth and Designation of All Things*, *Election and Grace*, and *The Heavenly and Earthly Mysteries* in or around 1622. He wrote *The Way of Christ* in 1623 and 1624. His longest work, *Mysterium Magnum*, was written between 1622 and 1624, and he wrote a short work called *The Key* in 1624. This flurry of writing once again was brought to the attention of Pastor Richter, and Boehme was told by the city council to leave town. By the end of the year, Richter was dead. Boehme returned home but died shortly afterwards.[25]

Perhaps Boehme would have stayed a local curiosity if not for the missionary zeal of his followers, particularly Abraham von Franckenberg, who wrote a biography on Boehme. There is evidence that Boehme's thought influenced a number of important historical figures ranging from Angelus Silesius to John Milton and Isaac Newton.[26]

---

24 Erb, "Introduction," 6.

25 Bernard McGinn, *Mysticism in the Reformation 1500–1650* (New York: Crossroad, 2016), 171.

26 Erb, "Introduction," 1.

ANGELUS SILESIUS

One of Boehme's more interesting followers was a man named Johannes Scheffler (1624–1677). Scheffler was born into a wealthy Lutheran family in the city of Breslau, the capital city of Silesia. As a young man Scheffler went to study medicine and philosophy, first in Strasbourg and then in Leiden. In Leiden he was introduced to a number of new religious ideas, but most notable were those of Jakob Boehme. He later cultivated a friendship with Boehme's biographer, Abraham von Franckenberg. Franckenberg eventually left Scheffler his library, which included many mystical works.

Scheffler had mystical experiences, which he wrote about in his texts *The Holy Joy of the Soul* and *The Cherubinic Wanderer*. These texts express a mystical sense of joy and peace. Eventually the mystical physician converted to Catholicism. He became a Franciscan and was ordained a priest in 1661, taking the name Angelus Silesius. As a jarring counter to his beautiful mystical writings, he became a vitriolic Counter-Reformation pamphleteer as well.

Not all looked so kindly on Boehme's writings, though. John Wesley, referring to *Mysterium Magnum*, said, "It is most sublime nonsense."[27] Boehme's writing can be difficult to read and even more difficult to comprehend. His works include concepts that are challenging to define and do not fit easily within a more traditional Christian theology. For example, Boehme writes of the Virgin Sophia, who is neither the Sophia of Scripture nor an equivalent to the Virgin Mary. However, many have found his writings powerful, and he is without

27 As quoted in McGinn, *Mysticism in the Reformation 1500–1650*, 172.

question one of the more influential Protestant mystics of the early modern era. His radical transformation from shoemaker to local prophet is also of note. Despite significant personal cost, the most obvious being his exile from his home and city, Boehme continued to follow his religious calling.

Can Boehme be properly called a mystic? Yes, but he is a rather unusual figure within Christian mysticism. His thought does not fit within the medieval sense of purgation, illumination, and union. Even when he uses these concepts, he does so in a way that runs counter to how other mystics understood the terms. In addition, there are elements of his thought that are unorthodox, and he pulls on a number of intellectual and religious traditions in his writings. However, he writes of a deep relationship with God, and he experienced deeply powerful encounters with God that without question changed his life. He had a transformative faith that affected not only his life but those who followed him, intrigued by this shoemaking mystic.

Marie of the Incarnation (1599–1672)

Born one year before Jakob Boehme's first illumination, Marie of the Incarnation spent the first part of her life in France as a wife and mother, working in business. Following a dramatic mystical experience, she became a missionary nun and sailed to what is now Canada, never returning to Europe. Somewhat obscure in the English-speaking world because her writings were available only in French for many years, she has been referred to as Canada's Teresa of Ávila, which communicates both her historical importance and her deep mystical relationship with God.

Marie of the Incarnation was born Marie Guyer in Tours, France, in 1599 to a middle-class family. The year before her birth, the Edict of Nantes was signed by King Henry IV, ending decades of religious conflict in France, and Marie grew up in a time of relative peace and spiritual resurgence, though the Thirty Years' War began when Maria was an adult. According to her own writings, at age seven she had a vision of Christ in which he asked her whether she would be his. After she told him she would, he returned to heaven.[28] This is a somewhat typical vision for a young saint, but since she wrote it herself, one cannot just discount it as hagiographic embellishment. While she did express some interest in becoming a nun, her family did not believe she had the temperament and arranged a marriage with a silk merchant named Claude Martin. Unfortunately, her husband died young, and Marie was left a widow with a baby boy and a failing business at age eighteen. Despite large debts, Marie decided to try to save the business.

On her way to work one day in March 1620 Marie had a life-changing mystical experience. She writes, "Then, in an instant, my inner eyes were opened and all the faults, sins, and imperfections that I had committed since my birth were shown to me in most vivid detail."[29] After this understanding, this moment of purgation, she saw herself immersed in Christ's blood, and she understood that it was for her that his blood had been shed. The vision is reminiscent of other mystics, particularly medieval mystics, who reported deep regret for their past actions before being able to unite with God. Marie continues to discuss how this vision affected her. The quote below is lengthy, but she writes of such a profound realization, one in which she understood that Christ would have died for only one soul, that it is worth reflecting on in its entirety:

> *No human language can express this: to look upon a God of infinite goodness and purity offended by a mere worm exceeds even horror itself. And then to think of a God made man, dying to atone for sin, shedding his precious blood to satisfy his Father and thus reconcile sinners to himself! In a word, it is impossible to express what the soul comes to understand*

---

28 Marie of the Incarnation, "The Revelation of 1654," in *Marie of the Incarnation: Selected Writings*, by Marie of the Incarnation, ed. Irene Mahoney, OSU (New York: Paulist Press, 1989), 41–42.

29 Marie of the Incarnation, "Revelation of 1654," 49.

> *in this marvel. And even beyond all this, to realize that one is personally guilty and that if one had been entirely alone the Son of God would have done exactly what he did for everyone. This truly wastes and, as it were, destroys the soul. These visions and what they evoke penetrate so deeply that in an instant they communicate everything with their own perfect efficacy. At that moment I felt transported beyond myself and transformed through the mercy of him who had wrought this wonderful grace.*[30]

Her recognition of guilt is a step in the process of understanding Christ's incredible love and mercy. She does not wallow in her sins; she is shown them to prepare her to receive graces from God. After her vision, she immediately went to confession, and she confessed every sin that had been revealed to her. She did not, however, tell her new confessor about the vision she had experienced. With her confessor's permission, she began forms of penance, such as wearing a hair shirt and, as she called them, unattractive clothes, to signal that her life in the world was over. She moved back into her parents' house because it was easier to achieve silence. After a year, she went to live with her sister for the next three or four years because her sister needed help. While she continued in the world, she had two things that helped her progress in her spiritual life. First was the book *Introduction to the Devout Life*, written by Francis de Sales. This text was discussed in chapter 5, but here we see a lay believer deeply affected by his writings. Second, Marie had a new confessor.[31]

Over the next number of years, Marie experienced growth in her spirituality. In addition to her flourishing prayer life, she received divine favors, such as feeling the presence of Christ, and she made vows of chastity, obedience, and poverty, which she believed were the foundations of Christ's earthly life. When she was about twenty-five,

30 Marie of the Incarnation, "Revelation of 1654," 49–50.

31 Marie of the Incarnation, "Revelation of 1654," 50–55.

she experienced a mystical union of sorts, a uniting of the hearts, as she describes it: "One time I felt that my heart was taken away and enclosed in another heart so that although there were still two hearts, they were so closely fitted together that they were like one." Later she experienced what can only be described as a mystical marriage: "Then, engulfed in the presence of this adorable Majesty, Father, Son, and Holy Spirit, adoring him in the awareness and acknowledgement of my lowliness, the Sacred Person of the Divine Word revealed to me that he was in truth the spouse of the faithful soul."[32] After this experience, she describes herself as completely changed. She increased her penances and busied herself with acts of charity to the neighbor in hopes of winning them for God. She describes her soul as completely transformed and says that she was living in a state of loving ecstasy.

At thirty-one, she entered a convent. While she had several options open to her in Tours, she chose the Ursulines because of their focus on the salvation of souls. There were two obstacles to her becoming a nun, however. Her son was only twelve years old, and he needed someone to care for him. Second, she did not have the money for a dowry, which was expected when a woman entered a convent. The archbishop approved her entrance without the money, and her sister and brother-in-law, for whom she had been working for the past decade, agreed to care for her son.[33] However, monastic life was not all that she had been hoping it would be. Leaving her son was painful, and after a lifetime of being out in the world, adjusting to contemplative life was more difficult than she anticipated.

At thirty-five, she had a dream that changed her life once again. In her dream, her spirit was carried through different lands around the world. After this she longed to be a missionary nun. She told her spiritual director, who was also rector of the Jesuits, and he told her that her vision could be realized if she went to Canada. It took some time to organize things, but eventually she left for Canada, arriving in August

---

32 Marie of the Incarnation, "Revelation of 1654," 71, 81.

33 Marie of the Incarnation, "Revelation of 1654," 94.

1639 along with two other Ursuline nuns and a wealthy laywoman named Madeleine de la Peltrie, who helped fund the operation.[34]

Marie founded the first Ursuline monastery in Quebec, opened a school for girls, and, after learning the local languages, composed a catechism in Huron and dictionaries in Huron and Algonquin. She was a prolific writer; much of what she wrote was to her son, who became a Benedictine monk, and he collected it and published her writings after her death in 1672, against her wishes.[35] Marie's descriptions of the indigenous Americans are difficult for the modern reader. She betrays the prejudices of her times in the language she uses, and their salvation, not necessarily their well-being, is her primary concern. The school was successful but not necessarily in the way the sisters had hoped. Over time the tribal populations decreased, but the number of colonists increased, and soon their school was filled with the children of colonists. This was a disappointment to the nuns because it was not why they had come, though Marie did believe that her teaching work still had value.[36]

When Marie died in 1672, the Ursuline monastery she helped to found was financially stable, with a steady supply of sisters who were being trained in Quebec. She left behind a robust collection of writings detailing her conversion experiences and missionary work, and she was declared a saint in 2014 by Pope Francis. Her canonization was an "equivalent canonization" because it involved a thorough study of her writings, record of holiness, and reports of favors granted through intercession, and it did not require a verification of miracles through her intercession. A report from the time called her the mother of the Canadian church.[37]

---

34 Marie of the Incarnation, "Revelation of 1654," 108–15, 136.

35 Irene Mahoney, OSU, "Introduction," in Marie of the Incarnation, *Marie of the Incarnation*, 5–7.

36 Mahoney, "Introduction," 34.

37 Cindy Wooden, "Laval, Marie de L'Incarnation Decreed Saints," *Catholic Register*, April 3, 2014, https://www.catholicregister.org/faith/item/17877-laval-marie-de-lincarnation-decreed-saints.

Marie of the Incarnation experienced not one but two dramatic conversion experiences resulting from mystical visions and dreams. The first resulted in her dramatic embrace of the religious life—it drew her into a desire for silence and contemplation. She tried to leave the world, first through returning to her parents' home and then by entering a convent. The second conversion event pulled her back into the world, though not to working in trade or business, like she once had; she now desired to work in the world as a missionary. In the seventeenth century, Canada was a world away from France, and she was never able to return to see her family and friends. She believed it was her divine call, and she followed it.

Phoebe Palmer (1807–1874)

Nearly two hundred years after Marie of the Incarnation established her Canadian mission, a Methodist named Phoebe Palmer was traveling through the United States and Canada, preaching at and eventually leading religious revivals. Palmer was a different sort of religious leader from Marie, though they both experienced mystical visions resulting in dramatic conversions that led to life-changing decisions to enter into ministry. Marie, as a missionary nun, worked with her monastic community, but Palmer, as a Protestant laywoman, was able to travel far and wide spreading her message.

Palmer was a writer, leader, social reformer, preacher, and sought-after revivalist. Her theology is closer to that of someone like Sojourner Truth, another American revivalist preacher, than the Catholic mystics of old. Her theology was affected by her commitment to both Methodism and Christian perfection, but there has recently emerged scholarship exploring Palmer as a genuine Christian mystic,[38]

38 The most important of these is Elaine A. Heath, *Naked Faith: The Mystical Theology of Phoebe Palmer* (Cambridge: Lutterworth, 2009).

and there is a strong case for arguing that she should be considered one of America's true mystical thinkers.

A moment on the holiness movement and Palmer's distinct theology is useful to understand Palmer's designation as a mystic. The holiness movement, which was developed in the United States in the nineteenth century, grew out of Methodism but was also influenced by other theological traditions such as monasticism, pietism, and the Society of Friends. One critical aspect of the holiness movement was a commitment to "Christian perfection," sometimes also called entire sanctification, which means achieving a sinless life. As demonstrated by other mystics, a commitment to a holy lifestyle is often an important aspect of spiritual growth, though many religious denominations would deny the possibility of living a sinless life due to humanity's fallen nature. Palmer took the idea of Christian perfection even further with her "shorter way," detailed below. However, the big difference between Palmer and the Catholic and Orthodox mystics was in how a believer achieved holiness. For Catholic and Orthodox mystics, holiness is a *process*. Christians can spend years tempering the passions and developing a profound relationship with God, and even then a holy life still involves struggle.

For Palmer and for those affected by her theology and writings, God expected perfect holiness from all believers, but it did not need to be a lengthy process. After Palmer's conversion, she developed her "shorter way" for others who were seeking it. The shorter way involves three steps: entire consecration, faith, and testimony. Entire sanctification means that a believer needs to put everything on the altar, which is Christ himself, and nothing can be held back. The second step is faith in the sanctification regardless of outward signs. For Palmer, who did not have a particularly emotional conversion experience (a notable difference from many other mystics), this was especially important. The final step is testimony. One cannot keep this blessing private; the gift of sanctification is meant to be shared with the world. As Palmer writes in her most popular book, *The Way of Holiness*: "Whatever my former deficiencies may have been, God requires that I should now be *holy*. Whether *convicted*, or otherwise, *duty is plain*. God requires *present* holiness."[39] Palmer did not come to these theological conclusions immediately. She spent years developing them. Her theology is markedly different from the medieval spiritual progress of purgation, illumination, and union, though there are echoes of it. She outlines a spiritual progress of sorts, though sanctification is the first step, followed by faith and then testimony. While older mystics often did write about their experiences as a sort of testimony, it was certainly not a required step of the progress.

A significant complication in examining Palmer as a mystic is her own aversion to mysticism. She once wrote, "I have no sympathy for mysticism in religion. Any attainment of grace, however lofty, that does not energize the soul and bring it into sympathy with Jesus in the great work of soul-saving, leading to holy activities, does not to my conceptions, reach the Bible standard of Christian holiness."[40] Placing Palmer within the mystical tradition when she herself rejects that designation is admittedly problematic. However, the issue for Palmer was that she did not believe in a spiritual elite, which she associated with the concept of mysticism. For her, the Bible was the ultimate authority. Interestingly, because she was so invested in a Bible-based Christianity, she was open to phenomena such as visions and prophetic dreams, which people would often classify as mystical in nature, because these do occur in Scripture. And Palmer had a visionary experience, which she interpreted as her call to ministry.[41] She specifically had a vision in which she came to recognize that holiness was a gift that came from God alone, after which she envisioned the community of saints, which strengthened her to testify to her faith.[42]

39 Phoebe Palmer, *The Way of Holiness* (New York, 1854), 7 (italics original).

40 Thomas C. Oden, ed., *Phoebe Palmer: Selected Writings* (New York: Paulist Press, 1988), 278.

41 Heath, *Naked Faith*, 51.

42 Heath, *Naked Faith*, 52.

To better understand Palmer and her mysticism, a brief examination of her life is helpful. She was born in New York in 1807 to Methodist parents. Her father had been converted at a camp meeting by John Wesley, the founder of Methodism, and Christianity and church life were a large part of Palmer's childhood. In her youth, Palmer demonstrated both piety and concern about not having a dramatic conversation experience, or a second blessing, as it was called in the fledgling holiness movement.[43] If Palmer had any desire to join the ministry as a youth, it is not known. Though it was not unheard of for Methodist women to preach, it was still an exceedingly uncommon practice at the time. Instead, she chose the typical life of a wife and married Walter Clarke Palmer in 1826. Also a Methodist, he had considered the ministry but felt a divine call to medicine.[44] The couple was financially comfortable; they had a happy marriage, and he supported her eventual ministry career. Yet a strong bond could not stop the tragedy that the young couple experienced early in their marriage. Their first two children, both boys, died before their first birthdays. Palmer was devastated and sought theological explanation for what had happened. She concluded that God had taken her sons because she had made an idol of them.[45]

In 1837 Palmer had an experience that would affect her theology and her future career as a preacher. She experienced the second blessing that she had been hoping and praying for. After this she wrote, "I felt . . . that the seal of consecration had been set, and that God had proclaimed me by the testimony of his Spirit, entirely his."[46] From that point forward her life was completely different. She developed her theology of the shorter way to help others receive their second blessing. She became a popular writer and published eighteen books, plus

---

43 Charles Edward White, *The Beauty of Holiness: Phoebe Palmer as Theologian, Revivalist, Feminist, and Humanitarian* (Eugene, OR: Wipf & Stock, 1986), 1–3.

44 White, *Beauty of Holiness*, 4.

45 White, *Beauty of Holiness*, 5–6.

46 White, *Beauty of Holiness*, 19.

articles, and edited the periodical *Guide to Holiness*.[47] *The Way of Holiness*, her most popular work, went through fifty printings by 1867, and it is estimated that worldwide sales were around one hundred thousand during Palmer's lifetime.[48] In addition, she wrote countless letters to those who sought spiritual directions from her.

She became one of the better-known revivalists of the era. For the first twenty years or so of her revivalist ministry, she usually attended revivals alone, while Walter stayed home to work and take care of their children, which is quite remarkable for the time. Eventually, though, Walter was able to quit his job, and the two worked together as revivalist preachers, though she was undoubtedly the more talented and sought-after preacher.

Palmer represents an interesting intersection of mystical theology and public ministry within a Protestant framework. What is so remarkable about her story is the radical change that occurred as a result of her mystical vision and subsequent second blessing. She went from a typical nineteenth-century life of a wife and mother to being a sought-after preacher and bestselling author who traveled through the United States, Canada, and Great Britain leading large revivals. In this way she was similar to Marie of the Incarnation in particular but also others within this chapter. She had the benefit of a loving spouse, who supported her rather countercultural career, but the motivations were her own. Another thing to note on Palmer is her pushing of gender roles of the time. In many ways she was a conservative Christian woman. She was not generally supportive of women's suffrage, and her reform activities were focused on moral purity as it was defined at the time. Yet, it was not typical for women to speak publicly, to preach, or to pursue a ministry career, especially while raising children. Her

---

47 Heath, *Naked Faith*, 11.

48 Susan Lindley Hill, *You Have Stept Out of Your Place: A History of Women and Religion in America* (Louisville: Westminster John Knox, 1996), 119; White, *Beauty of Holiness*, 29.

religious visions and experiences propelled her to do these things, and she defended these decisions vigorously.

Palmer is admittedly a complex mystical figure, especially due to her own hesitations about the term. Yet, she displayed enough tendencies of a typical mystic that she cannot be ignored. She also represents an important Protestant voice in a stream of Christian thought that tends to be dominated by Catholic and Orthodox figures. Her fusion of mystical thought and American revivalism, like Sojourner Truth, is another important and unusual tradition that is particularly important to remember for those living in the United States.

A Changed Life for a Modern World

In an increasingly secular world, at least in North America and Europe, these stories of radical transformation can provide an especially strong witness. Today people are less likely to grow up in a church, less likely to identify as Christian, and less likely to have biblical or theological literacy than in the decades and centuries past. Because of this, Christian figures who felt their call as a child or even as a teenager may not be as relatable as people who lived a secular life in the world prior to a conversion event. These individuals all lived typical (well, perhaps Ignatius's life was not *typical*, but it was common enough for Spanish nobility) lay lives before their conversion moments. They did not set out to the convent in their teenage years. Most had jobs and had families. They dealt with common human events such as marriage, parenting, learning a craft, active guild membership, and military operations. Their conversion events and subsequent calls to the religious life may be fantastic in some sense to us, but their own detailing of the events makes them more relatable still.

In our current world, in which so many people are deciding to leave the church, these individuals can show how to live a faithful life or even be a guide in conversion to the Christian faith. They demonstrate how someone can be called at any time in life and that mystical life is not just for the spiritual elite who were called from their youth to engage in a highly unrelatable life of seclusion. In fact, some of these individuals, Palmer in particular, were completely opposed to the idea of a mystical elite. The faithful life is open to everyone.

Suggested Reading List

Angela of Foligno. *Angela of Foligno: Complete Works*. Edited and translated by Paul Lachance, OFM. New York: Paulist Press, 1993.

Boehme, Jacob. *The Aurora*. Translated by John Sparrow. London: John M. Watkins, 1914.

———. *The Way to Christ*. New York: Paulist Press, 1978.

Catherine of Genoa. *Purgation and Purgatory: The Spiritual Dialogue*. Translated by Serge Hughs. Mahwah, NJ: Paulist Press, 1979.

Ignatius of Loyola. *A Pilgrim's Journey: The Autobiography of Ignatius of Loyola*. Edited and translated by Joseph N. Tylenda, SJ. San Francisco: Ignatius, 2001.

———. *The Spiritual Exercises of St. Ignatius*. Translated by Louis J. Puhl. New York: Vintage Spiritual Classics, 2000.

Marie of the Incarnation. *Marie of the Incarnation: Selected Writings*. Edited by Irene Mahoney, OSU. New York: Paulist Press, 1989.

8

CONTROVERSY

When you have completely stripped yourself of your own self, and all things and every kind of attachment, and have transferred, made over, and abandoned yourself to God in utter faith and perfect love, then whatever is born in you or touches you, within or without, joyful or sorrowful, sour or sweet, that is no longer yours, it is altogether your God's to whom you have abandoned yourself.

—Meister Eckhart, *The Complete Mystical Works of Meister Eckhart*

MOST OF THE people featured in this book fall within traditional church structures. Yes, some of them faced scrutiny or investigation, but by and large they lived as active members of a church, often as monastics, and many were declared saints or hailed as important leaders before and after death. The individuals included in this chapter, however, fall outside the mainstream. They faced more than scrutiny—they faced serious persecution, heresy accusations (and/or trials), and imprisonment, and one, Marguerite Porete, was executed for her beliefs. Given their tenuous status within Christian institutions, there are three important questions this chapter needs to address. First, why were other mystics accepted by church bodies and society while these mystics faced persecution? Second, how did these mystics, with their unorthodox beliefs and teachings or their perceived unorthodox beliefs, affect Christianity and society despite scrutiny or persecution? Third, how can their stories be of value today in our increasingly secular world?

The chapter begins with a laywoman, possibly a beguine, Marguerite Porete. She and her writings were condemned, but her book circulated for years anonymously. Next is an examination of one of the better-known mystics of the Middle Ages, Meister Eckhart. While a prominent and well-respected theologian, he faced heresy accusations later in life, and his legacy has been tainted by a pronouncement following his death that some of his writings were indeed heretical. George Fox and the Society of Friends, with their radical understanding of humanity and salvation, follow. While steeped in Scripture, Fox rejected foundational elements of traditional Christianity, such as clergy and even the necessity of the Bible, which caused society to look on him and his fledgling movement with great suspicion. A modern-day Friend, Rufus Jones, will also be briefly discussed. Emmanuel Swedenborg, Swedish polymath and mystic, provides a fascinating look at an alternative cosmology within the age of the Enlightenment. Finally, Simone Weil, a philosopher and a deeply faithful woman who rejected baptism, concludes the chapter. While these figures span time and place, they each represent a version of mystical thought that thrived outside the confines of church institutions. In an era with decreased church attendance, they model a deep faith apart from the establishment.

Marguerite Porete (1250–1310)

Marguerite Porete (sometimes spelled Margaret Porette) is often identified as a beguine, though her story is markedly different than those of from Hadewijch and Mechthild, whom we met in chapter 6. While the beguine movement in general faced scrutiny, neither Hadewijch nor Mechthild faced severe persecution from authorities. They were both skilled poets and writers who were able to combine their deep mystical theology with the written word, and they are both representatives of the deep mystical tradition that thrived within some beguine communities. Conversely, Porete was a highly controversial figure who was burned to death as a heretic for her book, *The Mirror of Simple*

Souls. Porete's book and legacy have lived on despite the best attempts to suppress it. It was not until 1946 that Italian medievalist Romana Guarnieri discovered in the Vatican archives that Porete was the author of *The Mirror*. This discovery prompted an explosion of rich scholarship on Porete in subsequent years.[1]

Outside her book, all surviving documents about her were written by her political enemies, so caution is needed when interpreting what they wrote, and historians know only the basics about Porete's life. She was likely born sometime around 1260 in Hainaut, and at the time of her death she lived near the town of Valenciennes, which today is in France. Nothing is known of her family. She wrote in the vernacular, not Latin, but she understood literary and theological concepts, so she must have had some education, which likely suggests she was born upper class, though this is not guaranteed. She is called a beguine in the trial records, though it is unclear to which, if any, community she belonged. It is also possible that the word was used pejoratively and she was not a member of any sort of beguine community. In chapter 123 of *The Mirror*, she has this to say:

> *Dear Love, what will the Beguines say*
> *and the religious,*
> *When they shall hear the excellence*
> *of your divine song?*
> *The Beguines say that I am all astray,*
> *and priest, and clerics, and Preachers,*
> *The Austin Friars, the Carmelites,*
> *and the Friars Minor*
> *Because of what I write of the being*
> *of Perfect Love.*[2]

---

1 David J. Kangas, "Dangerous Joy: Marguerite Porete's Good-Bye to the Virtues," *JR* 91, no. 3 (July 2011): 299.

2 Margaret Porette, *The Mirror of Simple Souls*, trans. Edmund Colledge, OSA, J. C. Marler, and Judith Grant (Notre Dame: University of Notre Dame Press, 1999), 153.

It would appear from this text that Porete faced opposition from a great number of religious groups due to her beliefs, including at least some beguines. While her status as a beguine is unclear, it is apparent she was not a nun, nor she did benefit from the protection or guidance of a monastic community.

She wrote *The Mirror* in French, probably in the 1290s, and she considered it her life's work. In some ways, the book fits with the larger genre of mystical writings penned by women in vernacular languages that emerged during this time. Porete writes about her quest for a mystical union with God, and love plays a central role throughout. She has similarities to both Mechthild and Hadewijch in the way they all treat the subject of love. However, Porete is the only one who was executed for her writings, so the question becomes: What did the religious authorities find so damning in her book?

Perhaps most pertinent, Porete did not base her message on visionary authority, which is in stark contrast to many of the mystics of this era, nor did she claim that God spoke through her. Through the text, "characters" such as "Love, the Soul, and Reason ask and answer questions about the state of nonbeing, annihilation in love, and the destruction of the will that allows the simple soul to be nowhere and nothing and hence in a state of nondifference with God, who is All."[3] An excerpt from chapter 81 of the text demonstrates her belief that nothingness—or, one could go as far as to argue, the annihilation of the self—is necessary for union with God:

> **Love**: *Now this Soul, says Love, has her true name from the nothingness in which she dwells. And since she is nothing, she is concerned for nothing, not for herself or for her neighbors or God himself. For she is so little that she*

---

3 Sean L. Field, *The Beguine, the Angel, and the Inquisitor: The Trials of Marguerite Porete and Guiard of Cressonessart* (Notre Dame: University of Notre Dame Press, 2012), 8.

> *cannot find herself; and every created thing is so far from her that she cannot sense it; and God is so great that she can comprehend nothing of him; and on account of this nothingness she has reached the certainty of knowing nothing and of wishing for nothing. And this nothing of which we speak, says Love, gives her everything and in no way can anyone have it.*[4]

Porete describes the soul as being nothing, dwelling in nothing, and being concerned for nothing. Scholars often describe Porete as teaching about the annihilation of the soul or the self.[5] While there is precedent regarding this type of theology—Evagrius of Pontus speaks of the soul becoming one with God, for example, though his understanding of union is less extreme—it is overall a minority stance within mystical tradition, and one, as stated previously, that has often brought scrutiny. In the more traditional understanding of mystical union, there is a joining of wills, not an annihilation of the creature's sense of self entirely. Porete also writes of the soul caring for nothing—not God or neighbor—which poses another problem. Love of God and neighbor is not only scriptural (Deut 6:4–5; Matt 22:36–40; Mark 12:30–31; Luke 10:27) but also a dominant theme in mystical theology and arguably one of the main tenets of the faith.

In addition to her theological statements, she rejects critical aspects of medieval Catholicism, such as the virtues. She explicitly states, "Virtues, I take my leave of you for evermore. And so my heart will have more joy and be more free. Your service is a lifelong yoke as well I see. . . . There was a time I was your serf but now I break away."[6] It was her statements on the virtues and the sacraments that caused the

---

4 Porette, *Mirror of Simple Souls*, 105.

5 For example, see Patrick Wright, "Marguerite Porete's Mirror of Simple Souls and the Subject of Annihilation," *Mystics Quarterly* 35, no. 3/4 (2009): 63–98.

6 Porette, *Mirror of Simple Souls*, 16.

most problems for her.[7] She was not the only Christian, nor mystic, to claim that she was no longer bound by the law or virtues or agreed-on morality, but again, people who did this generally found themselves in hot water with religious authorities. One could make the case on these statements that she was an antinomian, a term used to describe people who believe that Christians are no longer bound by the law or other moral or ethical expectations.

Her refusal to cooperate with authorities certainly did not help save her life, but growing hostilities toward the beguines and the presence of other heretical groups in the area may have influenced the decision to execute her as well.[8] Porete was condemned and her book ordered to be burned by the bishop of Cambrai sometime between 1296 and 1306, and she was told not to write or promote her ideas in public. She did not adhere to this sentence and found herself arrested again in 1308. She spent two years in jail, and after the inquisitor had a group of twenty-one theologians read excerpts from her book, she was sentenced to death.[9]

None of these explanations of why her writings were found heretical are given to justify the religious persecution she faced. Burning someone for their beliefs and writings is unequivocally wrong. Instead, these explanations are meant to explain why Porete received such a radically different response, especially compared to women such as Mechthild and Hadewijch, when on the surface the three have much in common. The difference in reception also demonstrates the fine line mystics had to walk, and for someone like Porete, who likely did not benefit from a robust learning community such as Helfta, the danger of writing something that might be deemed heretical was real and certainly terrifying.

---

7 Kent Emery Jr., "Foreword: Margaret Porete and Her Book," in Porette, *Mirror of Simple Souls*, xvii.

8 Field, *Beguine, the Angel*, 1–2.

9 Field, *Beguine, the Angel*, 5–6.

Despite the persecutions and the suppression of her work, *The Mirror* continued to circulate, though the author was assumed to be a man until the 1960s.[10] In fact, in a testament to the surprisingly lasting power of the text despite active suppression, there were thirteen versions of her writings that survived in four different languages: Middle French, Middle English, Italian, and Latin.[11] She has had a lasting impact on Christian spirituality, and she influenced other female religious writers, including Simone Weil.[12]

Meister Eckhart (ca. 1260–1328)

From autumn 1311 to summer 1313, Meister Eckhart held a position as *magister* for the second time, at the University of Paris. While there, he lived in the same house as Dominican inquisitor William of Paris, who had been responsible for the execution of Marguerite Porete only one year earlier.[13] Eckhart had a more positive opinion of Porete's writings than William of Paris. In fact, scholars have shown that Porete, among other beguines, influenced Eckhart's theology.[14] While Eckhart managed to avoid execution for his writings and preaching, he has long been a controversial figure in Christian history. He was accused of heresy during his life, and some of his works were condemned after his death. Even today there is cloud of suspicion surrounding his work. He

---

10 Wolfgang Riehle, *The Secret Within: Hermits, Recluses, and Spiritual Outsiders in Medieval England*, trans. Charity Scott-Stokes (Ithaca, NY: Cornell University Press, 2014), 135.

11 Riehle, *Secret Within*, 142.

12 Riehle, *Secret Within*, 136.

13 Bernard McGinn, *The Harvest of Mysticism in Medieval Germany* (New York: Crossroad, 2005), 99.

14 For a study of the impact of Porete on Eckhart, see Maria Lichtmann, "Marguerite Porete and Meister Eckhart: *The Mirror of Simple Souls* Mirrored," in *Meister Eckhart and the Beguine Mystics: Hadewijch of Bradant, Mechthild of Magdeburg, and Marguerite Porete*, ed. Bernard McGinn (New York: Continuum, 1994), 66–86.

was incredibly influential both within his life and briefly after, founding the so-called Rhineland school of mysticism. People continue to engage with his work, and while there are points of his thought that push the boundaries of medieval Christian theology, there are excellent reasons to engage with this medieval theologian and philosopher today.

There are many unknowns in Eckhart's biography.[15] Scholars have been able to piece together a general outline, though it must be acknowledged that there is some guesswork at play here. In fact, the first certain bit of biographical data available on Eckhart's life is from Easter 1294, when he preached a sermon in Paris while serving a two-year teaching assignment in which he lectured on Peter Lombard's *Sentences* (the standard textbook of systematic theology in the Middle Ages) at the University of Paris. The year 1260 is often given as the date of Eckhart's birth, but that is anything but assured—it is possible he was born before or even a little after that.[16] There is also some debate regarding his family and place of origins, though it is now generally assumed that he was the son of a feudal knight, a member of the lower nobility, from the German state of Thuringia, probably in Tambach.[17]

THE ORDER OF PREACHERS

Meister Eckhart was a member of the Order of Preachers, commonly called the Dominicans. The Order of Preachers was founded by Dominic de Guzmán (1170–1221), a Spanish priest. At the beginning of the thirteenth century, Dominic was sent on a diplomatic mission and on

15 For a robust discussion of his life and how scholars have pieced information together, see Walter Senner, OP, "Meister Eckhart's Life, Training, Career, and Trial," in *A Companion to Meister Eckhart*, ed. Jeremiah M. Hackett (Leiden: Brill, 2013), 7–81.

16 Senner, "Meister Eckhart's Life," 7–8.

17 Senner, "Meister Eckhart's Life," 10.

his way home traveled through southern France. He came across some Cistercian monks who had been tasked with combating the heresy of the Cathars, but they were not having much success. Domonic believed that the monks' failure stemmed from the monks' lifestyle, which was lavish compared to the asceticism, or plain living, of the Cathars. Dominic, who believed that good preaching and right living were the best way to combat heretical teachings, took on an ascetic lifestyle himself and began to organize bands of preachers. The order received papal approval in 1216. Besides Eckhart, other famous Dominicans include Thomas Aquinas and Catherine of Siena.

Eckhart joined the Dominican Order sometime in his late teenage years. It is believed he did some of his studies at Cologne while Albert the Great taught there (Albert, who more famously taught Thomas Aquinas, died in 1280, so Eckhart must have been there sometime before that). Eckhart was later sent to Paris to study theology, and he was promoted to lecturer in the fall of 1293. In the fall of 1294, he was called back to be the prior of his home convent at Erfurt. During this period, he wrote one of his earliest vernacular works, called *The Talks of Instruction*. In 1302 he was called to Paris once more to take up the external (i.e., non-French) Dominican chair of theology, which had been previously held by both Albert the Great and Aquinas. It was a short appointment, which was customary and does not speak to the quality of his work, and he returned to Germany to take the position of provincial for the newly created province of Saxonia. In 1311 he was moved back to Paris for a second term. This was when he lived with the inquisitor who had Porete executed. After two years, he moved to Strasburg, where he served as the vicar for the Dominican master general. During this period, Strasburg was a center of women's spirituality. There were seven Dominican women's convents in Strasburg—yes, seven. There were also other houses of beguines. Interactions with these religious women influenced Eckhart and his theology. In 1323, he moved to Cologne, though his time there was relatively brief and filled with controversy.[18]

By the time he was in Cologne, Eckhart was an old man, especially considering the life expectancy of his day. As demonstrated by the above recounting of the many prestigious positions he had held within the Dominican Order, one may wonder how charges of heresy came to be. It seems that there had been some concern about his teaching prior to official heresy charges. In a now-lost document, Eckhart responded to objections of his teaching around 1325–1326, and his immediate supervisors were satisfied with his answers. However, the archbishop of Cologne, Henry of Virneberg, was preparing his own case against the theologian, and in September 1326, Eckhart appeared before the diocesan inquisitorial commission to defend himself against the charges of heresy.

Eckhart had an interesting response to the accusations. He stated, "I am able to be in error, but I cannot be a heretic, for the first belongs to the intellect, and the second to the will."[19] Because the Dominicans were under papal authority and not the authority of local bishops, Eckhart argued that only the pope or the University of Paris (since he was a *magister theologiae*) could investigate him for heresy. Therefore, he appealed to the pope and then headed to Avignon, the current seat of the papacy. In turn, the pope, John XXII, appointed two commissions to investigate Eckhart. There is no need here to go into the particulars of the trial. It is sufficient to say that Eckhart died in January 1328, but the trial did not end with his death. In 1329, the pope issued a bull (*In argo dominico*) in which twenty-eight points of Echkart's teaching were condemned. The bull also absolved Eckhart himself of heresy because he professed his faith at the end of his life, admitting to his errors insofar as they could generate heretical opinions in the minds of the

18 McGinn, *Harvest of Mysticism*, 94–103.

19 As quoted in McGinn, *Harvest of Mysticism*, 104.

faithful.[20] While perhaps obvious, it is worth noting Eckhart did not die as a heretic; some his teachings were condemned, but he was not.

While it is undeniable that there is some controversy surrounding Eckhart's life, there has also been debate about whether he should be considered a mystic. Eckhart was a scholastic theologian and a philosopher, but he was also a friar and preacher. He did not write about mystical experiences in the way that Teresa of Ávila or Hildegard of Bingen did, but he does employ mystical themes in his writings. He was undeniably influenced by the Neoplatonic "negative way" and mystics such as Pseudo-Dionysius the Areopagite. The interior life was of critical importance to Eckhart. True unity with God was not achieved by works or piety. One must make a desert of oneself—to push out everything, even things considered good. The mind must not be active but passive, so God could do the work in the soul. He explains these themes in the following excerpt from his "Sermon 3":

> *When you have completely stripped yourself of your own self, and all things and every kind of attachment, and have transferred, made over, and abandoned yourself to God in utter faith and perfect love, then whatever is born in you or touches you, within or without, joyful or sorrowful, sour or sweet, that is no longer yours, it is altogether your God's to whom you have abandoned yourself. Tell me, whom does the spoken word belong to? To the speaker or the hearer? Though it falls to the hearer, it really belongs to the speaker who gave it birth. Here is an example. The sun casts its light into the air; the air receives the light and gives it to the earth, thus enabling us to distinguish different colors. Now, though the light is formally in the air, essentially it is in the sun: the light actually comes from the sun, where it originates, and not in the air. It is received by the air which passes it on to anything that is receptive to light. It is just the same with the soul.*

20 McGinn, *Harvest of Mysticism*, 105–7.

> *God bears the Word in the soul, and the soul conceives it and passes it on to her powers in varied guise: now as desire, now as good intent, now as charity, now as gratitude, or however it may affect you. It is all His, and not yours at all.*[21]

This passage is a good example of his mystical thought and of how God and the soul interact with each other, particularly how it is God's actions and the soul's reception and how one must abandon oneself to God. He does not go as far as Porete. He is not calling for nothingness or advocating an annihilation of the self here, but he is calling for a more drastic version of emptying of the self than many other mystics did.

Eckhart was rediscovered and revived in the nineteenth century, particularly by German scholars.[22] This revival largely represented Eckhart as a speculative, dialectical thinker and as a forerunner to the Protestant Reformers.[23] In the twentieth century, this interest in Eckhart continued. His role as a mystical preacher was highlighted, and he also was compared to Eastern philosophers. To demonstrate how modern scholars have used his work, the following quote highlights some of the ways he has been characterized in modernity. The eclectic nature of this list borders on the absurd. He has been called a "Thomist scholastic, Neoplatonic negative theologian; Rheinish mystic; freethinker; accused heretic, and even feminist, Marxist, ecologist who respects God in nature; the apostle of freedom and 'letting be;' postmodern transgressive deconstructionist,

---

21 Meister Eckhart, "Sermon 3," in *The Complete Mystical Works of Meister Eckhart*, by Meister Eckhart, trans. Maurice O'C. Walshe (New York: Herder & Herder, 2009), 51.

22 For a full analysis of nineteenth-century Eckhart reception, see Cyril O'Regan, "Eckhart Reception in the 19th Century," in Hackett, *Companion to Meister Eckhart*, 629–67.

23 Dermot Moran, "Meister Eckhart in 20th-Century Philosophy," in Hackett, *Companion to Meister Eckhart*, 669–70.

postmetaphysical theologian; the Eastern sage and the Zen Buddhist enlightened master."[24]

Clearly some of these interpretations are more influenced by twentieth-century intellectual movements than Eckhart's own life or writings, but the list demonstrates just how influential, in a variety of academic fields, this German preacher has become. Part of what made him suspect in the medieval era makes him so intriguing in modernity. This is one reason Eckhart is an important mystic to consider today. Both scholars and lay readers have been able to find in Eckhart a writer who can speak across time and space. He pushed boundaries and is not easy to categorize. He is not an easy theologian to approach—his writings can be difficult and obscure—but there is a beauty and rewarding aspect of his work that is worth the work.

George Fox (1624–1691), the Early Society of Friends, and Rufus Jones (1863–1948)

Approximately 350 years after Porete was burned at the stake for both her theology and her questioning of church practices, and Meister Eckhart was accused of heresy, another Christian group, led by George Fox, was pushing the boundaries of what both religious authorities and larger society found acceptable. This was the Society of Friends, better known to most as the Quakers. Today few people find the Quakers so radical, but in the seventeenth century, they caused much scandal. The early Quakers faced fierce condemnation for both their faith and their practices. Among insults recounted by scholar Hilary Hinds, some of the more colorful include "blasphemous heretical seducers," "grievous wolves," and the highly creative "spawn of Romish Frogs."[25] Their quaking at meetings prompted Anglican minister Francis Higginson to state that it was "Diabolical Raptures immediately proceeding from

---

24 Moran, "Meister Eckhart in 20th-Century Philosophy," 671–72.

25 Hilary Hinds, *George Fox and Early Quaker Culture* (Manchester: Manchester University Press, 2011), 1.

the power of Satan."[26] Needless to say, they had a public-relations problem. What was it that the Quakers did that caused such a stir? To find the answer, one must go back to the start of the movement and look at their founder, an Englishman named George Fox, and his earliest followers.

Fox was born in 1624 to a Puritan family in the village of Fenny Drayton.[27] He was of humble origin—a cobbler's apprentice, to be exact, making him the second mystical shoemaker discussed in this book (the other being Boehme). However, at the age of nineteen, dealing with what he called being "tempted almost to despair," he went on a spiritual quest. He traveled around experiencing different Christian traditions and seeking counsel from various religious leaders. After a few years, Fox had a profound experience that shaped the rest of his life. The vision he had was not out of the ordinary compared to other mystical visions. Fox had a religious epiphany, and Jesus Christ featured centrally in it:

> *And when all my hopes in them and in all men were gone, so that I had nothing outwardly to help me, nor could tell what to do, then, Oh then, I heard a voice which said, "There is one, even Christ Jesus, that can speak to thy condition", and when I heard it my heart did a leap for joy. Then the Lord did let me see why there was none upon the earth that could speak to my condition, namely, that I might give him all the glory . . . that Jesus Christ might have the pre-eminence, who enlightens, and gives grace, and faith, and power. . . . And I knew this experimentally.*[28]

---

26 Francis Higginson, *A Brief Relation of the Irreligion of the Northern Quakers* (London: printed by T. R. for H. R., 1653), 16, as quoted in Hinds, *George Fox and Early Quaker Culture*, 2.

27 Robynne Rogers Healey, "History of Quaker Faith and Practices: 1650–1808," in *The Cambridge Companion to Quakerism*, ed. Stephen W. Angell and Pink Dandelion (Cambridge: Cambridge University Press, 2018), 15.

28 George Fox, *The Journal of George Fox*, ed. J. L. Nickalls (Cambridge: Cambridge University Press, 1952), 11, as quoted in Healey, "History of Quaker Faith," 15.

Fox no longer needed to look to experts, and he knew he needed to put his trust in God. This mystical experience framed his theology. He did not find comfort and support from clergy or other religious leaders but through a personal encounter with the divine. Fox came to challenge more established and traditional forms of Christianity. God did not dwell in church buildings, he argued. Hymns, sermons, sacraments, creeds, pastors, and priests were all stumbling blocks to the Spirit. A Quaker religious service, therefore, takes place largely in silence. Anyone who feels the Holy Spirit moving them to speak could do so.[29]

Central to Fox's theology was the light of Christ. Every human being was enlightened by the divine light of Christ. If people followed this inner light, they would see their sinful nature and come to Christ. If they failed to follow the light, they would be lost. In some ways, this theology is not so far from the more traditional concept of the *imago Dei* (or the image of God, which is present in all people). Yet, what was radical was that one did not need to have access to Scripture or even knowledge of Christ to be saved.

Similarly, those claiming Christian belief who did not follow the light would not be saved. Fox also taught that humans did not need an intermediary to God. Since God spoke directly to humanity, there was no need for a priestly class. Everyone had access to God, everyone had inner light, and ultimately a priestly class and even the Bible were unnecessary for salvation.[30] The Quakers did not throw out the Bible; in fact, it was important, but ultimately one could find salvation outside it. The theology of the inner light led to radical egalitarianism, especially for the time. Gender norms were typically maintained, but there was a fundamental equality between men and women within the movement. There was no formal clergy, but women spoke in worship meetings, and many were missionaries for the fledgling movement.

29 Justo L. González, *The Story of Christianity*, vol. 2, *The Reformation to the Present Day* (New York: HarperOne, 2010), 252–53.

30 Thomas D. Hamm, *Quakers in America* (New York: Columbia University Press, 2003), 15–16.

Throughout the 1650s, Quakerism spread throughout England and Wales, and in a limited capacity in Ireland. The early Quakers were both charismatic and apocalyptic in their theology.[31] Meanwhile, opposition also grew, largely due their social and theological positions. Quakers were arrested and imprisoned. In 1656 the Quakers faced a crisis. A leading Quaker processed into Bristol re-creating Christ's entrance into Jerusalem. It caused an enormous scandal, which caused Fox to take firmer control over leadership and increasingly emphasize unity and order. Following this, Quaker pamphlets tended to emphasize apologetics rather than the apocalyptic.[32] More structure was introduced as time passed, and eventually Quakers were no longer considered the subversive radicals they once were. However, the emphasis on experience and communication with the Holy Spirit continued within the Society of Friends.

It was not just early Quakers who were mystical in their theology. An important modern mystical Quaker voice was Rufus Jones, with whom a young Howard Thurman spent a semester. Born in 1863 to an old Quaker family, Jones went on to have an impressive academic career, serving as a professor at Haverford College in Pennsylvania, teaching philosophy, psychology, ethics, and the development of Christian thought.[33] Over the course of his career, he wrote over fifty books and hundreds of articles, including articles for journals and magazines with wide readership such as *The Atlantic Monthly* and *Christianity Today*.[34] In 1917, in the midst of the First World War, a group of Quakers met in Philadelphia and formed a committee called the American Friends Service Committee, and Jones was elected as the

---

31 Healey, "History of Quaker Faith," 15–16.

32 Healey, "History of Quaker Faith," 16–17.

33 Mary Hoxie Jones, "Rufus Matthew Jones: Mystic," *Mystics Quarterly* 12, no. 1 (1986): 15, 17.

34 Matthew Hedstrom, "Rufus Jones and Mysticism for the Masses," *CrossCurrents* 54, no. 2 (2004): 34, 37.

chairman.[35] The American Friends Service Committee was a way for the Friends, who were pacifists, to serve their country nonviolently.[36] The organization won the Nobel Peace Prize in 1947.[37] Jones was not just a man of words; he put his faith into action.

Jones helped popularized mysticism in the early twentieth century. To illustrate this point, a 1948 issue of *Time* magazine ran an article titled "Mystics among Us," which featured Jones and a young Thomas Merton. The article states, "Both men re-emphasize two facts often forgotten: the world still has millions of mystics, and the most mystical human beings are often among the most practical as well."[38] Indeed, Jones was not teaching an elitist and unobtainable mysticism. For Jones, mysticism was a direct experience with God, but that experience was open to anyone, not just the privileged few. His mysticism was for everyday people. Scholar Matthew Hedstrom makes the astute observation that Jones was simply being a good Quaker, affirming the inner light.[39] That one can have a personal experience with God unmediated by clergy or the church is at the core of the Quaker faith.

Also important was what one was to do with that experience. "For Jones, the test of mystical experience was its social utility."[40] Again, this tied in with his Quaker roots. The Society of Friends had long been on the cutting edge of social movements, with Quakers often emerging as prominent leaders fighting for abolition, racial justice, and women's rights. Quakerism offers an accessible and egalitarian expression of mystical theology. This is not the mystical thought practiced by the

---

35 Janet Whitney, "Rufus Jones: Friend," *The Atlantic*, April 1954, https://www.theatlantic.com/magazine/archive/1954/04/rufus-jones-friend/642733/.

36 American Friends Service Committee, "History," accessed May 2, 2024, https://afsc.org/history.

37 "American Friends Service Committee: Facts," The Nobel Prize, https://www.nobelprize.org/prizes/peace/1947/friends-committee/facts/.

38 As quoted in Hedstrom, "Rufus Jones and Mysticism," 31.

39 Hedstrom, "Rufus Jones and Mysticism," 37.

40 Hedstrom, "Rufus Jones and Mysticism," 36.

elite few in their monasteries. It is a faith that is active and available to all who desire it.

Emmanuel Swedenborg (1688–1772)

Emmanuel Swedenborg's early years were in many ways typical of a privileged son who came of age in the midst of the European Enlightenment. Swedenborg, born Emmanuel Svedberg, was born in Stockholm, Sweden, in 1688. His father was a professor of theology and later a Lutheran bishop, and his mother was from a prominent family that was in the copper business, though she died when Swedenborg was still a child. Swedenborg's family respected Enlightenment ideals, but they were also deeply religious, and Swedenborg was capable of conversing about both the rational and the religious. He received an excellent education in Sweden and then traveled for five years, learning in England, the Netherlands, France, and Germany. At twenty-eight he received the king's royal patronage as the assessor extraordinary to the Board of Mines.[41] Swedenborg was scientifically and mechanically gifted, and this post provided him with both an income and an opportunity to research.[42]

In 1745, Swedenborg's life changed dramatically. While in London, he heard a voice telling him not to eat too much, and then he saw a vision in which vapor left his body and turned into worms, which then burned. For the next twenty-seven years, he claimed to be able to access the spirit world, which allowed him to converse with heavenly and demonic beings, who gave him a new understanding of Scripture. He said that he traveled, via the spirit realm, to other planets, including the planets in our solar system as well as those in distant systems, where

---

41 John S. Haller Jr., *Swedenborg, Mesmer, and the Mind/Body Connection: The Roots of Complementary Medicine* (West Chester, PA: Swedenborg Foundation, 2010), 6–10.

42 Ernst Benz, *Emanuel Swedenborg: Visionary Saint in the Age of Reason* (West Chester, PA: Swedenborg Foundation, 2002), 95.

he met and conversed with other beings.[43] He became known for his clairvoyant knowledge, with notable events such as communicating with the queen of Sweden's dead brother at her request. Yet, Swedenborg continued to operate in a Christian mindset. He claimed to have visited heaven (which a few other mystics have also claimed). While there, he was able to talk with his family, plus some of the more prominent figures in the Bible, such as Abraham, Isaac, Jacob, Esau, Rebecca, Moses, Aaron, and the apostles. He also claims to have met some of the early church fathers, who told him that this type of communication with heaven had been possible in the early days of Christianity but had been lost when Christianity was corrupted by "heathenish philosophy." All these experiences led Swedenborg to greater study of the Scriptures. He believed that he was chosen to make Scripture more understandable to the people because the Bible was too difficult for regular people to understand.[44] One may detect some elitism in that statement; he was, after all, upper class, well educated, and emerging as a spiritual leader of sorts.

In 1747, Swedenborg resigned from the Board of Mines, returned to London, and began writing *Secrets of Heaven*, which ended up being eight volumes and more than forty-five hundred pages. *Secrets of Heaven* was followed up by nearly twenty additional books. One particularly notable aspect of Swedenborg's theology is his description of heaven and hell, which are rather different from typical Christian understandings of each. Swedenborg wrote that angels and demons had once been human, and these beings continued to be near the living. After death, the soul went to an intermediate stage called the world of spirits. There the soul took on its true essence—whether that be good or evil. The good souls became angels in heaven, and the bad souls became devils in hell.[45]

---

43 Haller, *Swedenborg, Mesmer*, 33–34.

44 Haller, *Swedenborg, Mesmer*, 38.

45 Haller, *Swedenborg, Mesmer*, 41–43.

Unsurprisingly, Swedenborg's writings caused controversy. His ideas were not well received by most of his contemporaries, though he did gain a small but devoted group of followers. Swedenborg had no desire to establish a new church—he believed he was bringing a new understanding to the existing church. However, twelve years after his death, a group of followers founded the Church of the New Jerusalem, which has survived until today. In the early nineteenth century, the Swedenborgian Society was founded with the purpose of publishing and distributing his works.[46] He has had a notable amount of influence in contemporary religious thought. His cosmology, especially the belief that the spirit realm was near the living, was critical for the foundation of the spiritualist religions that emerged in the nineteenth century. He also influenced writers and scholars such as William Blake and Ralph Waldo Emerson.

In some ways Swedenborg functioned like many other Christian mystics. Following a profound experience, believing he was being commanded by God, he wrote about his visions with the purpose to helping others understand both God and the Scriptures better. However, there are profound differences from other mystics as well. His theology was unorthodox. He rejected the Trinity (he was more of a Unitarian); typical understandings of heaven, hell, and celestial beings; and books of the Bible. He was also accused by his detractors of denying atonement, Jesus's role in salvation, and justification by faith.[47] For these reasons, Swedenborg always stayed outside the mainstream when it came to Christian thought. However, he did provide an influential concept of a cosmology that has had profound impact on the popular religious imagination. It also led to the founding of the Swedenborg church and affected a host of other religious movements, particularly the nineteenth-century metaphysical movements. He also evinces a life of profound change and devotion. His theology, though unconventional, has appealed to and fascinated many. He is an important

46 González, *Story of Christianity*, 2:258.

47 Haller, *Swedenborg, Mesmer*, 50.

example of a mystic who came out of not only a Protestant, specifically Lutheran, tradition but an intellectual one.

Simone Weil (1909–1943)

It is Simone Weil's own insistence on her outsider status that places her among these other Christian figures who largely fall outside the mainstream. It is true that Weil refused baptism, and there are aspects of her theology that could be interpreted as unorthodox, but it was her own desire to remain outside, her refusal to cut herself off from any group—and thus her refusal to join any—that separated her. To Weil, her outsideness was essential to her witness. As one scholar writes about her, "To what then does she bear witness? To the uses of exile and suffering, to the glory of annihilation and absurdity, to the unforeseen miracle of love."[48] But what does that mean exactly, and how is Weil an important mystical figure for the modern era? To answer these questions, one must look at her life and writings to discover a most unusual mystic.

Weil was born in 1909 in Paris to a secular family of Jewish descent. Her father was a medical doctor, and her mother stayed home and took care of the children.[49] Her brother, André, became one of the most prominent mathematicians of the twentieth century. From a young age Weil was profoundly principled and almost shockingly inflexible. For example, at age five, she refused to eat any sugar as long as soldiers at the front lines were unable to get it.[50] War was a defining feature of her life—the First World War during her childhood and the Spanish Civil War as a young adult. She died during the Second World War in 1943 at thirty-four.

During her teenage years, she struggled with a spiritual crisis of sorts and suffered from what can only be called severe depression. She

48 Leslie A. Fiedler, "Introduction," in "Spiritual Autobiography," by Simone Weil, in *Waiting for God*, trans. Emma Craufurd (New York: HarperPerennial, 2001), xii.

49 Maria Clara Bingemer, *Simone Weil: Mystic of Passion and Compassion*, trans. Karen M. Kraft (Cambridge: Lutterworth, 2016), 1.

50 Fiedler, "Introduction," xv.

felt horribly inadequate intellectually compared to her brother, and her own intellectual success during her time at the University of Paris seemed to do little to comfort her or convince her of her own abilities. After graduation, she became a teacher in Le Puy, France, and there she engaged in various political and labor right activities. She made contact with trade unions and took an active part in their movements. She joined the national teachers' union and organized meetings for activists fighting for trade union unity. In addition to her teaching job and union activities, she gave free classes to local miners and wrote articles for the newspaper *L'Effort* and the union newsletter.[51] To be in solidarity with the working class, she refused to eat more than the rations of those who were on relief, giving any of her surplus foods to the needy.

Later, wanting to truly join the proletariat, she quit her teaching job and went to work in a Renault auto plant. Her health suffered, but she believed that the hardships of working-class life had entered her soul. This was not the only attempt she made to join those who were suffering. She later went to Spain to fight during the Spanish Civil War. There she was injured, and her parents came to rescue her from the field hospital and take her home. Later, during the Second World War, she dreamed up a particularly ridiculous plan to parachute into the Soviet Union, which thankfully never happened.[52] These anecdotes demonstrate Weil's desire to throw herself into causes in which she believed regardless of the absurdity of doing so or how it might have affected her health or well-being.

THE SPANISH CIVIL WAR (1936–1939)

The Spanish Civil War began when troops started an uprising against the democratically elected government in Spain on July 18, 1936; the coup d'état was only partially

51 Bingemer, *Simone Weil*, 14.

52 Fiedler, "Introduction," xviii–xx.

successful. This escalated into a civil war between the Republicans, who supported the elected government, and the Nationalists, who supported the military junta. A number of foreign powers became involved in the war, with the Nationalists receiving aid from both Nazi Germany and fascist Italy. The Republicans were supported by the Soviet Union. The United States, France, and the United Kingdom recognized the Republican government but did not intervene in the war. A number of people from noninterventionist countries, such as Simone Weil, went to Spain to fight in the war in international brigades. The Nationalists won, and General Francisco Franco ruled Spain until his death in 1975.

As Weil aged, she became more preoccupied with faith. In her "Spiritual Autobiography" she discusses various experiences that were important to her spirituality. After her time in Spain, her parents took her to Portugal, and she was "in pieces, soul and body." She believed herself to be a slave, and she came to the conviction that Christianity was the religion of slaves, "that slaves cannot help belonging to it, and I among others."[53] In 1937, particularly fond of Francis, she went to Assisi, and in 1938 she spent ten days at the Solesmes Abbey following all the liturgical services. These experiences deepened her understanding of human affliction[54] and God's love. They also deepened her habit of prayer and "firmly anchored her faith in an unexpected mystical experience of Christ's presence."[55] One cannot speak of her having a

53 Weil, "Spiritual Autobiography," 26.

54 The word she uses in French is *malheur*, which does not have a precise English translation.

55 Mario von der Ruhr, *Simone Weil: Late Philosophical Writings*, trans. Eric O. Springsted and Lawrence E. Schmidt (London: Continuum, 2006), 86.

dramatic conversion experience; rather, it was a gradual and deepening relationship with God.

Despite her draw to Christianity, she was unwilling to be baptized. She explained in a letter written to Father Perrin, the closest thing she ever had to a spiritual guide and confessor: "Christianity should contain all vocations without exception since it is catholic. In consequence the Church should also. But in my eyes Christianity is catholic by right but not in fact. So many things are outside it, so many things that I love and do not want to give up, so many things that God loves, otherwise they would not be in existence." Essentially, Weil is arguing that the church should be universal but is not. Since there are many things that fall outside Christianity, things that she and God both love, she does not want to be cut off them those by joining the church—instead, she wanted to remain an outsider, a witness to those also on the outside. She later explains: "I remain beside all those things that cannot enter the Church."[56] Weil also admits that she did not believe it was the will of God that she enter into the church.[57] The French editors of her work—lay theologian and friend Gustave Thibon, and priest and adviser Father Perrin, both Catholics—believed that had she lived longer she would have accepted baptism, but this may have been an overly optimistic view of her spiritual journey.[58] As Catholics, they both wanted Weil to accept baptism, but it is difficult to know whether she would have ever taken that step. Perhaps only if she explicitly felt God calling her to do so.

Her understanding of the sacraments was unorthodox, and since she refused baptism, despite her mystical theology, it is worth spending a moment on this topic. She believed the sacraments had value insofar as they allowed people to have contact with God. However, she believed that only those who were at a certain level of spirituality should participate in the sacraments. While this statement initially has

---

56 Weil, "Spiritual Autobiography," 31–33.

57 Simone Weil, "Hesitations Concerning Baptism," in *Waiting for God*, 6.

58 Fiedler, "Introduction," ix–x.

tinges of spiritual elitism, Weil complicates it by stating that she did not believe that she was worthy of the sacraments. She argued that this belief did not come from a sense of humility but a state of inadequacy.[59] On the one hand, there are echoes of other mystics in this statement. Countless before her confessed that they were sinners and undeserving of the favors that God offered them. On the other hand, the sacraments are a fundamental aspect of religious life, especially the Catholic life, and they are not reserved for the worthy.

Another way in which she is reminiscent of mystics of old but with a modern bent was in her commitment to asceticism. Gustave Thibon wrote the introduction to Weil's book *Gravity and Grace*, and in it he tells of when she came to live at his farm. He had been asked by Father Perrin because Weil, now excluded by laws from the university, wanted to go to the country to work as a farmhand. Thibon found her difficult, and they agreed on very little, but he came to respect her greatly. He states that he had no doubt about her religious vocation and that she demonstrated both her faith and detachment in her actions. Weil found his house too comfortable, so she moved into an old "half-ruined farm" that belonged to his in-laws. She was both "delicate and ill," yet she worked and ate little—she distributed her ration coupons to political prisoners.[60] He described the Gospels as her "daily spiritual food," but she also had deep veneration for writings of other faiths, not to mention her love of Plato, whom she interpreted in a fundamentally Christian manner.[61] While a commitment to an ascetic lifestyle is not universal among mystics, it is common, especially among the mystics who lived in antiquity and the Middle Ages. Catherine of Siena is a perfect example of a mystic who went without food and comforts for the sake of God. Yet, in the twentieth century, this willingness to suffer voluntarily seems out of place—perhaps even

59 Weil, "Hesitations Concerning Baptism," 5.

60 Gustave Thibon, "Introduction," in *Gravity and Grace*, by Simone Weil, trans. Arthur Wills (Lincoln: University of Nebraska Press, 1997), 6.

61 Thibon, "Introduction," 7.

more bizarre than the medieval mystic wearing metal crowns of thorns, wearing shirts made of hair, or eating only the Eucharist. Yet, Weil practiced an asceticism that wore her body down.

To read Weil is to enter a space where the profound and the absurd interact, sometimes on the same page. Her passion and love for humanity are palpable, as is her own sense of unworthiness, despite the fact that her writings betray her brilliance. Her commitment to her ideals was all encompassing—she did not compromise, which can feel both frustrating and refreshing. She chose to put herself in situations that were difficult, to put it mildly, putting both her health and safety at risk. She did not need to work in an auto factory or as a field hand, and she certainly did not need to go to Spain to fight in a war that was not hers. Yet, one can see a commitment to ideals that was extraordinary.

Controversial Mystics for a Modern World

To modern Americans, the idea that one would enter a monastery as a child, tend to a religious vocation from a young age, and then later teach the ideals of contemplation to others is largely outrageous. These things are simply not done anymore, and in the American context they were rarely done at all. While so many medieval mystics followed that path, it is important to remember that this is not the only model. The mystics featured in this chapter followed a different path, a path of searching and engaging with God outside the institutional church, or, in the case of Meister Eckhart, pushing the boundaries of an institutional church. This may indeed be a model going forward. At the present time, the American voluntary-organization model of church is on the decline. Americans are looking for meaning outside institutions. Many are distrustful of authority. People have not, however, stopped looking for God.

These mystics who took the road less traveled are a diverse lot, but they are models that could be helpful for those who feel uncomfortable in formal religious intuitions. For example, the beguines, discussed in both here and chapter 6, offer an example of religious community without the confines of a monastic rule and the oversight of an institution. Some scholars in the past have idealized this movement, though the beguines, like any community of human beings, faced challenges both internal and external. Eventually their movement was suppressed, but their faithful witness has left a lasting impact. In a similar fashion, the Society of Friends was formed with a radical vision of faith. Despite controversy and persecution, they transitioned from a movement to an established faith tradition, highly dependent on the work of the Holy Spirit. Both movements consisted of faithful people who came together to live around common values and beliefs, and both movements were open to experiential forms of Christianity.

The beguines and the Friends offer a model of communal worship and living, but others in this chapter represent a more individualistic understanding of mystical faith, though none were truly solitary figures. Eckhart, the most traditional Christian included in this chapter, was indeed a friar and preacher. It was not his life that set him apart but aspects of his theology. Though his creativity caused issues in his life, he has been a particularly influential mystic, especially in more academic circles, in the modern era. Swedenborg's theology is the most original of the group, and in many ways he truly did carve his own path, but he was still concerned with other people and their ability to understand Scripture. Finally, Weil provides an example of a modern mystic who in nontraditional terms embraced a life of self-sacrifice and asceticism while choosing to stay on the outside of a faith that she believed was not as universal as it should be.

Suggested Reading List

Eckhart, Meister. *The Complete Works of Meister Eckhart*. Translated and edited by Maurice O'C. Walshe. New York: Herder & Herder, 1979.

Fox, George. *The Journal*. Edited by Nigel Smith. New York: Penguin Classics, 1999.

Porette, Margaret. *The Mirror of Simple Souls*. Translated by Edmund Colledge, OSA, J. C. Marler, and Judith Grant. Notre Dame: University of Notre Dame Press, 1999.

Swedenborg, Emanuel. *Heaven and Its Wonders and Hell from Things Heard and Seen.* London: Swedenborg Society, 1992.

Weil, Simone. *Gravity and Grace.* Translated by Arthur Wills. Lincoln: University of Nebraska Press, 1997.

———. *Waiting for God.* Translated by Emma Craufurd. New York: HarperPerennial, 2001.

CONCLUSION

Mysticism in Modernity

[Jesus] set before me the book of nature; I understood how all the flowers He has created are beautiful, how the splendor of the rose and the whiteness of the lily do not take away the perfume of the little violet or the delightful simplicity of the daisy. I understood that if all flowers wanted to be roses, nature would lose her springtime beauty, and the fields would no longer be decked out with little wild flowers.

And so it is in the world of souls, Jesus' garden. He willed to create great souls comparable to Lilies and roses, but He has created smaller ones and these must be content to be daisies or violets destined to give joy to God's glances when He looks down at his feet. Perfection consists in doing his will, and being what he wills us to be.

—St. Thérèse of Lisieux, *Story of a Soul: The Autobiography of St. Thérèse of Lisieux*

THIS CONCLUSION RETURNS to the image of a garden, written about by a Carmelite nun. This time, however, the writer is not the great sixteenth-century Spanish mystic and reformer Teresa of Ávila but a young French woman named Thérèse of Lisieux,[1] who died at age twenty-four, never knowing what type of influence she would have on modern Catholicism. She did not engage in a grand program of church reform like Teresa of Ávila; in fact, her short life was in many regards

1 She was born Marie Françoise-Thérèse Martin.

unremarkable and almost entirely separate from the world. She entered the Carmelite monastery at Lisieux, France, when she was only fifteen. About a year and a half before her death, at the request of her sister, who was also the mother superior of her convent, Thérèse wrote her autobiography, which she called the "way of a spiritual childhood."[2] Within the first few pages of her book, Thérèse describes Jesus's garden, which is filled with different souls. Each of the souls are presented as different flowers, everyone bringing a certain beauty to the whole. Through the book, Thérèse writes about her "little way," a life of trust in God and self-surrender.[3] The little way consists of performing little virtues as opposed to the grandiose acts sometimes exhibited by the mystics of old.

It was only after Thérèse's death that her impact and legacy became apparent. This unlikely path to fame started with her convent's decision to disseminate her autobiography after her death. Quickly, miracles were being attributed to Thérèse. By 1914, the sisters were receiving about five hundred letters a day, and between 1915 and 1925, an average of four hundred people per day visited her tomb. In 1925, less than thirty years after her death, she became a canonized saint, and her book had been translated into thirty-five languages.[4]

Thérèse became and continues to be a wildly popular religious figure. In discussing her impact on American Catholics, scholar Maura Hearden writes of how both clergy and laity became devoted to Thérèse. The clergy saw in her a "antidote for modernism," and for the laity, largely composed of poor, immigrant, working-class Americans, she was a saint for the common person. Thérèse served as a "source of hope and courage for the thousands who led hard, hidden, and thankless lives."[5] By promoting Thérèse, priests and other religious leaders

---

2 Maura Hearden, "Catholic America's Love Affair with the Little Flower," *American Catholic Studies* 116, no. 3 (2005): 41.

3 Hearden, "Catholic America's Love Affair," 41.

4 Hearden, "Catholic America's Love Affair," 43–44.

5 Hearden, "Catholic America's Love Affair," 39–40.

were promoting the concept of "interior prayer—a set of spiritual practices designed to produce a more deeply personal and experiential connection to God by appropriating a more intimate style of piety."[6] Thérèse in many ways was a different type of Catholic saint. As a Carmelite nun, she lived away from the world, but there is a simplicity and approachability to her faith that is replicable. While Thérèse did report some visions, her story is not one of dramatic miracles and flashy shows of piety. Her type of mysticism is unassuming and quiet but nonetheless a faithful witness. And perhaps more importantly for modern Christians, it seems doable. Her story teaches that one can be faithful in small ways, and those small things are no less important than more grandiose manifestations of piety.

Thérèse is as an important hinge figure for modernity. Like the mystics of old, she was a cloistered nun who reported miraculous events in her own life. In that way she is more like the medieval or early modern mystics. On the other hand, she paid attention to personal piety and interior prayer, and she exhibited a highly approachable and replicable type of faith that has been incredibly influential in modern religion. She is a precursor to someone like Thomas Merton, who was able to write popular books and bring an ancient form of spirituality to the masses, but nonetheless the seed of this modern mysticism is here with her.

So . . . There Are Still Mystics?

The short answer is yes! As seen in previous chapters, which include several mystics who lived during the twentieth century, the mystical impulse in Christianity is still strong, especially if mysticism is defined primarily as relationship. Yet, it is important to recognize that modern mysticism is not identical to the mysticism one might have come

---

6 James P. McCartin, "The Sacred Heart of Jesus, Thérèse of Lisieux, and the Transformation of U.S. Catholic Piety, 1865–1940," *U.S. Catholic Historian* 25, no. 2 (2007): 54.

across in late antiquity, the Middle Ages, or even early modernity. There are some similarities, of course; the mystics of old influenced modern mystics, both explicitly and implicitly. Yet, Christianity is adaptable, and Christian mysticism too has adapted to the modern age. Because mysticism is unruly and hard to define, any discussion of its modern form will fall into generalizations, but there are salient features that are worth highlighting, two particularly notable ones being increased interest of the laity and an increased commitment to ecumenical engagement.

Of the modern mystics discussed in previous chapters, Evelyn Underhill, Rufus Jones, Howard Thurman, and Thomas Merton all wrote about mysticism at a popular level. None believed that Christian mysticism was for a religious elite, and their work had great impact on laypeople and even some non-Christians. To look back a little further, in the nineteenth-century mystics, Phoebe Palmer and Sojourner Truth were highly concerned with spreading the gospel and increasing personal piety of everyday people as well. This impulse to reach everyday believers did not die out with the end of the twentieth century. If anything, today's renewed interest in mysticism speaks to the continued interest in modern mystical thought. For example, one of the best-known modern contemplatives is Richard Rohr, a Franciscan, who founded his Center for Action and Contemplation in 1987 because he saw "a deep need for the integration of both action and contemplation."[7] Its mission is to "introduce Christian contemplative wisdom and practice that support transformation and inspire loving action."[8] This is not an organization seeking to serve a spiritual elite. No longer is mysticism seen as the activity of a class of super-Christians, who can devote all their time and effort to it. It is a strain of faith that can be and should be accessible to all Christians.

---

7 Center for Action and Contemplation, "Who We Are," accessed March 1, 2024, https://cac.org/about/who-we-are/.

8 Center for Action and Contemplation, "What We Do," accessed May 1, 2024, https://tinyurl.com/3tua6vjz.

Another salient feature of modern mysticism is an increase in ecumenism. As the world has become more connected, there is a desire and need to look toward the neighbor who may practice a different faith. A few of the mystics previously discussed embody this ecumenical spirit. Edith Stein, who was born Jewish, continued to engage with Judaism throughout her life, showing deep respect for the faith into which she was born. Her last recorded words were a reference to going to die for her people. Thurman engaged with mystical thought coming from a variety of religious traditions. Merton too had deep interfaith leanings. While he showed an interest in a number of Asian religions, his primary ecumenical conversation partner was Buddhism. In his book *Mystics and Zen Masters*, he writes:

> *In reality, when we examine them more closely, the great contemplative traditions of East and West, while differing sometimes quite radically in their formulation of their aims and in their understanding of their methods, agree in thinking that by spiritual disciplines a man [*sic*] can radically change his life and attain to a deeper meaning, a more perfect integration, a more complete fulfillment, a more total liberty of spirit than are possible in the routines of purely active existence centered on money-making.*[9]

There is a recognition that there are both similarities and value in looking at mystical traditions of other faiths. This does not mean that Merton viewed Buddhist and Christian forms of mysticism as the same thing; he did not. However, he does recognize common ground.

Another important twentieth-century mystic for whom ecumenical dialogue was vital was Raimon Panikkar. Panikkar was born in 1918 in Barcelona to a Spanish Catholic mother and an Indian father who was Hindu. He received a doctorate in philosophy and

9 Thomas Merton, *Mystics and Zen Masters* (New York: Farrar, Straus & Giroux, 1961), vii–viii.

literature from the University of Madrid in 1946, and a doctorate in chemistry, again from Madrid, in 1958, and finally a third doctorate in theology from the Pontifical Lateran University in Rome in 1961. He held teaching positions at Harvard and the University of California at Santa Barbara. Toward the end of his life, he moved back to Spain and founded Vivarium, a center where he taught, held seminars, and worked in interfaith dialogue.[10] He became an expert not only in Christianity but also in Hinduism and Buddhism, and he declared himself to be both a Christian and a Hindu.[11] While this ecumenism was not without controversy, it does speak to the general atmosphere of openness that present in modern mystical thought. While cultures have always interacted and influenced each other, the changes that occurred from globalization in the twentieth and twenty-first centuries are unparallel in human history. With more interaction between cultures, more understanding between faiths, and more ecumenical and interfaith dialogues occurring, the opportunities to explore similarities and differences between mystical traditions have expanded.

Pentecostalism: A New Type of Mysticism?

This book cannot truly examine mysticism in the modern era without at least considering whether Pentecostalism and other forms of charismatic Christianity can or should be associated with Christian mysticism.[12] This movement undoubtedly has some commonalities with mysticism, though there are enough distinctive aspects that there is

---

10 Milena Carrara Pavan and Rowan Williams, "Raimon Panikkar: Life and Work," in *Raimon Panikkar: A Companion to His Life and Thought*, ed. Peter C. Phan and Young-chan Ro (Cambridge: Lutterworth, 2018), 1–2.

11 Pavan and Williams, "Raimon Panikkar," 6.

12 For a very helpful discussion of the complicated relationship between Pentecostalism, other forms of charismatic Christianity, and evangelicalism, see Amos Yong, "Evangelicals, Pentecostals, and Charismatics: A Difficult Relationship or Promising Convergence?," Fuller Studio, accessed May 2, 2024, https://fullerstudio.fuller.edu/evangelicals-pentecostals-and-charismatics/.

room for legitimate disagreement and debate on this topic. However, it is an important conversation because no religious movement has had a bigger impact on modern global Christianity than Pentecostalism. This movement did not emerge in a vacuum, though historical accounts often depict it as something quite novel. In the eighteenth and nineteenth centuries, though particularity in the nineteenth, there was an explosion of more emotional forms of Christianity. For example, during the Second Great Awakening, there were revivals, mass conversion events, and an increase in reported miraculous events such as speaking in tongues or being slain in the spirit. Both Sojourner Truth and Phoebe Palmer fit into the larger religious landscape of nineteenth-century revivalism, and their theologies fit within this more emotional and conversion-focused framework, though neither can be considered charismatics.

This emotionalism and experiential Christianity of the nineteenth century culminated in the explosion of Pentecostalism in the twentieth century. The Azusa Street revival, led by holiness preacher William Seymour in 1906, is largely considered the beginning of the global Pentecostal movement, though an argument can be made for more of a polygenesis since there were similar events in both the United Kingdom and Latin America around the same time. Pentecostalism emphasizes direct personal experiences with God and the active role of the Holy Spirit in the world. Scholars now estimate that around six hundred million Christians identify as Pentecostal or charismatic, which is more than a quarter of the world's Christians. Remarkably, this is up from an estimated fifty-eight million in 1970.[13] Globally

13 The numbers vary a little, which makes sense considering the nature of the movement. Pentecostalism and other forms of charismatic Christianity are not a well-defined church but a collection of different denominations and movements that share tendencies. For more information, see Pew Research Center, "Global Christianity"; Todd M. Johnson, Gina A. Zurlo, and Becky Yang Hsu, *World Christian Encyclopedia*, 3rd ed., ed. David B. Barrett and George Thomas Kurian (Edinburgh: Edinburgh University Press, 2020), 26.

speaking, the movement has had particular impact in Latin America since the 1970s, Africa since the 1980s, and Asia since the 1990s.

An interesting question is whether Pentecostalism and charismatic forms of Christianity should be considered Protestant. While not directly related to mysticism, the question helps situate the movement. On the one hand, Pentecostalism emerged from a particular stream of Protestantism, mainly the holiness movement. On the other hand, there are aspects of the Pentecostal movement that do not necessarily align with traditional Protestant thought. Complicating this picture is that there are Protestant, Catholic, and Orthodox Christians all who also identify as Pentecostal or charismatic. Perhaps a helpful middle ground would be to accept that a large percentage of Pentecostals and charismatics identify as Protestant, but the movement cannot be solely limited to a Protestant framework.

As for the basic tenets of Pentecostalism, it is important to remember that it is a rather loose movement, so firm definitions and criteria are challenging. While there is no Pentecostal statement of faith, there are some basic premises that most Pentecostals and charismatics would agree on. Similarly, mysticism is a difficult-to-define term, as seen throughout this book. Therefore, it is exceedingly difficult to compare two tough-to-define, loose movements. Discussions will inevitably be based on generalizations, which is admittedly problematic. Nonetheless, there are tendencies and themes in both traditions that can be compared.

The first Pentecostal/charismatic theme is an emphasis on a personal and transformative relationship with Jesus Christ (as one is born again in Christ). The language is steeped in a nineteenth-century Protestant revivalist mentality, but if one unpacks the statement, a relationship with God sits at the core. That is mystical. Now, one thing that is not explicit here is spiritual progress, which is such an important aspect of mysticism. All language about purgation, illumination, and union is gone, but in Pentecostalism there is often an understanding that there is a process to becoming born again (even if that process happens very quickly), and that process includes recognizing oneself as a sinner (reminiscent of purgation), and then a transformative conversion moment, and then hopefully a transformed life. This progression is not identical to these older forms of mystical thought, but there are echoes of mysticism here.

Another aspect of Pentecostal/charismatic thought is the centrality, power, and activity of the Holy Spirit in the world and in the lives of believers. As one scholar puts it, "Pentecostals assume a Spirit-drenched world so that what may appear as textualized in Scripture is in some sense anticipated and realized—and thus witnessed—in their worship settings. Miracles are recorded in Scripture, *and* they are available now."[14] A specific and prominent example of this activity would be the phenomenon of baptism in the Holy Spirit, in which the Holy Spirit descends on a believer. One could possibly associate baptism in the Holy Spirit with the concept of mystical union, though the terminology is admittedly different, and the theology behind these two events generally differs as well. Regardless, for Pentecostals and charismatics, the Holy Spirit is seen as actively moving in the world and an important part of their lived experience. Believing in both the miraculous and in a God who is active in the lives of believers has long been part of Christian belief, though modernity has curtailed this belief, especially in the West. Yet, the phenomenal growth of charismatic forms of Christianity may speak to the larger disillusionment with such rationalistic forms of Christianity.

Third, Pentecostal/charismatic Christians tend to believe that the gifts of the Holy Spirit are alive and well. Believers may speak in tongues (which is often the hallmark of Pentecostalism, but not always) or engage in other miraculous phenomenon such as prophecy, faith healing, and exorcisms. Again, these phenomena are not limited to charismatic Christianity, but they play a more prominent

14 Daniel Castelo, *Pentecostalism as a Christian Mystical Tradition* (Grand Rapids: Eerdmans, 2017), 127 (emphasis original).

role than in many other modern Christian traditions. Scholar of Pentecostalism Harvey Cox makes an interesting connection between speaking in tongues and mystical union. In his book *Fire from Heaven*, he writes:

> *I believe that the inner significance of speaking in tongues or praying in the spirit can be found in something virtually every spiritual tradition in human history teaches in one way or another: that the reality religious symbols strive to express ultimately defies even the most exalted human language. Virtually all the mystics of every faith have indicated that the vision they have glimpsed, though they try desperately to describe it, finally eludes them. . . . Confronted with this verbal paralysis, what can people do? They sing, they rhapsodize, they invent metaphors; they soar into canticles and doxologies. But ultimately, words fail them and they lapse into silence. Or they speak in tongues.*[15]

Cox is leaning into the otherness of God and the inability of language to adequately convey religious truths and experiences. When looking through the long history of mystical visions, for example, there is frequently a feeling that the mystic cannot quite put into words their own experiences with the divine. This does seem to be a genuine commonalty between Pentecostals and mystics of old. That said, speaking in tongues and other miraculous phenomena may be a way in which mysticism and Pentecostalism look similar, but the theology behind the manifestations is not necessarily the same. The mystics of old often viewed the miraculous as gifts or tangential to their faith. Pentecostals would agree that they are gifts, but there is often a heavier expectation among modern Pentecostals that these gifts of the Spirit be more

---

15 Harvey Cox, *Fire from Heaven: The Rise of Pentecostal Spirituality and the Reshaping of Religion in the Twenty-First Century* (Reading, MA: Addison-Weseu, 1995), 92.

prevalent than mystics of old would have accepted and that they are more accessible to everyday Christians.[16]

Theologian Daniel Castelo, in his book *Pentecostalism as a Christian Mystical Tradition*, argues that Pentecostalism is indeed a form of modern mysticism. He writes, "What primarily makes Pentecostalism a mystical tradition of the church catholic is its persistent, passionate, and widespread emphasis on encounter, which at some level is relatable through the language of union."[17] He does rightly acknowledge there is difference in terminology, however. He notes that modern Pentecostals would likely pause at or even reject some of the terminology that is common in mystical literature. Yet, he argues for a "family resemblance" between Pentecostalism and Christian mysticism.[18]

This "family resemblance" argument is particularly convincing. No, the two movements are not identical, and they do emerge from distinct theologically traditions, but there are commonalities that should be acknowledged. Both modern Pentecostal/charismatic Christianity and Christian mysticism emphasize experience, relationship, and a God who is active in the world and in the lives of believers. The particulars of how this plays out in theology, liturgy, faith practices, and lived experience do vary tremendously, though.

Secular Mysticism?

While I briefly touched on this topic in the introduction, it is worth noting again that religion, though not necessarily belief in God, in America is in decline. Americans are fleeing religious institutions, and

16 The three basic parameters I use are highlighted in Robert W. Hefner, "Introduction: The Unexpected Modern—Gender, Piety, and Politics in the Global Pentecostal Surge," in *Global Pentecostalism in the 21st Century*, ed. Robert W. Hefner (Bloomington: Indiana University Press, 2013), 2.

17 Castelo, *Pentecostalism as a Christian Mystical Tradition*, 80.

18 Castelo, *Pentecostalism as a Christian Mystical Tradition*, 75–77.

they are doing so at shocking rates.[19] In the past, places of worship offered a place for people to come together for a common mission, for spiritual nourishment, and for socialization, and those spaces are in decline. There is no shortage of books, articles, blogs, podcasts, and so on focusing on the topic of decline of the American church, and a full discussion of the causes of decline is unnecessary here.[20] There are plenty of hypotheses about why Americans, especially younger Americans, are fleeing the institutional church, and there are undoubtedly a plethora of different reasons why individuals decide to leave or to never attend. However, when considering the phenomenon on a whole, it is evident that church bodies are no longer meeting the spiritual needs of many Americans. And if churches and other places of worship are no longer filling that role, where are people turning for spiritual nourishment and community? Or are people simply no longer having those needs met? It seems likely, for some, that their spiritual needs are simply not being met. For others, in the absence of a meaningful faith community, a form of secular mysticism has become popular in American culture—one that simply does not offer the life-giving benefits that faithful mysticism does.

The concept of a secular mysticism admittedly sounds like a contradiction. And if one takes the definition of mysticism as relationship with God, then no, a mysticism without God is simply not possible. However, if one were to define mysticism in terms of spiritual progress, especially with a spiritualism that is agnostic in nature (think spiritual but not religious), then a secular mysticism starts to emerge. One could take it a step further and remove any sort of higher power, and a

---

19 It is not only religious institution that are in decline but all voluntary organizations. Rates of volunteering in the US have been in decline for two decades. For more information, see Linda Poon, "Why Americans Stopped Volunteering," Bloomberg, September 11, 2021, https://www.bloomberg.com/news/articles/2019-09-12/america-has-a-post-9-11-volunteerism-slump.

20 See a recent projection of the decline in "Modeling the Future of Religion in America."

form of secular mysticism emerges in which one views personal growth as a type of mystical path.[21]

This attention to secular varieties of mysticism is worth discussing. As an example of a particularly popular type of self-improvement, wellness culture could be understood as a secular form of mysticism. There is a sense of progress to it. If one eats right, does the right exercises, does that juice cleanse, engages in the right mindfulness exercises, then one will be better, healthier, more spiritual. But this type of spirituality is not rooted in a transcendent God who breaks into reality. It is rooted in one's own ability, and when one fails—because ultimately everyone will fail at some point—it is *your* failure. Everyone will get sick, everyone will age, and eventually everyone will die. There is no exception. While it is important to take care of oneself, wellness as a spiritual ideal is a false god offering ephemeral promises.

Other types of secular mysticism could involve increasing personal wealth, growing in personal happiness, creating one's own personal brand and online presence; the list could go on and on. These secular varieties, while popular, will never be able to replace the long tradition of Christian mysticism rooted in relationship and prayer. There are lots of spiritual people out there looking for something. This type of mysticism without God appeals to those who have rejected a more traditional Christian framework. This secular mysticism, though it will always be a hollow substitute, also demonstrates the desire of all people, whether religious or not, to strive for something greater than themselves.

The Future of Christian Mysticism

One of the main purposes of this book is to demonstrate that Christian mysticism is not some abstract or eccentric strain of thought that

---

21 For a full exploration of this idea, see Andy Root, *The Church in an Age of Secular Mysticisms: Why Spiritualities without God Fail to Transform Us* (Grand Rapids: Baker Academic, 2023).

runs tangential to the faith. Christian mysticism is relatable and accessible and sits at the very center of Christianity. Christianity without mysticism has the tendency to become either moralistic or mere sentimentality. Mysticism elevates relationship and love. While mysticism can look radically different, whether desert monastics or modern activists, attention to prayer, relationship, and love permeates the lives and actions of the mystics. While there has undoubtedly been a rich history of Christian mysticism, is this still relevant? Does Christian mysticism offer anything for the future of the church?

In an era when people are leaving organized religion, mysticism offers a different way to be in relationship with God and with one another. This is not to justify or promote the exodus from Christian churches. The mystics were generally embedded in religious institutions. But it is to offer up a personal and experiential stream of faith that may be appealing to many. It is also a challenge to institutional churches to embrace this long and robust history of experiential Christianity because it may just be what draws in new Christians or even brings disillusioned Christians back into the pews.

Mysticism offers up a different way of looking at the world. It places value on human beings as children of God. Ultimately, the gift of Christian mysticism in the modern age is that it pulls us out of ourselves. It shows us that we can never be enough to save ourselves. It exposes that hollow goal of continual self-improvement and continual productivity. It demonstrates humanity's dependence on a loving God who breaks into our lives and offers both salvation and transformation. Mysticism is not about our actions or our successes. It is about God's actions and God's love. Mysticism should center us in our love of God and help us turn toward our neighbor. It is about being in relationship with the creator of the universe, not because we are worthy, not because we deserve it, but because we are loved anyway.

EPILOGUE

Becoming Mystics

In Louisville, at the corner of Fourth and Walnut, in the center of the shopping district, I was suddenly overwhelmed with the realization that I loved all those people, that they were mine and I theirs, that we could not be alien to one another even though we were total strangers. . . . There is no way of telling people that they are all walking around shining like the sun.

—Thomas Merton, *Conjectures of a Guilty Bystander*

ONE OF THE fundamental aims of this book is to demonstrate that Christian mysticism is not some abstract or eccentric strain of thought that runs tangential to the faith. Christian mysticism is relatable and accessible and sits at the very center of Christianity. Christianity without mysticism has the tendency to become either moralistic or mere sentimentality. Mysticism elevates relationship and love. Throughout the previous chapters, we have seen that this can play out in a plethora of different ways. From desert monastics to modern activists, mystics have all engaged in mystical prayer, and while it can look radically different in different contexts, this attention to relationship and love permeates the lives and actions of these individuals. Not everyone is going to completely embrace the mystical lifestyle, but there are aspects of it that are beneficial to everyone. Regardless of one's level of interest in engaging in mystical prayer and the mystical tradition, there are a number of ways to learn and engage. There are more passive ways, such as reading mystical texts or Scripture, and there are more active ways, such as engaging in a variety of spiritual practices.

Reading the mystics is a great next step in learning more. This book provides reading lists at the end of each chapter and a robust bibliography as well. It is beneficial to read a variety of different texts from different authors from different time periods to get a good feel for the diversity found among the mystics. When I teach seminary students about Christian mysticism, I am always surprised at how one text will be transformative to one student while barely registering with another. Then a completely different text will have the opposite effect. I have yet to be able to predict which texts will appeal to which students! During my teaching, I have found that texts from Bernard of Clairvaux, Julian of Norwich, Johannes Tauler, and Thomas Merton tend to be particularly appealing. *The Cloud of Unknowing* always has a fan base as well. But there are so many mystical writings, and these are only scratching the surface.[1] Other particularly engaging texts include those from Teresa of Ávila, Francis de Sales, Edith Stein, Thérèse of Lisieux, and Howard Thurman. If not apparent already, Teresa of Ávila and Bernard of Clairvaux are my own personal favorites. All these aforementioned texts tend to be more accessible to nonexperts. Whereas some mystical texts are genuinely difficult to read, others are quite relatable, especially if one is reading a more modern translation. Reading a combination of older texts and newer texts can be a positive way in which to engage with this tradition as well, since one will be able to see similarities and differences through time.

While reading the mystics is an excellent way to get to know the tradition, spiritual practices are also helpful and often edifying. Below is a list of different historical practices that tend to promote mystical prayer. When I teach a course on Christian mysticism, I require each student to keep a prayer journal and try each of the historic spiritual practices listed below. Overwhelmingly, students note that the prayer

---

1 While I am Catholic, I teach at an Evangelical Lutheran Church of America seminary, and most of my students are from mainline Protestant traditions. This is not a tradition that has typically embraced mystical thought as much as Catholic and Orthodox traditions. Often students are curious but not necessarily familiar with the mystics, but many of them want to know more.

and spiritual practices were the most powerful part of their learning. Each of the following practices has been mentioned in previous sections of the book, but what follows is a more practical guide.

The first practice is the oldest and the simplest to bring into daily life, and that is reciting the Jesus Prayer. The most common version of the prayer is simply, "Lord Jesus Christ, Son of God, have mercy on me, a sinner." An even simpler version is, "Lord Jesus, have mercy on me." This prayer dates back to at least the sixth century, but some form of it is likely much, much older. The basic premise is to repeat this prayer while concentrating on one's breath. Many people find this an incredibly calming prayer practice.[2] This is the prayer that features prominently in the nineteenth-century book *The Pilgrim's Tale*, the prayer that the pilgrim learned to pray ceaselessly. While most of us are not looking to pray ceaselessly, it is such an easy prayer that it is relatively simple to fit into an already-busy life.

The practice of *lectio divina* is admittedly more involved than the Jesus Prayer, but it is a helpful way to encounter God through Scripture. It is an essential component of the Rule of Benedict, and many, many mystics have utilized this practice through the centuries. It can be valuable for modern lay Christians as well. The process involves a slow and mediative reading of a Bible passage multiples times. Critical to this exercise is the understanding that it is not textual analysis. It is the place where one encounters God. One should ask questions such as: What is God trying to communicate this these words? How am I reacting to these words? Then pray about those thoughts and feelings. *Lectio divina* becomes more of a conversation with God through Scripture than a passive reading.[3]

---

2 For a robust discussion of this prayer and practice, see Rossi, "Saying the Jesus Prayer."

3 See a helpful and accessible explanation of the practice in Stephen Barany, "How to Practice Lectio Divina, Pray with Scripture," McGrath Institute for Church Life, University of Notre Dame, May 2, 2019, https://mcgrathblog.nd.edu/how-to-practice-lectio-divina-praying-with-scripture.

Praying the Ignatian examen in the evenings can also be a beneficial practice. This is part of Ignatius of Loyola's larger work *The Spiritual Exercises*, but it stands alone as a daily practice of reflection and prayer. There are many versions of this exercise available, including free versions online, but the essence of it is encounter with God. Through this practice, one reflects on one's day, shows gratitude, and acknowledges and commits to make up for any mistakes or wrongdoing. The process involves putting oneself in God's presence, reviewing one's day—including recalling specific moments when one was drawing closer to God or moving further away from God—and then looking toward tomorrow.[4]

While there are countless other prayers and prayer practices, these three are historically grounded and have played a role in Christian mysticism throughout the centuries. However, one should not feel limited to these. A prayerful walk, active participation in a church service, or even listening to a prayer app on one's phone (of which there are many), just to name a few, can help one grow closer to God. Figuring out what works for one individually is essential since everyone is different and there is no one-size-fits-all solution when it comes to prayer and spiritual practices.

While the word *mystic* might still occasionally conjure up images of levitating saints and ascetic hermits, it is important to understand that mystical prayer and practice are open to everyone. It is not the work of an elite class of Christians, nor is it an obscure thread of Christian thought that had its heyday in the Middle Ages and then slipped into obscurity. Mysticism has always been an important aspect of the Christian faith, and it continues to be so today. It places love and relationship at the center of the Christian witness, and it offers an experiential and exciting way to be in relationship with God.

---

4 While there are many versions of this around, a simple explanation from the Jesuits is extremely helpful. See "The Ignatian Examen," The Jesuits, https://www.jesuits.org/spirituality/the-ignatian-examen/. In addition to the classic examen, there are a variety of more topic-specific versions of the examen available there as well.

BIBLIOGRAPHY

"About the Catholic Worker Movement." The Catholic Worker Movement, accessed August 9, 2023. https://catholicworker.org/about-the-catholic-worker-movement/.

Ahlgren, Gillian T. W. *Enkindling Love: The Legacy of Teresa of Avila and John of the Cross*. Minneapolis: Fortress, 2016.

American Friends Service Committee. "History." Accessed May 2, 2024. https://afsc.org/history.

"American Friends Service Committee: Facts." The Nobel Prize. https://www.nobelprize.org/prizes/peace/1947/friends-committee/facts/.

Angela of Foligno. *The Book of Blessed Angela*. Edited and translated by Paul Lachance, OFM. New York: Paulist Press, 1993.

Anonymous. *The Cloud of Unknowing and the Book of Privy Counseling*. Edited by William Johnston. New York: Image Books, 1996.

Asciuto, Nicoletta. "Light and Mystical Writing: T. S. Eliot's Poetic Practice in Four Quartets." *Religion & Literature* 52/53, no. 3 (2020): 47–69.

Athanasius of Alexandria. *Life of St. Anthony*. Translated by E. Ellershaw. Philadelphia: Dalcassian, 2019.

Augustine of Hippo. *Confessions*. Translated by Henry Chadwick. Oxford: Oxford University Press, 2008.

———. *On the Trinity*. Edited by D. P. Curtin. Translated by Arthur West Hadden. Philadelphia: Dalcassian, 2018.

Barany, Stephen. "How to Practice Lectio Divina, Pray with Scripture." McGrath Institute for Church Life, University of Notre Dame, May 2, 2019. https://mcgrathblog.nd.edu/how-to-practice-lectio-divina-praying-with-scripture.

Barrett, Julia, and A. A. Lukowski. "Wedded to Light: The Life, Letters, and Legend of St. Catherine of Siena." *The Journal of the Midwest Modern Language Association* 41, no. 1 (2008): 1–9.

Barry, Patrick, OSB. "Introduction to the Rule of St. Benedict," in *Saint Benedict's Rule*, by Benedict, translated by Patrick Barry, OSB, 1–42. Mahwah, NJ: Hidden Springs, 2004.

Benedict. *Saint Benedict's Rule*. Translated by Patrick Barry, OSB. Mahwah, NJ: Hidden Springs, 2004.

Benedict XIV. *Novembris in Festo S. Gertrudis Virginis, et Abbatissoe Ordinis S. Benedicti.* Rome: Typis Joseph Francesci Ferri, 1739. https://archive.org/details/wotb_6743650/page/n1/mode/2up.

Benz, Ernst. *Emanuel Swedenborg: Visionary Saint in the Age of Reason.* West Chester, PA: Swedenborg Foundation, 2002.

Berger, David. "The Attitude of St. Bernard of Clairvaux toward the Jews." *PAAJR* 40 (1972): 89–108.

Bernard of Clairvaux. *On Loving God.* Translated by Jean Leclercq. Kalamazoo, MI: Cistercian Publications, 1995.

———. *Sermons on the Song of Songs.* 4 vols. Translated by Kilian Walsh and Irene M. Edmonds. Spencer, MA: Cistercian Press, 1971–1980.

Bestul, Thomas H. "*Meditatio*/Meditation." In *The Cambridge Companion to Christian Mysticism*, edited by Amy Hollywood and Patricia Z. Beckman, 157–66. Cambridge: Cambridge University Press, 2012.

Bingemer, Maria Clara. *Simone Weil: Mystic of Passion and Compassion.* Translated by Karen M. Kraft: Cambridge: Lutterworth, 2016.

Bochen, Christine M. "Introduction: Awakening the Heart." In *Thomas Merton: Essential Writings*, edited by Christine M. Bochen, 11–49. Maryknoll, NY: Orbis Books, 2000.

Boehme, Jacob. *The Aurora.* Translated by John Sparrow. London: John M. Watkins, 1914.

———. *The Way to Christ.* New York: Paulist Press, 1978.

Bonaventure. *The Life of Saint Francis.* London: J. M. Dent and Co, and Aldine House, n.d.

———. *Works of Bonaventure: Journey of the Mind to God; The Triple Way, or, Love Enkindled; The Tree of Life; The Mystical Vine; On the Perfection of Life, Addressed to Sisters.* N.p.: Mockingbird, 2020.

Brown, Peter. *Augustine of Hippo: A Biography.* Berkeley: University of California Press, 2000.

Butcher, Carmen Acevedo. *A Life of St. Benedict: Man of Blessing.* Brewster, MA: Paraclete, 2006.

———. *St. Hildegard of Bingen: A Spiritual Reader.* Brewster, MA: Paraclete, 2013.

Bynum, Caroline W. "Vita: Gertrude of Helfta." *Harvard Magazine*, May–June 2012. https://www.harvardmagazine.com/2012/03/vita-gertrude-of-helfta.

Casey, Michael. "Reading Saint Bernard." In *A Companion to Bernard of Clairvaux*, edited by Brian Patrick McGuire, 62–107. Leiden: Brill, 2011.

Casiday, Augustine. *Evagrius Ponticus.* London: Routledge, 2006.

———. "Hesychasm." In *The Cambridge Dictionary of Christian Theology*, edited by Ian McFarland et al., 211. Cambridge: Cambridge University Press.

Cassian, John. *The Conferences*. Translated by Boniface Ramsey, OP. New York: Paulist Press, 1997.

———. *The Institutes*. Translated by Boniface Ramsey, OP. New York: Paulist Press, 2000.

Catherine of Genoa. *Purgation and Purgatory: The Spiritual Dialogue*. Translated by Serge Hughs. Mahwah, NJ: Paulist Press, 1979.

Catherine of Siena. *The Dialogue*. Translated by Suzanne Noffke. New York: Paulist Press, 1980.

Catholic Church. *Catechism of the Catholic Church: Revised in Accordance with the Official Latin Text Promulgated by Pope John Paul II*. Washington, DC: United States Catholic Conference, 2000.

Center for Action and Contemplation "What We Do." Accessed May 1, 2024. https://tinyurl.com/3tua6vjz.

———. "Who We Are." Accessed March 1, 2024. https://cac.org/about/who-we-are/.

Childs, Donald J. "T. S. Eliot: From Varieties of Mysticism to Pragmatic Poesis." *Mosaic: A Journal for the Interdisciplinary Study of Literature* 22, no. 4 (1989): 99–116.

Chryssavgis, John. *John Climacus: From the Egyptian Desert to the Sinaite Mountain*. Burlington, VT: Ashgate, 2004.

Climacus, John. *The Ladder of Divine Ascent*. Translated by Colm Luibheid and Norman Russell. New York: Paulist Press, 1982.

Costelo, Daniel. *Pentecostalism as a Christian Mystical Tradition*. Grand Rapids: Eerdmans, 2017.

Cox, Harvey. *Fire from Heaven: The Rise of Pentecostal Spirituality and the Reshaping of Religion in the Twenty-First Century*. Reading, MA: Addison-Weseu, 1995.

Cropper, Margaret. *The Life of Evelyn Underhill: An intimate Portrait of the Groundbreaking Author of Mysticism*. Woodstock, VT: Skylight Paths, 2003.

Cullen, Christopher M. *Bonaventure*. Oxford: Oxford University Press, 2006.

Day, Dorothy. *The Long Loneliness: The Autobiography of the Legendary Catholic Social Activist*. San Francisco: HarperSanFransisco, 1997.

Duffy, Eamon. *Ten Popes Who Shook the World*. New Haven: Yale University Press, 2011.

Dulles, Avery. "Preface." In *The Spiritual Exercises of St. Ignatius*, translated by Louis J. Puhl, xiii–xxiii. New York: Vintage Spiritual Classics, 2000.

Dysinger, Luke. "Beholding Christ in the Other and in the Self: Deification in Benedict of Nursia and Gregory the Great." In *Deification in the Latin Patristic Tradition*, edited by Jared Ortiz, 253–271. Washington, DC: Catholic University of America Press, 2019.

Eckhart, Meister. *The Complete Works of Meister Eckhart.* Edited and translated by Maurice O'C. Walshe. New York: Herder & Herder, 1979.

Egan, Harvey. *An Anthology of Christian Mysticism.* Collegeville, MN: Liturgical Press, 1991.

Eire, Carlos. *The Life of Saint Teresa of Avila.* Princeton: Princeton University Press, 2019.

———. *They Flew: A History of the Impossible.* New Haven: Yale University Press, 2023.

Eliot, T. S. *Four Quartets.* Orlando: Harcourt Books, 1943.

———. "The Love Song of J. Alfred Prufrock." The Poetry Foundation. https://www.poetryfoundation.org/poetrymagazine/poems/44212/the-love-song-of-j-alfred-prufrock.

———. *The Waste Land.* Edited by Michael North. New York: Norton, 2001.

Emery, Kent, Jr. "Foreword: Margaret Porete and Her Book." In *The Mirror of Simple Souls,* by Margaret Porette, translated by Edmund Colledge, OSA, J. C. Marler, and Judith Grant, vii–xxxiii. Notre Dame: University of Notre Dame Press, 1999.

Erb, Peter. "Introduction." In *The Way to Christ,* by Jacob Boehme, 1–26. New York: Paulist Press, 1978.

Evagrius of Pontus. "The Great Letter." In *Evagrius Ponticus,* by A. M. Casiday, 63–78. London: Routledge, 2006.

———. "On Prayer." In *Evagrius Ponticus,* by A. M. Casiday, 185–202. London: Routledge, 2006.

Evans, Christopher. "How the Social Gospel Movement Explains the Roots of Today's Religious Left." The Conversation, July 17, 2017. https://theconversation.com/how-the-social-gospel-movement-explains-the-roots-of-todays-religious-left-78895.

Evans, G. R. *Bernard of Clairvaux.* Oxford: Oxford University Press, 2000.

Faith+Lead. *Faithful Innovation Leader Companion.* St. Paul: Faith+Lead of Luther Seminary, 2021.

Fiedler, Leslie A. "Introduction." In "Spiritual Autobiography," by Simone Weil, in *Waiting for God,* translated by Emma Craufurd, vii–xxxiv. New York: Harper-Perennial, 2001.

Field, Sean L. *The Beguine, the Angel, and the Inquisitor: The Trials of Marguerite Porete and Guiard of Cressonessart.* Notre Dame: University of Notre Dame Press, 2012.

Fox, George. *The Journal.* Edited by Nigel Smith. New York: Penguin Classics, 1999.

———. *The Journal of George Fox.* Edited by J. L. Nickalls. Cambridge: Cambridge University Press, 1952.

Francis of Assisi. *The Writings of St. Francis*. Translated by Father Paschal Robinson. Philadelphia: Dolphin, 1906.

Friedrich, Markus. *The Jesuits*. Translated by John Noël Dillon. Princeton: Princeton University Press, 2022.

Gallyon, Margaret, ed. *The Visions, Revelations and Teachings of Angela of Foligno: A Member of the Third Order of St Francis*. Liverpool: Liverpool University Press, 2012.

Gertrud the Great of Helfta. *Spiritual Exercises*. Edited and translated by Gertrud Jaron Lewis and Jack Lewis. Kalamazoo, MI: Cistercian Publications, 1989.

Gertrude of Helfta. *The Herald of Divine Love*. Edited and translated by Margaret Winkworth. New York: Paulist Press, 1993.

———. *Spiritual Exercises*. Edited and translated by Gertrud Jaron Lewis and Jack Lewis. Kalamazoo, MI: Cistercian Publications, 1989.

González, Justo. *The Story of Christianity*. Vol. 1, *The Early Church to the Dawn of the Reformation*. New York: HarperOne, 2010. Vol. 2, *The Reformation to the Present Day*. New York: HarperOne, 2010.

Gonzalez, Xochitl. "What Happened to Empathy?" *The Atlantic*, October 12, 2023. https://www.theatlantic.com/ideas/archive/2023/10/american-empathy-digital-isolation-humanity/675615/.

Gordon, Lyndall. *T. S. Eliot: An Imperfect Life*. New York: Norton, 1998.

Gregory the Great. *The Dialogues of Gregory the Great: Book Two: Saint Benedict*. Translated by Myra L. Uhlfelder. Indianapolis: Bobbs-Merrill, 1967.

———. *Morals on the Book of Job*. Translated by John Henry Parker, JGF, and J. Rivington. Oxford: Oxford University Press, 1844.

Griffin, Emilie. "Introduction." In *Evelyn Underhill: Essential Writings*, by Evelyn Underhill, edited by Emilie Griffin, 17–33. Maryknoll, NY: Orbis Books, 2003.

Guigo II. *The Ladder of Monks: A Letter on the Contemplative Life and Twelve Meditations*. Translated by Edmund Colledge and James Walsh. Kalamazoo, MI: Cistercian Publications, 1981.

Gunn, Cate, and Liz Herbert McAvoy. "Introduction: 'No Such Thing as Society'? Solitude in Community." In *Medieval Anchorites in Their Communities*, edited by Cate Gunn and Liz Herbert McAvoy, 1–12. Rochester, NY: Boydell & Brewer, 2017.

Hadewijch. *The Complete Works*. Translated by Mother Columba Hart, OSB. New York: Paulist Press, 1980.

Haller, John S., Jr. *Swedenborg, Mesmer, and the Mind/Body Connection: The Roots of Complementary Medicine*. West Chester, PA: Swedenborg Foundation, 2010.

Hamm, Thomas D. *Quakers in America.* New York: Columbia University Press, 2003.

Harvey, Paul. *Howard Thurman and the Disinherited: A Religious Biography.* Grand Rapids: Eerdmans, 2020.

Healey, Robynne Rogers. "History of Quaker Faith and Practices: 1650–1808." In *The Cambridge Companion to Quakerism*, edited by Stephen W. Angell and Pink Dandelion, 13–30. Cambridge: Cambridge University Press, 2018.

Hearden, Maura. "Catholic America's Love Affair with the Little Flower." *American Catholic Studies* 116, no. 3 (2005): 39–54.

Heath, Elaine A. *Naked Faith: The Mystical Theology of Phoebe Palmer.* Cambridge: Lutterworth, 2009.

Hedstrom, Matthew. "Rufus Jones and Mysticism for the Masses." *CrossCurrents* 54, no. 2 (2004): 31–44.

Hefner, Robert W. "Introduction: The Unexpected Modern—Gender, Piety, and Politics in the Global Pentecostal Surge." In *Global Pentecostalism in the 21st Century*, edited by Robert W. Hefner, 1–36. Bloomington: Indiana University Press, 2013.

Herbstrith, Waltraud. *Edith Stein: A Biography.* Translated by Father Bernard Bonowitz, OCSO. San Francisco: Harper & Row, 1985.

Herrera, R. A. *Silent Music: The Life, Work, and Thought of St. John of the Cross.* Grand Rapids: Eerdmans, 2004.

Hesychios the Priest. "On Watchfulness and Holiness." In *Philokalia: The Eastern Christian Spiritual Texts, Selections, Annotated and Explained*, translated by G. E. H. Palmer, Philip Sherrard, and Bishop Kallistos Ware. Woodstruck VT: Skylight Paths, 2006.

Higginson, Francis. *A Brief Relation of the Irreligion of the Northern Quakers.* London: Printed by T. R. for H. R., 1653.

Hildegard of Bingen. *Scivias.* Translated by Mother Columba Hart and Jane Bishop. New York: Paulist Press, 1990.

Hill, Susan Lindley. *You Have Stept Out of Your Place: A History of Women and Religion in America.* Louisville: Westminster John Knox, 1996.

Hillis, Gregory. "Remembering Thich Nhat Hanh, the Buddhist Monk Who Thomas Merton Called a Brother." *America the Jesuit Review*, January 24, 2022. https://www.americamagazine.org/faith/2022/01/24/thich-nhat-hanh-thomas-merton-242268.

Hinds, Hilary. *George Fox and Early Quaker Culture.* Manchester: Manchester University Press, 2011.

House, Adrian. *Francis of Assisi: A Visionary Life.* Mahwah, NJ: Hidden Springs, 2001.

Hughes-Edwards, Mari. *Reading Medieval Anchoritism: Ideology and Spiritual Practices.* Cardiff: University of Wales Press, 2012.

"The Ignatian Examen." The Jesuits. https://www.jesuits.org/spirituality/the-ignatian-examen/.

Ignatius of Loyola. *A Pilgrim's Journey: The Autobiography of Ignatius of Loyola.* Edited and translated by Joseph N. Tylenda, SJ. San Francisco: Ignatius, 2001.

———. *The Spiritual Exercises of St. Ignatius.* London: Burns & Lambert, 1860.

Jacobs, Alan. "Thomas Merton, the Monk Who Became a Prophet: Fifty Years after His Death, Merton's Contradictions Have Made His Work All the More Instructive." *The New Yorker,* December 28, 2018. https://www.newyorker.com/books/under-review/thomas-merton-the-monk-who-became-a-prophet.

John of the Cross. *John of the Cross, Selected Writings.* Edited by Kieran Kavanaugh. New York: Paulist Press, 1987.

———. *The Poems of Saint John of the Cross.* Translated by Willie Barnstone. Bloomington: Indiana University Press, 1968.

Johnson, Paul E., and Sean Wilentz. *The Kingdom of Matthias: A Story of Sex and Salvation in 19th Century America.* Oxford: Oxford University Press, 1994.

Johnson, Todd M., Gina A. Zurlo, and Becky Yang Hsu. *World Christian Encyclopedia.* 3rd ed. Edited by David B. Barrett and George Thomas Kurian. Edinburgh: Edinburgh University Press, 2020.

Jones, Jeffrey M. "Belief in God in U.S. Dips to 81%, a New Low." Gallup, June 17, 2022. https://news.gallup.com/poll/393737/belief-god-dips-new-low.aspx.

Jones, Mary Hoxie. "Rufus Matthew Jones: Mystic." *Mystics Quarterly* 12, no. 1 (1986): 14–18.

Julian of Norwich. *Julian of Norwich: Revelations of Divine Love.* Edited by Barry Windeatt. Oxford: Oxford University Press, 2016.

———. *Revelations of Divine Love, the Short Text.* Translated by Elizabeth Spearing. London: Penguin Books, 1998.

———. *Revelations of Divine Love, the Long Text.* Translated by Elizabeth Spearing. London: Penguin Books, 1998.

———. *The Writings of Julian of Norwich: A Vision Showed to a Devout Woman and A Revelation of Love.* Edited by Nicholas Watson and Jacqueline Jenkins. University Park: Pennsylvania State University Press, 2006.

Kangas, David J. "Dangerous Joy: Marguerite Porete's Good-Bye to the Virtues." *JR* 91, no. 3 (July 2011): 299–319.

Khazan, Olga. "Why People Are Acting So Weird." *The Atlantic,* March 2022. https://www.theatlantic.com/politics/archive/2022/03/antisocial-behavior-crime-violence-increase-pandemic/627076/.

Koester, Nancy. *We Will Be Free: The Life and Faith of Sojourner Truth*. Grand Rapids: Eerdmans, 2023.

Konstantinovsky, Julia S. *Evagrius Ponticus: The Making of a Gnostic*. Burlington, VT: Ashgate, 2009.

Lachance, Paul, OFM. "Introduction." In *Angela of Foligno: Complete Works*, by Angela of Foligno, edited and translated by Paul Lachance, OFM, 15–46. New York: Paulist Press, 1993.

LaHaye, Tim, and Jerry B. Jenkins. *Left Behind*. Carol Stream, IL: Tyndale House, 1995.

The Legend of St. Francis by Three Companions. London: J. M. Dent and Co, and Aldine House, n.d.

Lewis, Gertrud Jaron, and Jack Lewis. "Introduction." In *Gertrud the Great of Helfta, Spiritual Exercises*, edited and translated by Gertrud Jaron Lewis and Jack Lewis, 1–18. Kalamazoo, MI: Cistercian Publications, 1989.

Lichtmann, Maria. "Marguerite Porete and Meister Eckhart: *The Mirror of Simple Souls* Mirrored." In *Meister Eckhart and the Beguine Mystics: Hadewijch of Bradant, Mechthild of Magdeburg, and Marguerite Porete*, edited by Bernard McGinn, 66–86. New York: Continuum, 1994.

Louth, Andrew. "Apophatic and Cataphatic Theology." In *The Cambridge Companion to Christian Mysticism*, edited by Amy Hollywood and Patricia Z. Beckman, 137–46. Cambridge: Cambridge University Press, 2012.

Luongo, F. Thomas. "Birgitta and Catherine and Their Textual Communities." In *Sanctity and Female Authorship: Birgitta of Sweden and Catherine of Siena*, edited by Maria H. Oen and Unn Falkeid, 14–34. New York: Routledge, 2020.

———. *The Saintly Politics of Catherine of Siena*. Ithaca, NY: Cornell University Press, 2006.

Maddocks, Fiona. *Hildegard of Bingen: The Woman of Her Age*. New York: Doubleday, 2001.

Mahoney, Irene, OSU. "Introduction." In *Marie of the Incarnation: Selected Writings*, edited by Irene Mahoney, OSU, 5–40. New York: Paulist Press, 1989.

Marie of the Incarnation. "The Revelation of 1654." In *Marie of the Incarnation: Selected Writings*, edited by Irene Mahoney, OSU, 41–178. New York: Paulist Press, 1989.

Mastroianni, A. M., and D. T. Gilbert. "The Illusion of Moral Decline." *Nature* 618 (2023): 782–89.

Matter, E. Anna. "Lectio Divina." In *The Cambridge Companion to Christian Mysticism*, edited by Amy Hollywood and Patricia Z. Beckman, 147–56. Cambridge: Cambridge University Press, 2012.

McCartin, James P. "The Sacred Heart of Jesus, Thérèse of Lisieux, and the Transformation of U.S. Catholic Piety, 1865–1940." *U.S. Catholic Historian* 25, no. 2 (2007): 53–67.

McCaslin, Susan. "Vision and Revision in Four Quartets: T. S. Eliot and Julian of Norwich." *Mystics Quarterly* 12, no. 4 (1986): 171–78.

McGinn, Bernard. *The Beginnings of Western Mysticism*. New York: Crossroad, 1991.

———. *The Essential Writings of Christian Mysticism*. New York: Random House, 2006.

———. *Foundations of Mysticism*. New York: Crossroad, 1991.

———. *The Growth of Mysticism: Gregory the Great through the 12th Century*. New York: Crossroad, 1994.

———. *The Harvest of Mysticism in Medieval Germany*. New York: Crossroad, 2005.

———. *Mysticism in the Reformation 1500–1650*. New York: Crossroad, 2016.

McGuire, Brian Patrick. *Bernard of Clairvaux: An Inner Life*. Ithaca, NY: Cornell University Press, 2020.

———. "Bernard's Life and Works: A Review." In *A Companion to Bernard of Clairvaux*, edited by Brian Patrick McGuire, 18–61. Leiden: Brill, 2011.

McIntosh, Mark A. *Mystical Theology*. Malden: MA: Wiley-Blackwell, 1998.

Mechthild of Magdeburg. *The Flowering Light of the Godhead*. Translated by Frank Tobin. New York: Paulist Press, 1998.

Meconi, Honey. *Hildegard of Bingen*. Champaign: University of Illinois Press, 2018.

Merton, Thomas. *Contemplation in a World of Action*. 2nd ed. Notre Dame: University of Notre Dame Press, 1998.

———. *Mystics and Zen Masters*. New York: Farrar, Straus & Giroux, 1961.

———. *Seeds of Destruction*. New York: Farrar, Straus & Giroux, 1987.

———. *Seven Story Mountain*. New York: Harcourt, Brace & World, 1948.

———. "The Way of Nonviolence." In *Thomas Merton's Essential Writings*, edited by Christine M. Bochen, 122–34. Maryknoll, NY: Orbis Books, 2000.

Meyendorff, John. *Gregory Palamas and Orthodox Spirituality*. Translated by Adele Fiske. New York: St. Vladimir's Seminary Press, 1974.

Moran, Dermot. "Meister Eckhart in 20th-Century Philosophy." In *A Companion to Meister Eckhart*, edited by Jeremiah M. Hackett, 669–70. Leiden: Brill, 2013.

Morris, Bridget. *St. Birgitta of Sweden*. Woodbridge, UK: Boydell, 1999.

Mulder-Bakker, Anneke B. *Lives of the Anchoresses: The Rise of the Urban Recluse in Medieval Europe*. Philadelphia: University of Pennsylvania Press, 2005.

Oden, Thomas C., ed. *Phoebe Palmer: Selected Writings*. New York: Paulist Press, 1988.

Oen, Maria H., and Unn Falkeid, eds. *Sanctity and Female Authorship: Birgitta of Sweden and Catherine of Siena*. New York: Routledge, 2020.

O'Regan, Cyril. "Eckhart Reception in the 19th Century." In *A Companion to Meister Eckhart*, edited by Jeremiah M. Hackett, 629–67. Leiden: Brill, 2013.

Origen. "Commentary on the Song of Songs." In *An Anthology of Christian Mysticism*, edited by Harvey Egan, SJ, 25–29. Collegeville, MN: Liturgical Press, 1991.

———. *Spirit and Fire: A Thematic Anthology of His Writings*. Edited by Hans Urs von Balthasar. Translated by Robert J. Daly, SJ. Washington, DC: Catholic University of America Press, 1984.

"Our History." Trappist Brothers & Sisters: Cistercians of the Strict Observance, accessed July 13, 2023. https://www.trappists.org/history-of-the-trappists/history-trappists/.

Palamas, Gregory. *The Triads*. Edited by John Meyendorff. Translated by Nicholas Gendle. New York: Paulist Press, 1983.

Palmer, Phoebe. *The Way of Holiness*. New York, 1854.

Panikkar, Raimon. *The Rhythm of Being*. Gifford Lectures. Maryknoll, NY: Orbis Books, 2010.

Paul VI. "Proclamacíon de Santa Teresa de Jesús como Doctora de la Iglesia." The Vatican, September 27, 1970. https://www.vatican.va/content/paul-vi/es/homilies/1970/documents/hf_p-vi_hom_19700927.html.

Pavan, Milena Carrara, and Rowan Williams. "Raimon Panikkar: Life and Work." In *Raimon Panikkar: A Companion to His Life and Thought*, edited by Peter C. Phan and Young-chan Ro, 1–18. Cambridge: Lutterworth, 2018.

Pentikovsky, Aleksei. "Introduction." In *The Pilgrim's Tale*, edited by Aleksei Pentikovsky, translated by T. Allan Smith, 1–36. New York: Paulist Press, 1999.

Peters, Greg. *The Story of Monasticism: Retrieving an Ancient Tradition for Contemporary Spirituality*. Grand Rapids: Baker Academic, 2015.

Pew Research Center. "Global Christianity—A Report on the Size and Distribution of the World's Christian Population." December, 19, 2011. https://www.pewforum.org/2011/12/19/global-christianity-exec/.

———. "Modeling the Future of Religion in America." Pew Research Center Report, September 13, 2022. https://www.pewresearch.org/religion/2022/09/13/how-u-s-religious-composition-has-changed-in-recent-decades/.

Philokalia: The Eastern Christian Spiritual Texts, Selections, Annotated and Explained. Translated by G. E. H. Palmer, Philip Sherrard, and Bishop Kallistos Ware. Woodstock, VT: Skylight Paths, 2006.

Poon, Linda. "Why Americans Stopped Volunteering." Bloomberg, September 11, 2021. https://www.bloomberg.com/news/articles/2019-09-12/america-has-a-post-9-11-volunteerism-slump.

Poor, Sara S. *Mechthild of Magdeburg and Her Book: Gender and the Making of Textual Authority*. Philadelphia: University of Pennsylvania Press, 2004.

Porette, Margaret. *The Mirror of Simple Souls.* Translated by Edmund Colledge, OSA, J. C. Marler, and Judith Grant. Notre Dame: University of Notre Dame Press, 1999.

Pseudo-Dionysius. *The Complete Works.* Translated by Colm Luibhéid. New York: Paulist Press, 1987.

Putnam, Robert D. *Bowling Alone: The Collapse and Revival of American Community.* New York: Simon & Schuster, 2000.

Rabin, Roni Caryn. "Ask Well: The Health Benefits of Meditation." *New York Times,* November 10, 2015. https://archive.nytimes.com/well.blogs.nytimes.com/2015/11/10/ask-well-the-health-benefits-of-meditation/.

Raboteau, Albert J. *American Prophets: Seven Religious Radicals and Their Struggle for Social and Political Justice.* Princeton: Princeton University Press, 2016.

Raymond of Capua. *The Life of St. Catherine of Siena.* Dublin: James Duffy, n.d.

Rennie, Kriston R. "Second World War Fight to Protect Monte Cassino Abbey Was a Battle over Europe's History." The Conversation, August 4, 2020. https://theconversation.com/second-world-war-fight-to-protect-monte-cassino-abbey-was-a-battle-over-europes-history-138697.

Ricken, David Laurin. "Decree on the Authenticity of the Apparitions of 1859 at the Shrine of Our Lady of Good Help." December 8, 2010. https://www.gbdioc.org/images/stories/Evangelization_Worship/Shrine/Documents/Shrine-of-Our-Lady-of-Good-Help.pdf.

Riehle, Wolfgang. *The Secret Within: Hermits, Recluses, and Spiritual Outsiders in Medieval England.* Translated by Charity Scott-Stokes. Ithaca, NY: Cornell University Press, 2014.

Robertson, Duncan. "The Experience of Reading: Bernard of Clairvaux 'Sermons on the Song of Songs.'" *Religion & Literature* 19, no. 1 (1987): 1–20.

Root, Andy. *The Church in an Age of Secular Mysticisms: Why Spiritualities without God Fail to Transform Us.* Grand Rapids: Baker Academic, 2023.

Ross, David. "Church of St Julian and Shrine, Norwich." Britain Express, accessed May 1, 2024. https://www.britainexpress.com/counties/norfolk/norwich/st-julian.htm.

Rossi, Albert S. "Saying the Jesus Prayer." St. Vladimir's Orthodox Theological Seminary, accessed May 1, 2024. https://www.svots.edu/saying-jesus prayer#:~:text=We%20are%20to%20breath%20naturally,slowly%20and%20reverently%20and%20attentively.

Ruhr, Mario von der. *Simone Weil: Late Philosophical Writings.* Translated by Eric O. Springsted and Lawrence E. Schmidt. London: Continuum, 2006.

"The Rule." Order of Saint Benedict, accessed July 13, 2023. https://tinyurl.com/48sbcy2t.

The Russian Primary Chronicle Laurentian Text. Edited and translated by Samuel Hazzard Cross and Olgerd P. Sherbowitz-Wetzor. Cambridge: Crimson, 1953.

Sahlin, Claire L. *Birgitta of Sweden and the Voice of Prophecy.* Rochester, NY: Boydell, 2001.

Sales, Francis de. *Introduction to the Devout Life.* Edited and translated by John K. Ryan. New York: Image Books, 1989.

———. *On the Love of God.* Translated by H. L. Sidney Lear. London: Rivingtons, 1888.

Sauer, Michelle M. "Introduction: Anchoritism, Liminality, and the Boundaries of Vocational Withdrawal." *Journal of Medieval Religious Cultures* 42, no. 1 (2016): v–xii.

Schmidt, Margot. "Preface." In *The Flowering Light of the Godhead,* by Mechthild of Magdeburg, translated by Frank Tobin, xxv–xxxvii. New York: Paulist Press, 1998.

Senner, Walter. "Meister Eckhart's Life, Training, Career, and Trial." In *A Companion to Meister Eckhart,* edited by Jeremiah M. Hackett, 7–81. Leiden: Brill, 2013.

Shackleton, Sir Ernest. "The Extra Man." In *The Waste Land,* by T. S Eliot, edited by Michael North, 60. New York: Norton, 2001.

Sinkewicz, Robert E., "Introduction." In *Evagrius of Pontus: The Greek Classic Corpus,* edited and translated by Robert E. Sinkewicz, xvii–xl. Oxford: Oxford University Press, 2003.

Smith, Gregory A. "About Three-in-Ten U.S. Adults Are Now Religiously Unaffiliated." Pew Research Forum, December 14, 2021. https://www.pewforum.org/2021/12/14/about-three-in-ten-u-s-adults-are-now-religiously-unaffiliated/.

Smith, Luther E., Jr. "Introduction: The Call to Prophetic Spirituality." In *Howard Thurman, Essential Writings,* edited by Luther E. Smith Jr., 13–33. Maryknoll, NY: Orbis Books, 2006.

Southern, R. W. *Western Society and the Church in the Middle Ages.* Baltimore: Penguin Books, 1979.

Stein, Edith. *Essential Writings.* Edited by John Sullivan, OCD. Maryknoll, NY: Orbis, 2002.

———. *Life in a Jewish Family: An Autobiography 1891–1916.* Edited by L. Gelber and Romaus Leuven. Translated by Josephine Koeppel. Washington, DC: Institute of Carmelite Studies, ICS Publications, 1999.

———. "The Mystery of Christmas." *Plough,* December 25, 2022. https://www.plough.com/en/topics/culture/holidays/christmas-readings/the-mystery-of-christmas#.

———. *The Science of the Cross.* Translated by Josephine Koeppel, OCD. Washington, DC: ICS, 2002.

———. *Selected Writings.* Edited by Marian Maskulak, CPS. New York: Paulist Press, 2016.

Sterling, Peter, and Michael L. Platt. "Why Deaths of Despair Are Increasing in the US and Not Other Industrial Nations—Insights from Neuroscience and Anthropology." *JAMA Psychiatry* 79, no. 4 (2022): 368–74.

Stewart, Columba. *Cassian the Monk*. Oxford: Oxford University Press, 1998.

Stoudt, John Joseph. *Jacob Boehme: His Life and Thought*. New York: Seabury, 1968.

Sullivan, John. "Introduction." In *Essential Writings*, by Edith Stein, edited by John Sullivan, OCD, 17–34. Maryknoll, NY: Orbis, 2002.

Summers, Juana. "America Has a Loneliness Epidemic. Here Are 6 Steps to Address It." NPR, May 2, 2023. https://tinyurl.com/3utuz79u.

Swedenborg, Emanuel. *Heaven and Its Wonders and Hell from Things Heard and Seen*. London: Swedenborg Society, 1992.

Taylor, Charles. *A Secular Age*. Cambridge: Belknap, 2007.

"Teresa Benedict of the Cross, Edith Stein (1891–1942)." The Holy See, accessed January 21, 2024. https://www.vatican.va/news_services/liturgy/saints/ns_lit_doc_19981011_edith_stein_en.html.

Teresa of Ávila. *The Book of My Life*. Translated by Mirabai Starr. Boston: New Seeds, 2007.

———. *The Interior Castle*. Translated by Kieran Kavanaugh, OCD, and Otilio Rodriguez, OCD. Washington, DC: ICS, 2020.

———. *The Way of Perfection*. Translated by Paula Hutson. Brewster, MA: Paraclete, 2009.

Thérèse of Lisieux. *Story of a Soul: The Autobiography of St. Thérèse of Lisieux*. 3rd ed. Translated by John Clark, OCD. Washington, DC: ICS, 1996.

Thibon, Gustave. "Introduction." In Simone Weil, *Gravity and Grace*, translated by Arthur Wills, 3–48. Lincoln: University of Nebraska Press, 1997.

Thurman, Howard. *The Creative Encounter*. New York: Harper & Row, 1954.

———. "Men Who Have Walked with God: The Mystics." In *The Way of the Mystics*, edited by Peter Eisenstadt and Walter Early Fluker, 1–9. Maryknoll, NY: Orbis, 2021.

———. "Mysticism and Social Change: Rufus Jones." In *The Way of the Mystics*, edited by Peter Eisenstadt and Walter Early Fluker, 141–60. Maryknoll, NY: Orbis, 2021.

———. *With Head and Heart: The Autobiography of Howard Thurman*. San Diego: Harcourt, Brace, 1979.

Tobin, Frank. "Introduction." In *The Flowering Light of the Godhead*, by Mechthild of Magdeburg, translated by Frank Tobin, xxv–xxxvii. New York: Paulist Press, 1998.

Truth, Sojourner. "Ain't I a Woman?" The Sojourner Truth Project, accessed May 2, 2024. https://tinyurl.com/3enfc655.

———. *The Narrative of Sojourner Truth.* Battle Creek, MI: Review and Herald Office, 1884.

Underhill, Evelyn. *Mysticism: A Study in the Nature and Development of Spiritual Consciousness.* Grand Rapids: Christian Classics Ethereal Library, 1911.

———. *Practical Mysticism.* Columbus, OH: Ariel, 1914.

———. *Practical Mysticism: A Little Book for Normal People and Abba Meditations on the Lord's Prayer.* Edited by John F. Thorton and Susan B. Varenne. New York: Vintage Spiritual Classics, 2003.

U.S. Department of Health and Human Services. "New Surgeon General Advisory Raises Alarm about the Devastating Impact of the Epidemic of Loneliness and the Isolation in the United States." May 3, 2023. https://www.hhs.gov/about/news/2023/05/03/new-surgeon-general-advisory-raises-alarm-about-devastating-impact-epidemic-loneliness-isolation-united-states.html.

Weil, Simone. *Gravity and Grace.* Translated by Arthur Wills. Lincoln: University of Nebraska Press, 1997.

———. *Waiting for God.* Translated by Emma Craufurd. New York: HarperPerennial, 2001.

White, Charles Edward. *The Beauty of Holiness: Phoebe Palmer as Theologian, Revivalist, Feminist, and Humanitarian.* Eugene, OR: Wipf & Stock, 1986.

Whitney, Janet. "Rufus Jones: A Friend." *The Atlantic Monthly,* April 1954. https://www.theatlantic.com/magazine/archive/1954/04/rufus-jones-friend/642733/.

Winkworth, Margaret. "Introduction." In *The Herald of Divine Love,* by Gertrude of Helfta, edited and translated by Margaret Winkworth, 5–46. New York: Paulist Press, 1993.

Wojciechowski, Jennifer Hornyak. "The Ecstatic and the Everyday." Faith+Lead Blog, January 17, 2024. https://faithlead.org/blog/the-ecstatic-and-the-everyday/.

———. *Women and the Christian Story: A Global History.* Minneapolis: Fortress, 2022.

Wooden, Cindy. "Laval, Marie de L'Incarnation Decreed Saints." *The Catholic Register,* April 3, 2014. https://www.catholicregister.org/faith/item/17877-laval-marie-de-lincarnation-decreed-saints.

Wright, Patrick. "Marguerite Porete's Mirror of Simple Souls and the Subject of Annihilation." *Mystics Quarterly* 35, no. 3/4 (2009): 63–98.

Yong, Amos. "Evangelicals, Pentecostals, and Charismatics: A Difficult Relationship or Promising Convergence?" Fuller Studio, accessed May 2, 2024. https://fullerstudio.fuller.edu/evangelicals-pentecostals-and-charismatics/.

INDEX